GOLD FROM THE LAND OF ISRAEL

A New Light on the Weekly Torah Portion

From the Writings of
Rabbi Abraham Isaac HaKohen Kook

GOLD FROM THE LAND OF ISRAEL

A New Light on the Weekly Torah Portion

From the Writings of
Rabbi Abraham Isaac HaKohen Kook

Rabbi Chanan Morrison

URIM PUBLICATIONS

Jerusalem • New York

Gold from the Land of Israel: A New Light on the Weekly Torah Portion –
From the Writings of Rabbi Abraham Isaac HaKohen Kook
By Rabbi Chanan Morrison

First Edition.
ISBN 965-7108-92-6

Urim Publications, P.O. Box 52287, Jerusalem 91521 Israel
Lambda Publishers Inc.
3709 13th Avenue Brooklyn, New York 11218 U.S.A.
Tel: 718-972-5449, Fax: 718-972-6307, mh@ejudaica.com

www.UrimPublications.com

"The name of the first [river] is Pishon. It surrounds the entire land of Chavilah, where there is gold. And the gold of that land is good." (Gen. 2:11–12)

"Where there is gold" – this refers to the words of Torah, which are more desirable than much fine gold.
"And the gold of that land is good" – this teaches that there is no Torah like the Torah of the Land of Israel.[1] (*Bereishit Rabbah* 16:4)

"Gibeon" from the *Dictionary of the Bible* (Hartford, Conn., 1867), p. 290.

---

[1] For more on the special qualities of the Torah of the Land of Israel, see "*Bereishit*: The Torah of *Eretz Yisrael*."

For my father, ע״ה, who taught me integrity and responsibility

For my mother, ע״ה, who taught me sensitivity

And for my wife, תבדל״א, who taught me to give.

CONTENTS

Preface

I consider myself a reasonably rational person, but sometimes one makes decisions based on factors that only become clearer later on. My decision to study at Mercaz HaRav seemed natural enough at the time, but looking back, I can see that objective criteria would have perhaps indicated a different choice.

In the spring of 1981, I spent a few weeks searching for a suitable yeshivah in Israel for the coming year. Together with several friends, we toured various institutions, until we made our last stop, the Jerusalem yeshivah founded by Rabbi Abraham Isaac Kook in 1924.

I will never forget that first visit to Mercaz HaRav.[1] Over the years, I have visited and studied in a wide variety of yeshivot in America and in Israel, great and small, "black-hat" and "knitted-kippah," Zionist, non-Zionist, and anti-Zionist. But this building in the Kiryat Moshe neighborhood of Jerusalem possessed some intangible quality – a vibrant idealism, an electricity in the air – that I have never encountered elsewhere. It was as if an aura of the supernal light mentioned so often in Rav Kook's writings had somehow descended and enveloped his yeshivah.

By that time, of course, Rav Kook[2] was no longer alive. Even his son, Rabbi Tzvi Yehudah Kook, already in his early 90's, was so ill that

---

[1] The yeshivah's official name is the "Central Universal Yeshivah" – an indication of the institution's central role in Rav Kook's vision for the spiritual revitalization of the Jewish people. Rav Kook, however, lacked the financial backing needed to establish a proper yeshivah. Instead, he initiated its modest beginning as a small group (or center, *Mercaz*) of yeshivah students associated with *HaRav*, as the chief rabbi of *Eretz Yisrael* was deferentially referred. The name *Mercaz HaRav* stuck, despite the yeshivah's transformation over the years into one of the largest and most influential Torah academies in Israel.

[2] In this book, "Rav Kook" always refers to Rabbi Abraham Isaac HaKohen Kook (1865–1935), the first Chief Rabbi of pre-state Israel. For an account of his

the only class he was still able to teach was a Saturday night lecture at his home. (He passed away the following year.) Nonetheless, there was something special about the atmosphere at Mercaz HaRav that enchanted me. I admit, the decision to enter Mercaz HaRav was not fully based on rational, logical factors. I cannot claim that I was drawn by the scholarship of the faculty or the erudition of the lectures, since I had not been in the country long enough to fully understand classes in Talmud delivered in rapid-fire Hebrew. And I had never even studied any of Rav Kook's writings. But the special atmosphere that I felt there, a wonderful combination of seriousness and joy, of "rejoicing in trembling," convinced me that this is where I wanted to study.

In the yeshivah, one seemed to absorb the Torah philosophy of Rav Kook by osmosis. At other yeshivas, I had sensed the holiness in the Torah study and prayer, but this was a holiness that came from one's private connection to God. In Mercaz HaRav, one felt that his personal *avodat Hashem* (service of God) was part of the spiritual connection between the soul of the nation and the God of Israel. When studying in the *Beit Midrash*, there was an atmosphere of excitement and creative energy, a sense that we were part of a much larger entity. Our intellectual efforts were not just about our own private spiritual growth; we were helping establish the spiritual foundations of the nation.

In truth, these impressions did not come from nowhere. Rabbi Tzvi Yehudah Kook was an educator par excellence, and made sure his father's Torah philosophy pervaded the yeshivah milieu, through his lectures, the pamphlets edited by Rabbi Shlomo Aviner ("*Sichot HaRav Tzvi Yehudah*"), and the classes of his disciples. It was impossible for a student to spend more than a short time at the yeshivah without imbibing such concepts as "This people I have formed for Myself [in order that]

---

life, see *An Angel Among Men* by Rabbi Simcha Raz, translated by Rabbi Moshe Lichtman (Jerusalem: Kol Mevaser, 2003). I have provided a summarized timeline of Rav Kook's life in an appendix.

they will speak my praises,"[3] the Jewish people as "a heart among the nations,"[4] and the *Keitz HaMeguleh*, the manifest commencement of the era of redemption.[5]

There were, of course, regular lectures in Rav Kook's writings. Three in particular enabled me to access these sublime realms of divine lights and ideals. Rabbi Shlomo Aviner's Sunday night lectures in *Orot HaTorah*, with his high-pitched French-accented Hebrew and entertaining sense of humor, were a wonderful introduction to the basic concepts in Rav Kook's thought. My second introduction was an early morning study session with Rabbi Moshe Kantman.[6] Before morning prayers, we would study *Orot HaTeshuvah*, Rav Kook's treatise on the subject of repentance. As the Jerusalem sun sent its morning rays into the yeshivah library where we sat, we read Rav Kook's poetic description of "currents of penitence… flaring out like the waves of fire on the sun's surface," flooding the universe with an unimaginably varied gamut of hues and colors (4:1). I could almost feel the warmth of these spiritual waves of *teshuvah* washing over me, and would bask in the confluence of physical and metaphysical light.

---

[3] From Isaiah 43:21, defining the national mission of the Jewish people as sanctifying God's name in the world.

[4] From Rabbi Yehudah HaLevi's classic work, *The Kuzari* (II:36), indicating the organic connection between the Jewish people and the other nations.

[5] Based on *Sanhedrin* 98a. When the Land of Israel bursts forth in agricultural productivity, this is a clear sign of redemption, as the land metaphorically greets the returning nation with its fruits and produce.

[6] Rabbi Kantman is worthy to be the subject of a book in his own right. Born in pre-war Holland, he survived the Holocaust by posing as a Protestant clergyman. He made *aliyah* to Israel after the war, and, drawn one day to the music of learning as he walked near Mercaz HaRav, he began studying there. At age 48, he commenced rabbinical training at the yeshivah, and completed the five-year program – twice. Despite requests by Rabbi Shapira, the head of the yeshivah, to give classes, Rabbi Kantman prefers studying one-on-one with younger students. At the advanced age of 85, he still dances up a storm at the weddings of the yeshivah students.

My third major introduction was a class in *Orot* delivered by Rabbi Yehoshua Zuckerman early Shabbat morning in the original yeshivah building on Rav Kook Street. A small cadre of yeshivah students would briskly make their way across a still sleepy Jerusalem, walking in the middle of streets empty of their usual busy traffic. In a room adjacent to Rav Kook's study, we listened as Rabbi Zuckerman explained the Rav's expositions on the special inner bond connecting the people of Israel to their land, the unique spiritual gifts of the Land of Israel, the cosmic significance of Israel's national rebirth, and our national mission.

Rabbi Tzvi Yehudah Kook often quoted the Aramaic translation of Isaiah 12:3, "And you shall joyfully draw water from the springs of redemption." According to *Targum Yonatan*, this "water" is a metaphor for Torah: "You will joyfully receive a new teaching [of Torah] from the elite of the righteous." In other words, the era of redemption will require a new approach to Torah.[7] A worldview that only deals with the spiritual aspirations of the individual was no longer sufficient. The generation of nation-builders needs a Torah that examines the soul of the nation and its divine mission. How fortunate we are, Rabbi Tzvi Yehudah would exclaim, to have merited learning this renewed Torah from the select righteous!

*   *   *

Rav Kook, upon whose writings this work is based, was blessed with a lyric soul. In his hands, even prose was magically transformed into a form of poetry. The great Hebrew poet Haim Nahman Bialik once commented that, while his style was perhaps more elegant than Rav Kook's, that was due to his meticulous efforts at polishing his sentences. Rav Kook, on the other hand, wrote only once – *kulmus rishon* – without erasing or correcting.

---

[7] Hence, the inspiration for this book's subtitle, "A New Light on the Weekly Torah Portion."

I believe that a straight translation of Rav Kook's writings, besides the near impossibility of maintaining their original poetic resonance, would fail to achieve the author's aim. Rav Kook sought to present the inner teachings of Torah, especially the philosophical concepts expressed by the Talmudic sages in the *Aggadah* and the Midrash, in a literary format that would appeal to the people of his time. A literal translation creates a work containing elements of early 20th century Hebrew literature together with classical rabbinical scholarship. Neither of these styles particularly speaks to the contemporary English-speaking reader, certainly not without extensive notes. Therefore I have forgone any attempt to translate,[8] preferring to summarize the basic ideas and present them in a succinct style that will be accessible to the modern reader, even one lacking an extensive background in Hebrew language and literature. My hope is that many readers will be inspired to study Rav Kook's writings in their beautiful poetic Hebrew.[9]

The translation of Biblical and Talmudic sources is my own. When translating verses from the Pentateuch, I was heavily influenced by Rabbi Aryeh Kaplan's excellent translation in the "Living Torah," although I found that it was often necessary to translate more literally so that the reader will be able to grasp the Talmudic and Midrashic exegesis (and sometimes Rav Kook's own original interpretation of the text). While I have tried as much as possible to limit Hebrew expressions in this book,[10] I have avoided certain terms that have taken on non-Jewish connotations

---

[8] With the exception of five short passages that I have chosen as an introduction to each of the Five Books of Moses.

[9] Rav Kook was aware, of course, that his writings were not light reading. He once remarked, "Studying my philosophical works, such as *Orot*, requires great effort and hard work. They cannot be read on the sofa like a newspaper" (*Shivchei HaRe'iyah*, p. 246). When asked why he does not write in a simpler, more popular style, Rav Kook responded, "In the near future, someone will write [my ideas] in a popular fashion, and they will be widely understood and accepted. But I do not think that I am the one to do this" (ibid., p. 233).

[10] I have compiled a short glossary of Hebrew terms in an appendix.

in English (such as "priests" and "saints"), preferring in these cases to retain the original Hebrew words (*kohanim* and *tzaddikim*).

As for myself, I can only quote Moses' admission, "I am not a man of words." When I began writing these short essays, they were meant simply to be a way of maintaining contact with former students via email. To my great surprise, however, they seem to have taken on a life of their own. They found their way on to various websites and newsletters, and an email distribution list of a few students mushroomed over the years into thousands. For the sake of this book, I have tried to polish them up a bit, so that the writing style will not embarrass the richness of ideas contained within.

In these difficult and trying times, it is especially crucial that we clarify and deepen our connection to the Torah and the Land of Israel. I hope my efforts in bringing Rav Kook's thought to the English-speaking audience will help promote a renewal of our inner ties, on both the individual and national levels, to Torah and *Eretz Yisrael*.

Chanan Morrison
Mitzpeh Yericho, Israel
1 Shevat 5766 / January 30, 2006
http://RavKook.n3.net

The Conversation of the Patriarchs[1]

One spark from the lives of the Patriarchs, from their holiness and from the sublime, divine power of their greatness, gives an ever-increasing light that revives the people of Israel in the end of days with a permanent renascence. And with them, gradually, the entire world. This spark is greater and more sublime than all of the revealed holiness to be found within the framework of faith and religiosity, Torah and *mitzvot*, of the replicated continuation derived from offshoots of the descendants. "The conversation of the Patriarch's servants is superior to the Torah of their descendants."[2] This "Patriarchal conversation" gives life to the final generation with a hidden love.

---

[1] This short essay is based on the Midrashic remark that the Torah is more verbose in retelling the conversations of Abraham's servant (in his search for a wife for Isaac) than in its legal sections, where important laws may be derived even from a single letter. According to Rav Kook, this phenomenon is due to the cosmic importance of the Patriarch's activities in settling the Land and founding the people of Israel. With the return of the Jewish people to their land, the apparently mundane activities of once again settling the Land and reestablishing national institutions of government, economy, language, etc., take on a significance, on par with the practical *mitzvot*. This connection of holy occupation shared by the Patriarchs and the generation of redemption is reflected in the daily prayer, "He remembers the kindnesses of the Patriarchs and brings a redeemer to their offspring."

[2] *Bereishit Rabbah* 60.

Like "a candle in the midday sun,"[3] the paltry lights are dispelled. The chutzpah, inside of which God's spirit proudly beckons, drives them off.[4] The truly great *tzaddikim* recognize this secret and will defend the holy. In their sublime wholeness, they will connect the Torah of the children to the conversation of the Patriarchs and their servants....[5] [This connection] is the redemption of the descendants.

(*Orot*, pp. 66–67)

---

[3] *Chulin* 60b.

[4] The Mishnah in *Sotah* 49b describes the generation before the redemption as one in which "brazenness will increase." This chutzpah, according to Rav Kook, will serve a positive function by driving away small faith in order to make way for a greater, truer light.

[5] The task of the truly righteous is to bridge and harmonize between the current acts of national revival and the Torah and its *mitzvot*.

Tasty Fruit Trees[1]

The account in the Torah describing Creation and the beginnings of humanity is not particularly encouraging. We read of Adam's sin, the murder of Abel, the origins of idol worship, the corrupt generation of the Flood, and so on.

The Kabbalists used the term *shevirat hakeilim*, breaking of the vessels, to describe the many difficulties that occurred in the process of creating the world. With this phrase, they wished to convey the idea that the limited physical realm was incapable of accepting all of the spiritual content that it needed to contain. Like a balloon pumped with too much air, it simply burst.

The Midrash (*Bereishit Rabbah* 5:9) relates that these failings were not only with the human inhabitants of the universe, but also with the heavenly bodies (a power struggle between the sun and the moon) and even with earth itself. The "vessels broke" on many different levels.

What was the "rebellion of the earth"?

God commanded the earth to give forth "fruit trees producing fruit" (Gen. 1:11). The earth, however, only produced "trees producing fruit" (Gen. 1:12). God's intention, the Midrash explains, was that the trees would be literally fruit trees – i.e., the taste of the fruit would be in the tree itself. Were one to lick the bark of an apple tree, for example, it would taste like apple. What does this mean? Why should the trees taste like their own fruit?

---

[1] Adapted from *Orot HaTeshuvah* 6:7.

Appreciating the Path

Rav Kook explained that the Midrash is describing a fundamental flaw of nature. One of the basic failings of our limited world is that we are unable to appreciate the means – the path we take towards a particular goal – as much as we value the goal itself. We set for ourselves many goals, both short-term and long-term; and we are usually excited, even inspired, by the vision of accomplishing our final objectives. But how much exhilaration do we feel in our laborious, day-to-day efforts to attain these goals?[2]

A number of factors – the world's material character, life's transient nature, and the weariness of spirituality when confined to a physical framework – contribute to the current state of affairs, so that we can only sense true fulfillment after attaining the ultimate goal.

God's intention, however, was that the soul would be able to feel some of the inspiration experienced when contemplating a sublime goal also during the process of achieving that end. This is the inner meaning of the Midrash: the means (the fruit tree) should also contain some of the taste, some of the sense of satisfaction and accomplishment, that we experience in the final goal (the fruit).

In the future, the flaws of Creation will be corrected, including the sin of the earth. The world's physical nature will no longer obstruct the resplendent light of the ideal while it is being accomplished through suitable means. Then we will be able to enjoy genuine awareness of the ultimate purpose that resides within all preparatory activity.

---

[2] For example, one may be inspired to write a book, but it is uncommon that the tedious chores of proofreading, checking sources, etc., are anticipated eagerly and enthusiastically.

Bereishit

The Age of the Universe[1]

Contradictions between science and Torah appear particularly irreconcilable with respect to the Torah's description of the creation of the world and the beginnings of mankind. Are these accounts meant to be taken literally? Should we believe that the universe came into existence some 5,760 years ago? Must we reject the theory of evolution out of hand?

In a letter written in Jaffa in 1905, Rav Kook responded to questions concerning evolution and the geological age of the world. He put forth four basic arguments:

1. Even to the ancients, it was well known that there were many periods that preceded our counting of nearly six thousand years for the current era. According to the Midrash (*Bereishit Rabbah* 3:7), "God built worlds and destroyed them" before He created the universe as we know it. Even more astonishing, the *Zohar* (*Vayikra* 10a) states that there existed other species of human beings besides the "Adam" who is mentioned in the Torah.

2. We must be careful not to regard current scientific theories as proven facts, even if they are widely accepted. Scientists are constantly raising new ideas, and all of the scientific explanations of our time may very well come to be laughed at in the future as imaginative drivel.

3. The fundamental belief of the Torah is that God created and governs the universe. The means and methods by which He acts, regardless of their complexity, are all tools of God, Whose wisdom is

---

[1] Adapted from *Igrot HaRe'iyah* vol. I, pp. 105–7.

infinite. Sometimes we specifically mention these intermediate processes, and sometimes we simply say, "God formed" or "God created."

For example, the Torah writes about "the house that King Solomon built" (I Kings 6:2). The Torah does not go into the details of Solomon speaking with his advisors, who in turn instructed the architects, who gave the plans to the craftsmen, who managed and organized the actual building by the workers. It is enough to say, "Solomon built." The rest is understood, and is not important. So too, if God created life via the laws of evolution, these are details irrelevant to the Torah's central message, namely, the ethical teaching of a world formed and governed by an involved Creator.

4. The Torah concealed much with regard to the process of creation, speaking in parables and ciphers. The act of creation – which the mystics refer to as *Ma'aseh Bereishit* – clearly belongs to the esoteric part of Torah (see *Chaggigah* 11b). If the Torah's account of creation is meant to be understood literally, what then are its profound secrets? If everything is openly revealed, what is left to be explained in the future?

God limits revelations, even from the most brilliant and holiest prophets, according to the ability of that generation to absorb the information. For every idea and concept, there is significance to the hour of its disclosure. For example, if knowledge of the rotation of the Earth on its axis and around the sun had been revealed to primitive man, his courage and initiative may have been severely retarded by a fear of falling. Why attempt to build tall structures on top of an immense ball turning and whizzing through space at high velocity? Only after a certain intellectual maturity, and scientific understanding about gravity and other compensating forces, was humanity ready for this knowledge.

The same is true regarding spiritual and moral ideas. The Jewish people struggled greatly to explain the concept of Divine providence to the pagan world. This was not an easy idea to market. Of what interest should the actions of an insignificant human be to the Creator of the universe? Belief in the transcendental importance of our actions is a central principle in Judaism, and was disseminated throughout the world by her daughter religions. But if mankind had already been aware of the true dimensions of the cosmos, and the relatively tiny world that we inhabit, could this fundamental concept of Torah have had any chance in spreading? Only now, that we have greater confidence in our power and control over the forces of nature, is awareness of the grandiose scale of the universe not an impediment to these fundamental ethical values.

To summarize:

- Ancient Jewish sources also refer to worlds that existed prior to the current era of six thousand years.
- One should not assume that the latest scientific theories are eternal truths.
- The purpose of the Torah is a practical one – to have a positive moral influence on humanity, and not to serve as a primer for physicists and biologists. It could very well be that evolution, etc., are the tools by which God created the world.
- Some ideas are intentionally kept hidden, as the world may not be ready for them, either psychologically or morally.

The Torah of *Eretz Yisrael*[1]

"And the gold of that land is good." (Gen. 2:12)

Why is the Torah suddenly interested in the quality of gold? Was this verse written for prospectors of rare metals?

The Midrash (*Bereishit Rabbah* 16:4) explains that the land referred to is *Eretz Yisrael* (the Land of Israel), and the precious commodity is none other than the Torah itself. The Midrash then declares, "This teaches that there is no Torah like the Torah of the Land of Israel."

This is a pretty remarkable statement. Is there really a different Torah in the Land of Israel? And in what way is it superior to the Torah studied outside of Israel?

Details and General Principles

According to Rav Kook, the Torah of *Eretz Yisrael* is fundamentally different in its method and scope. The Torah of the Diaspora focuses on the details – specific laws and rules. The Torah of the Land of Israel, on the other hand, uses a more holistic approach. It connects those details with their governing moral principles.

This approach is particularly needed in our time of national renascence. We must reveal the truth and clarity of our divine treasure. We must demonstrate the beauty and depth of practical *mitzvot*, by endowing them with the light of the mystical and philosophical side of the

---

[1] Adapted from *Orot HaTorah*, chap. 13.

Torah. And the true depths and foundations of Torah can only be experienced in the Land of Israel.

The Individual and the Nation

The contrast in Torah between the *prat* and the *klal*, the details and the whole, also exists on a second level.

The Torah of the Diaspora concerns itself with developing the spiritual potential of the individual. The Torah of *Eretz Yisrael*, on the other hand, relates to the nation as a whole. This Torah deals with physical and spiritual needs of a nation who, as an organic whole, sanctify God's name in the world. The Torah of *Eretz Yisrael* occupies itself with a long list of national institutions belonging to this special people, including kings and prophets, the Temple and *Sanhedrin*, Levites and *kohanim*, Sabbatical and Jubilee years.

All of the ideals that are dispersed and diluted in the Diaspora, become relevant and united in the Land of Israel. In *Eretz Yisrael*, the life of the individual derives its existential meaning from the nation's crowning destiny and is uplifted through the nation's spiritual elevation.

Noah

The Walk of the Righteous[1]

Not all *tzaddikim* are equal. Different individuals attain different levels of holiness and righteousness. The Torah calls our attention to these distinctions when it describes Noah and Abraham with similar yet slightly different phrases.

Regarding Noah, the Torah states that he "walked with God" (Gen. 6:9). To Abraham, on the other hand, God commanded, "Walk before Me" (Gen. 17:1). Noah walked *with* God, while Abraham walked *before* God. What is the difference? Which is better?

Interestingly, we find in the Torah a third expression for living a holy life. The Torah charges us to "walk after the Lord, your God" (Deut. 13:5). Where does "walking *after* God" fit in?

Repairing the Universe

We must first examine this metaphor of "walking." Why not "standing with God" or "running with God"?

After Adam sinned and the natural order underwent a drastic shift, God did not seek to correct the world instantaneously. Rather, humanity was to gradually correct itself, repairing the universe in stages until "the earth will be filled with awareness of God" (Isaiah 11:9). This is the inner significance of the "walk" of the righteous: a slow but steady moral progression.

Similarly, the Sages wrote[2] that prophecy is not revealed to the world all at once, but in a measured fashion, according to our ability to

---

[1] Adapted from *Midbar Shur*, pp. 101–103.

receive and assimilate it. This principle is true for all forms of divine wisdom. Enlightenment is granted to each generation in a measure appropriate for that generation, in order to uplift it and prepare it for the future.

Before the Torah's revelation at Sinai, the world was not ready to receive its full light. Enlightenment is only bestowed according to the world's capacity to accept it. Nonetheless, the universe always contained a hidden potential for its future spiritual level, when it could absorb the Torah's light.

Two Paths of Progress

How does this explain the difference between the "walk" of Noah and Abraham? Before Sinai, there were two paths of spiritual growth. The first path was to perfect oneself according to the spiritual state appropriate for that generation. This is called "walking *with* God": perfecting oneself in accordance with the divine ideals and aspirations that were ordained for that time.

A higher path was to aspire to a level beyond the normal state for that era. This was an extraordinary spiritual effort, in order to prepare for and hasten the highest level of enlightenment – that of the Torah itself. This striving for the spiritual betterment of future generations is referred to as "walking *before* God," or walking ahead of God.

The Torah tells us that Noah "walked *with* God." Noah was just and good according to the standards ordained for his time. For this reason, the Torah emphasizes that Noah was "faultless in his generation." His level of righteousness corresponded to the moral expectations for his generation.

Abraham, on the other hand, sought to awaken the entire world to integrity and holiness. Abraham "walked *before* God," preparing the world

---

[2] "Rabbi Acha said: even prophecy that rests on the prophets does so in a [set] measure" (*Vayikra Rabbah* 15:2).

for the greatest enlightenment, the Torah. Since Abraham helped ready the world for the Torah, the Sages wrote that he fulfilled the Torah before it was given (*Yoma* 28b).

Striving for Sinai

What about the third form of walking, "walking *after* God"? Once the Torah was given, and God revealed the purest divine light, we struggle to merit the pristine light that was revealed and subsequently hidden from us. It is impossible for us to reach the enlightened state of Sinai without first correcting our various faults. Therefore, we cannot be expected to "walk with God," and certainly not "before God." All we can hope for is to "walk *after* God" – to strive after the historic level of enlightenment that was revealed at Sinai. In our efforts to reach this level, we prepare ourselves to approach this state of enlightenment, until God "renews our days as of old" (Lamentations 5:21).

Noah

Permission to Eat Meat[1]

After God destroyed His world by water, making a fresh start with Noah and his family, God told Noah,

> Every moving thing that lives shall be food for you. Like plant vegetation [which I permitted to Adam], I have now given you everything.... Only of the blood of your own lives will I demand an account. (Gen. 9:3, 5)

Up until this point, humanity was expected to be vegetarian. But after Noah and his family left the ark, God allowed them to eat everything – except other people. Why was permission to eat animals given at this time?

Temporary Allowance

Given the violence and depravity of the generation of the Flood, it was necessary to make allowances for humanity's moral frailty. If mankind was still struggling with basic moral issues – such as not murdering his fellow human – why frustrate him with additional prohibitions on less self-evident issues?

After the Flood, God lowered the standards of morality and justice He expected of humanity. We would no longer be culpable for slaughtering animals; we would only be held accountable for harming

---

[1] Adapted from *Talelei Orot*, ch. 8 (quoted by Nechama Leibowitz, *Iyunim Besefer Bereishit*, pp. 55–6). See also *Otzerot HaRe'iyah* vol. II, pp. 88–92.

other human beings. Then our moral sensibilities, which had become cold and insensitive in the confusion of life, could once again warm the heart.

If the original prohibition against meat had remained in force, then, when the desire to eat meat became overpowering, there would be little distinction between feasting on man, beast, or fowl. The knife, the axe, the guillotine, and the electric pulse would cut them all down, in order to satiate the gluttonous stomach of "cultured" man. This is the advantage of morality when it is connected to its Divine Source: it knows the proper time for each objective, and on occasion will restrain itself in order to conserve strength for the future.

In the future, this suppressed concern for the rights of animals will be restored. A time of moral perfection will come, when "No one will teach his neighbor or his brother to know God – for all will know Me, small and great alike" (Jeremiah 31:33). In that era of heightened ethical awareness, concern for the welfare of animals will be renewed.

Preparing for the Future

In the interim, the *mitzvot* of the Torah prepare us for this eventuality.

The Torah alludes to the moral concession involved in eating meat, and places limits on the killing of animals. If "you desire to eat meat," only then may you slaughter and eat (Deut. 12:20). Why mention the "desire to eat meat"? The Torah is hinting: if you are unable to naturally overcome your desire to eat meat, and the time for moral interdiction has not yet arrived – i.e., you still grapple with not harming those even closer to you (fellow human beings) – then you may slaughter and eat animals.

Nonetheless, the Torah limits which animals we are allowed to eat, only permitting those most suitable to human nature.[2] The laws of

---

[2] According to Maimonides (*Guide for the Perplexed* III: 48), the animals permitted for food are those most suitable for the human body, and "no doctor will doubt this." Nachmanides disagreed, explaining that the permitted animals are the ones

shechitah (ritual slaughtering) restrict the manner of killing animals to the quickest and most humane. With these laws, the Torah impresses upon us that we are dealing with a living creature, not some automaton devoid of life. And after slaughtering, we are commanded to cover the blood, as if to say, *"Cover up the blood! Hide your crime!"*

These restrictions will achieve their effect as they educate the generations over time. The silent protest against animal slaughter will become a deafening outcry, and its path will triumph.

---

most suitable for the human *soul*. On Lev. 11:13, he wrote that "birds of prey will always be impure, for the Torah distanced them [from us as food] since their blood is warm in their cruelty... and they put cruelty in the heart [of those who eat them].... It is likely that the animals are similarly [prohibited], since those that chew their cud and have split hooves do not prey."

Noah

The Rainbow in the Clouds[1]

After the Flood, God informed Noah:

> I will make My covenant with you, and all flesh will
> never again be cut off by the waters of a flood.
> This is the sign of the covenant that I am placing
> between Me, you, and every living creature that is
> with you, for all generations: I have set My
> rainbow in the clouds... The rainbow will be in the
> clouds, and I will see it to recall the eternal
> covenant. (Gen. 9:11–16)

How does the rainbow symbolize God's covenant never again to
destroy the world by a flood? Why does the Torah emphasize that the
rainbow is "in the clouds"? And most importantly, what is the meaning of
this promise never again to flood the world? Does this imply that the
Flood was unjust? Or did God change His expectations for the world?

The rainbow is not just a natural phenomenon caused by the
refraction of light. The "rainbow in the clouds" represents a paradigm
shift in humanity's spiritual development.

Pre-Flood Morality
Before the devastation of the Flood, the world was different than the
world we know; it was younger and more vibrant. Its physical aspects
were much stronger, and people lived longer lives. Just as the body was

---

[1] Adapted from *Ein Ayah* vol. II, p. 318–9.

more robust, the intellect was also very powerful. People were expected to utilize their intellect as a guide for living in a sensible, moral fashion. The truth alone should have been a sufficient guide for a strong-willed individual. Ideally, awareness of God's presence should be enough to enlighten and direct one's actions. This was the potential of the pristine world of the Garden of Eden.

Rampant violence and immorality in Noah's generation, however, demonstrated that humanity fell abysmally short of its moral and spiritual potential. After the Flood, God fundamentally changed the nature of ethical guidance for the human soul. The sign that God showed Noah, the "rainbow in the clouds," is a metaphor for this change.

Greater Moral Guidance

The rainbow represents divine enlightenment, a refraction of God's light, as it penetrates into our physical world. Why does the Torah emphasize that the rainbow is "in the clouds"? Clouds represent our emotional and physical aspects, just as clouds are heavy and dark (the Hebrew word *geshem* means both "rain" and "physical matter"). The covenant of the "rainbow in the clouds" indicates that the Divine enlightenment (the rainbow) now extended from the realm of the intellect, where it existed before the Flood, to the emotional and physical spheres (the clouds). God's rainbow of light now also penetrated the thick clouds of the material world.

How was this accomplished? The Divine light became "clothed" in a more physical form – concrete *mitzvot*. God gave to Noah the first and most basic moral code: the seven laws of the Noahide code.[2] These commandments served to bridge the divide between intellect and deed, between the metaphysical and the physical.

---

[2] The seven commandments given to Noah were: 1. No idolatry; 2. No blasphemy; 3. No murder; 4. No stealing; 5. No eating limbs from a live animal; 6. No incest or adultery; 7. Establish a court system (*Sanhedrin* 56b).

We can now understand God's promise never again to flood the world. After the Flood, a total destruction of mankind became unnecessary, as the very nature of human ethical conduct was altered. Our inner spiritual life became more tightly connected to our external physical actions. As a result, the need for such a vast destruction of life, as occurred in the Flood, would not be repeated. Of course, individuals (and even groups and nations) retain the free choice to sink to the level of savages and barbarians. But the degree of immorality will never again reach the scope of Noah's generation, where only a single family deserved to be saved.

Leich Lecha

"Be Complete!"[1]

When Abraham was 99 years old, God appeared to him, announcing the *mitzvah* of *brit milah* (circumcision).

> He said, "I am God Almighty. Walk before Me and be complete. I will make a covenant (*brit*) between Me and you." (Gen. 17:1–2)

What was Abraham's immediate reaction? He literally fell on his face. The Talmud (*Nedarim* 32b) writes that when Abraham heard God command him, "walk before Me and be complete," his entire body began to shake. Abraham was confused and mortified. *"Perhaps there is something improper in my actions?"* But Abraham calmed down when God began to command him to circumcise himself and his household. Why was Abraham comforted to hear that God was referring to *brit milah*?

A Higher Prophetic Level
We perceive the outside world through various gateways. These include the five physical senses, and our powers of intellect and reason. And there exists an additional portal – the faculty of prophecy. We cannot truly fathom this unique gift, the product of a hidden connection between the soul and the body. For this reason, prophecy, unlike pure intellectual activity, involves the powers of imagination, desire, and other baser aspects of the mind.

---

[1] Adapted from *Olat Re'iyah* vol. I, pp. 396–7.

When God charged Abraham, "Be complete," Abraham feared that he was lacking in his intellectual dedication in serving God. This would be a fault for which a righteous individual like Abraham would certainly be held accountable.

But when Abraham heard that God was referring to the *mitzvah* of circumcision, his concerns were put to rest. *Brit milah* serves to refine the special connection between body and soul. It deals with a sphere that is beyond human comprehension – and accountability. God's command was not that Abraham needed to rectify some error or character flaw, but rather to bestow upon him a unique covenant, one which would enable him to attain a purer, higher level of prophecy.

With this gift, Abraham would be able to "walk before God." The word *hit'halech* ("walk") is in the reflexive tense; Abraham would be able to "walk himself," as it were, and progress on his own, before God.

Leich Lecha

Sanctity in Space[1]

> Abraham rose early in the morning, to the place
> where he had [previously] stood before God.
> (Gen. 19:27)

What does it mean that Abraham "stood before God"? The Talmud understood this phrase to refer to prayer.[2]

A Set Place for Prayer

From the fact that Abraham returned to the place where he had prayed in the past, the Sages deduced that Abraham had designated a particular spot for prayer.

> Rabbi Helbo said: Anyone who has a set location
> for his prayers will be assisted by the God of
> Abraham. And when he dies, they will say about
> him, "What a pious individual! What a humble
> person! He was a disciple of our forefather
> Abraham." (*Berachot* 6b)

In what way is a person who sets aside a place for prayer a humble individual? What makes him a disciple of Abraham? Why is it so praiseworthy to always pray in the same location?

---

[1] Adapted from *Ein Ayah* vol. I, p. 25.
[2] The central prayer is called the *Amidah*, meaning "standing," since it is recited while standing.

Spatial Holiness

We are accustomed to the idea that holiness is a function of space. Different places have different degrees of sanctity. The synagogue is holier than the *Beit Midrash* (house of study), the *Beit Midrash* is holier than an ordinary home, and an ordinary home is holier than the bathhouse. Levels of sanctity are also a geographic reality. The Land of Israel is holier than outside of Israel, Jerusalem is holier than other parts of Israel, the Temple Mount is holier than the rest of Jerusalem, and so on.

When examined by cold logic, however, our sense of holiness in space raises questions. Does not God's glory fill the entire universe? Are not the limitations of space and location irrelevant to God? Why should it matter if I pray to him in the synagogue – or in the bathhouse? What difference is there to God between the inner sanctum of the holy Temple and a Los Vegas casino?

Elevating the Imagination

Rav Kook explained that a fundamental truth is at work here: whatever contributes to our ethical and spiritual improvement merits divine providence. Our moral perfection is dependent not only on the intellect, but on the refinement of all of our faculties, including our powers of imagination. Anything that elevates our emotions and imagination, directing them towards good deeds and refined character traits, merits divine providence.

A set location for prayer is a powerful mechanism for uplifting the imagination. Sanctity of place greatly enhances our sense of holiness. Because of its importance in developing this aspect of human nature, there is divine providence to help us succeed in this area.

Intellectual Humility

What makes this conduct humble? The essence of religious humility is preventing the intellect from belittling matters of spiritual value, even though logically they appear to be baseless. We live not by the intellect alone. Good deeds are the ultimate measure of true living, and our actions are greatly influenced by our imagination and feelings.

Abraham exemplified this form of intellectual modesty. He arrived at belief in the Creator through his powers of logic and reasoning.[3] But when he was tested in the *Akeidah*, the Binding of Isaac, Abraham relied solely on his faith in God. He chose to disregard all arguments of reason and logic. Anyone who follows in Abraham's footsteps, and sets aside a special location for prayer, is elevating his imaginative and emotive powers. He is a disciple of Abraham, emulating his traits of humility and piety.

---

[3] See Maimonides, *Mishneh Torah*, Laws of Idolatry 1:9.

Leich Lecha

Mamrei's Advice[1]

The Sages made an astounding statement about Abraham and the *mitzvah* of *brit milah* (circumcision). According to the Midrash (*Tanchuma VaYeira* 3), Abraham only circumcised himself after consulting with his friend Mamrei. "Why did God reveal Himself to Abraham on Mamrei's property? Because Mamrei gave Abraham advice about circumcision."

Could it be that Abraham, God's faithful servant, entertained doubts whether he should fulfill God's command? What special difficulty did circumcision pose that, unlike the other ten trials that Abraham underwent, this *mitzvah* required the counsel of a friend?

Abraham's Dilemma

Abraham was afraid that if he circumcised himself, people would no longer be drawn to seek him out. The unique sign of *milah* would set Abraham apart from other people, and they would naturally distance themselves from him. Additionally, people would avoid seeking his instruction out of fear that Abraham might demand that they too accept this difficult *mitzvah* upon themselves. As the Midrash in *Bereishit Rabbah* (sec. 47) says, "When God commanded Abraham to circumcise, he told God, 'Until now, people used to come to me; now they will no longer come!'"

This side effect of *brit milah* deeply disturbed Abraham. It negated the very goal of Abraham's life and vision – bringing the entire world to recognize "the name of God, Lord of the universe" (Gen. 21:33). If

---

[1] Adapted from *Midbar Shur*, p. 197.

isolated, Abraham would no longer be able to carry on with his life's mission.

This then was Abraham's dilemma. Perhaps it was preferable not to fulfill God's command to circumcise himself. On the personal level, Abraham would lose the spiritual benefits of the *mitzvah*, but the benefit to the entire world might very well outweigh his own personal loss.

Mamrei's Advice

Mamrei advised Abraham not to make calculations regarding a direct command from God. God's counsel and wisdom certainly transcend the limited wisdom of the human mind.

For his sage advice, Mamrei was rewarded *midah kneged midah* (in like measure). Since Mamrei respected the ultimate importance of God's commands, placing them above human reasoning, he was honored with the revelation of divine prophecy on his property.

God's Plan

In fact, Abraham's fears of isolation were realized. From the time of Isaac's birth, people began to avoid him. Abraham himself sent away the children of his concubines "from before his son Isaac" (Gen. 25:6), and God commanded him to send away Ishmael.

All of this was God's plan. God wanted Abraham to concentrate his energies in educating Isaac. For in Isaac resided the seed for repairing and completing the entire world. It was necessary to first nurture the initial sanctity of the Jewish people. The enlightenment and elevation of the world that Abraham so desired be realized through the spiritual influence of his children.

Vayeira

The Salt of Sodom[1]

The Torah vividly contrasts the kindness and hospitality of Abraham's household with the cruelty and greed of the citizens of Sodom. When visitors arrived at Lot's home, the entire city, young and old, surrounded the house with the intention of molesting his guests. Lot's attempts to appease the rioters only aggravated their anger.

Washing after Meals

The Talmud makes an interesting connection between the evil residents of Sodom and the ritual of washing hands at meals. The Sages decreed that one should wash hands before eating bread, as a form of ritual purification, similar to partial immersion in a *mikveh* (ritual bath). The rabbinical decree to wash hands before meals is based on the purification the *kohanim* underwent before eating their *terumah* offerings.

The Talmud in *Chulin* 105b, however, gives a rather odd rationale for *mayim acharonim*, washing hands after the meal. The Sages explained that this washing removes the salt of Sodom, a dangerous salt that can blind the eyes. What is this Sodomite salt? What does it have to do with purification? How can it blind one's eyes?

The Selfishness of the Sodomites

In order to answer these questions, we must first understand the root source of Sodom's immorality. The people of Sodom were obsessed with fulfilling their physical desires. They concentrated on self-gratification to

---

[1] Adapted from Ein Ayah vol. I, p. 21.

such a degree that no time remained for kindness towards others. They expended all of their efforts in chasing after material pleasures, and no energy was left for helping the stranger.

Purifying the Soul While Feeding the Body

A certain spiritual peril lurks in any meal that we eat. Our involvement in gastronomic pleasures inevitably increases the value we assign to such activities, and decreases the importance of spiritual activities, efforts that truly perfect us. As a preventative measure, the Sages decreed that we should wash our hands before eating. Performing this ritual impresses upon us the imagery that we are like the priests, eating holy bread baked from *terumah* offerings. The physical meal we are about to partake suddenly takes on a spiritual dimension.

Despite this preparation, our involvement in the physical act of eating will reduce our sense of holiness to some degree. To counteract this negative influence, we wash our hands after the meal. With this ritual cleansing, we wash away the salt of Sodom, the residue of selfish preoccupation in sensual pleasures. This dangerous salt, which can blind our eyes to the needs of others, is rendered harmless through the purifying ritual of *mayim acharonim*.

Vayeira

Combating Evil[1]

A careful reading of the Torah's account clearly indicates that Lot did not deserve to be saved on his own merits alone:

> When God destroyed the cities of the plain, God remembered Abraham; and He sent out Lot from the upheaval when He overturned the cities in which Lot lived. (Gen. 19:29)

Why was Lot not rescued on the basis of his own merits? He certainly did not participate in the infamous Sodomite cruelty towards visitors. Why was he allowed to escape only because "God remembered Abraham"?

Challenging Sodom

The need for God to destroy Sodom shows the importance of *chesed* (kindness) in our world. It demonstrates the extent of ruin that results from a society lacking this critical trait.

In any ideological conflict, opposition to a particular position can take one of two forms. Some people may reject a position on the basis of its expected consequences. But if they only denounce and point out its negative aspects, they are only partially confronting the objectionable position. True opposition is only achieved when we can present a positive alternative that promises to govern society in a better and more just fashion.

---

[1] Adapted from *Ein Ayah* vol. II, p. 250.

The problem with Sodom was not just that the people of Sodom were cruel. Rather, the very fabric of the Sodomite society was corrupt, based on their abhorrence of kindness. They based their municipal regulations on an ideology of selfishness and self-interest.

Lot and Abraham

To combat Sodom, it was not enough to merely reject their philosophy. It was necessary to present a comprehensive blueprint for a society guided by the traits of kindness and generosity.

Lot rejected the cruel ways of Sodom. By virtue of his association with Abraham, Lot recognized the importance of *chesed*. On a private level, he invited strangers and tried to protect them. But Lot was unable to present an alternative vision of society based on kindness.

Abraham, on the other hand, was a different story. His life was centered on developing and promoting the ideal of *chesed*. Abraham established *chesed* as a fixed and organized trait for both the individual and the community. As God Himself testified,

> For I have known [Abraham], that he will command his children and his household after him, and they will keep God's ways, doing righteousness and justice. (Gen. 18:19)

For this reason, Lot did not deserve to be saved from Sodom on his own merits. Unlike his uncle Abraham, he presented no alternative vision, and did not properly contest the Sodomite ideology of cruelty.

How to Fight Evil

This is an important lesson for us. Our rejection of ideologies that contradict the Torah's ethical ideals should not be limited to negative criticism. It is insufficient to merely point out the harmful or false aspects of an ill-conceived plan. Rather, we need to open an offensive front by

47

presenting a positive outlook based on true values – just as Abraham and his vision of *chesed* stood in direct opposition to the Sodomites' philosophy of egocentric cruelty.

Vayeira

The Binding of Isaac[1]

The great merit of Abraham's trial of the *Akeidah* (the Binding of Isaac) is mentioned repeatedly in our prayers. It is a theme of central importance to Judaism. Yet one could ask a simple question: What is so profound, so amazing about the *Akeidah*? After all, it was common among certain pagan cults to sacrifice children (such as the idolatry of Molech). In what way did Abraham show greater love and self-sacrifice than the idol-worshippers of his time?

Monotheism on Trial

Rav Kook addressed this issue in a letter penned in 1911. The absolute submission that idolatry demanded – and received – was not just a result of primitive mankind's fearful attempts to appease the capricious gods of nature. Even the most abject paganism reflects the truth of the soul's deep yearnings for closeness to God. Even the most abase idolatry is profoundly aware that the Divine is more important than anything else in life.

With the introduction of Abraham's refined monotheism in the world, it was necessary to counter the objection of paganism: can the Torah's abstract concept of God compete with the tangible reality of idols? Can monotheism produce the same raw vitality, the same passionate devotion, as paganism? Or is it merely a cold, cerebral religion – theologically correct, but tepid and uninspiring?

---

[1] Adapted from *Igrot HaRe'iyah* vol. II, p. 43.

Through the test of the *Akeidah*, Abraham demonstrated to the world that, despite the intellectual refinement of his teachings, his approach lacked none of the religious fervor and boundless devotion to be found in the wildest of pagan rites. His refined Torah could match idolatry's passion and fire without relying on primitive imagery and barbaric practices.

Chayei Sarah

Princess of Her People and the Entire World[1]

Universal Message

God changed both Abraham and Sarah's names: from Abram to Abraham, and from Sarai to Sarah. What is the significance of this name change? The Talmud in *Berachot* 13a explains that both changes share a common theme.

The name *Abram* means "father of Aram." At first, Abraham was only a leader of the nation of Aram, but in the end, he became a spiritual leader for the entire world. Thus, he became *Avraham – Av hamon goyim*, the father of many nations.

The name *Sarai* means "my princess." In the beginning, she was only a princess for her own people. In the end, though, she became *Sarah – "the* princess" – the princess of the entire world.

In other words, the teachings of Abraham and Sarah were transformed from a local message to a universal one. Yet the Talmud tells us that there was a fundamental difference in these name changes. One who calls Abraham by his old name has transgressed a positive commandment. No such prohibition, however, exists for using Sarah's old name. Why?

Abraham's Thought, Sarah's Torah

Rav Kook distinguished between the different approaches of these two spiritual giants. Abraham's teachings correspond to the philosophical heritage of Judaism. He arrived at belief in the Creator through his powers

---

[1] Adapted from *Ein Ayah* vol. I, p. 69.

of logic and reasoning, and used arguments and proofs to convince the people of his time. As Maimonides (Laws of Idolatry 1:9, 13) wrote, "The people would gather around him and question him about his words, and he would explain to each one according to his capabilities, until he returned him to the way of truth."

The Torah of Sarah, on the other hand, is more closely aligned with good deeds, proper customs, and practical *mitzvot*. Thus, the Midrash (*Bereishit Rabbah* 60:15) emphasizes the physical signs of her service of God – a cloud hovering at the entrance to the tent, a blessing in the dough, and a lamp burning from one Sabbath eve to the next.

The philosophical content of Judaism is universal in nature. Abraham's ideals – monotheism, *chesed*, helping others – are relevant to all peoples. It is important that Abraham be recognized as a world figure in order to stress the universal nature of his teachings. He must be called *Abraham*, "the father of many nations."

Practical *mitzvot*, on the other hand, serve to strengthen and consolidate the national character of the Jewish people. From Sarah, we inherited the sanctity of deed. These actions help develop the unique holiness of the Jewish people, which is required for the moral advancement of all nations. In this way, Sarah's Torah of practical deeds encompasses both the national and universal spheres. Sarah, while "the princess" of the world, still remained "my princess," the princess of her people.

Chayei Sarah

Burial in the Double Cave[1]

According to tradition, Sarah was not the first person to be buried in the *Machpelah* cave in Hebron; already buried there were Adam and Eve. Subsequently three more couples joined them: Abraham and Sarah, Isaac and Rebecca, Jacob and Leah.

Why was this burial cave called *Machpelah*? *Machpelah* means "doubled." The Talmud in *Eiruvin* 53a explains that it is a double cave, containing two rooms or two floors. The Talmud tells of one scholar who risked entering the cave. He found the *Avot* (the Patriarchs and Matriarchs) in one room, and Adam and Eve in the second.

What is the significance of the *Machpelah* cave having two rooms? In general, what is the function of burial?

Two Paths

There are two paths of spiritual growth and enlightenment, each with its own advantages. The first path utilizes our natural faculties of reasoning and analysis. When functioning properly, our powers of intellect can achieve wonderful results. They enable us to acquire precious character traits, and serve God through an inner awareness.

However, the mind is bound to and influenced by the body. When the body is drawn by cravings for physical pleasures, the mind also loses its direction. These physical desires can distort our perceptions and warp our reasoning, and we are left without guidance to enlightened living.

---

[1] Adapted from *Midbar Shur*, pp. 259–262.

Therefore, God created a second method for spiritual growth: the Torah. The Torah is independent of the physical body, unaffected by its proclivities and desires. It is an immutable guide to the path of integrity and holiness. Certainly the powers of the human mind can never provide for the same level of sanctity as that attained through the God-given instructions of the Torah and its *mitzvot*.

Yet, the path of the human intellect retains a special advantage. The observance of *mitzvot*, while very lofty, has no direct influence on the body itself. The body is still attracted to physical desires, and remains at odds with the Torah's spiritual goals.

Optimally, the two methods should be combined. If performance of *mitzvot* can awaken the heart and inspire the mind, a harmony is established between our physical actions and our inner awareness. Since the mental faculties are part of our basic nature, when the mind connects with the Torah, the physical side also becomes integrated with the precepts of the Torah. This refinement of the body could not have occurred without combining together the Torah with our natural powers of intellect and reason.

Death and Burial

After the sin of Adam, death was decreed upon humanity. This was not an arbitrary punishment. The purpose of death is to separate body and soul, enabling both to be repaired and refined. The soul, unburdened with the body's physical desires, is mended and refined in the World of Souls.

The body also requires spiritual correction. It too was formed in God's image, and has tremendous spiritual power when it complements the holiness of the soul. While the soul is corrected in the World of Souls, the body is repaired through burial, as it returns to its original elements.

Refining the Body

What does this have to do with the *Machpelah* cave? Burial in the double cave is a metaphor for the two methods by which the body is refined and elevated.

The first method, utilizing human intelligence and reason, is exemplified by Adam and Eve. The first man and woman were created with the highest level of pristine talents and powers. With their robust mental faculties, Adam and Eve embody the use of native intellect and reasoning for spiritual advance.

The Patriarchs and Matriarchs, on the other hand, were the origin of the Jewish people, paving the way for the Torah's revelation at Sinai. They represent the second spiritual guide, that of the Torah.

The double burial cave of *Machpelah* combined together these two paths. One room contained Adam and Eve, the pinnacle of natural intellectual capability. The second room hosted the *Avot*, the progenitors of the Torah. The name of the city, Hebron, comes from the word *hibur* ("connection"), hinting at the combination of both paths of elevating the body.

Chayei Sarah

Isaac's Afternoon Prayer[1]

> Isaac went out to meditate (*lasu'ach*) in the field toward evening. (Gen. 24:63)

The meaning of the word *lasuach* is unclear, and is the subject of a dispute among the Biblical commentators. The Rashbam[2] wrote that it comes from the word *si'ach*, meaning "plant." According to this interpretation, Isaac went to oversee his orchards and fields. His grandfather Rashi,[3] however, explained that *lasu'ach* comes from the word *sichah*, meaning "speech." Isaac went to meditate in the field, thus establishing the afternoon prayer.

Why does the Torah not use the usual Hebrew word for prayer? And is there a special significance to the fact that Isaac meditated in the afternoon?

The Soul's Inner Prayer

Rav Kook often expanded concepts beyond the way they are usually understood. Thus, when describing the phenomenon of prayer, he made a startling observation: "*The soul is always praying. It constantly seeks to fly away to its Beloved.*"

This is certainly an original insight into the essence of prayer. But what about the act of prayer that we are familiar with? According to Rav Kook, what we call "prayer" is only an external expression of this inner

---

[1] Adapted from *Ein Ayah* vol. I, p. 109.
[2] Rabbi Samuel ben Meir, twelfth-century Bible commentator and Talmudist.
[3] Rabbi Shlomo Yitzchaki (1040–1105).

prayer of the soul. In order to truly pray, we must be aware of the constant yearnings of the soul.

The word *lasu'ach* sheds a unique light on the concept of prayer. By using a word that also means "plant," the Torah is associating the activity of prayer to the natural growth of plants and trees. Through prayer, the soul flowers with new strength; it branches out naturally with inner emotions. These are the natural effects of prayer, just as a tree naturally flowers and sends forth branches.

Why was Isaac's meditative prayer said in the afternoon? The hour that is particularly suitable for spiritual growth is the late afternoon, at the end of the working day. At this time of the day, we are able to put aside our mundane worries and concerns, and concentrate on our spiritual aspirations. Then the soul is free to elevate itself and blossom.

Toldot

Harnessing the Power of Esau[1]

We know little about the birth of most Biblical personalities. Yet, the Torah describes in detail the birth of Jacob and Esau and their respective naming.

> The first one came out reddish, hairy all over like a fur coat. They named him Esau. Then his brother came out, his hand grasping Esau's heel. He named him Jacob. (Gen. 25:25–26)

The name Esau means *made* or *completed*. From day one, Esau was full of strength and energy. The name Jacob (*Ya'akov*) refers to the fact that he was holding on to Esau's heel (*ekev*). Later on, Jacob is named a second time; here too, his name refers to his relationship with his brother Esau. The night before meeting up with Esau, he struggles with a mysterious stranger. This stranger – according to some, Esau's guardian angel – informs him:

> Your name will no longer be said to be Jacob, but Israel. You have struggled with angels and men, and you have prevailed. (Gen. 32:29)

What is the inner meaning of Jacob's names? What is the significance of his grasping on to Esau's heel? Why does he have two names?

---

[1] Adapted from *Ein Ayah* vol. I, p. 68.

Restraint versus Control

Just as there are both positive and negative forces in the world, so too, every person is a composite of positive and negative traits. We need these negative forces, however; without their power and vitality, many goals and aspirations would lack the energy necessary to be realized.

Esau represents the raw, base forces in the world. His reddish complexion indicated the violent and brutal nature of his personality. Jacob did not prevent Esau from coming into the world; after all, the world needs Esau and his raw power. Rather, Jacob held on to Esau's heel, holding him back. The name *Jacob* refers to this aspect of restraint, reining in the fierce forces.

Ultimately, however, our goal is not to simply hold back these negative forces. We aspire to gain control over them and utilize them, like a hydroelectric dam that harnesses the vast energy of a raging waterfall for the production of electricity. For example, the Talmud tells us that a person with blood-thirsty tendencies should become a *shochet* (ritual slaughterer) or a *mohel*, thus sublimating his violent nature for noble purposes. This higher aspiration is represented by Jacob's second name, *Israel*, which comes from the root-word *sar*, meaning "to rule."

The name *Jacob* is appropriate when the Jews are in the Diaspora. There, they serve as a moral conscience to partially restrict the wild and violent forces in the world. But when redeemed and living in their own land, the Jewish people are able to attain the higher level of *Israel*. Then they have the opportunity to demonstrate how a nation may utilize its material capabilities for constructive and ethical goals.

Jacob's Hand on Esau's Heel[1]

The account of Jacob stealing blessings from his father raises many perplexing questions. How could Isaac not be aware of the true nature of his twin sons? Why did he insist on blessing his apparently wicked son Esau? And why was it necessary for Jacob to get the blessings that his father intended for his brother?

The Rights of the First-Born

We need to first analyze the concept of *bechorah*, the right of the first-born. Why should the family inheritance be determined by order of birth, without taking into account the relative merits of the heirs? The Talmud in *Baba Batra* 133b discusses this issue, advising against switching the inheritance, even if the first-born is wicked and his sibling is righteous. Why? The commentators explain that we should not make decisions based on the current situation; in the future, worthy children may come from the evil son.

Still, why not give preference to the son whom we know to be righteous and will use the inheritance for proper objectives? Why let the evil son utilize this wealth for corrupt purposes, just because of a possibility that he may have upright children?

Segulah Selection

Twelfth-century philosopher Rabbi Yehudah HaLevi explained the concept of *segulah* – how a particular people is chosen by God. The

---

[1] Adapted from *Midbar Shur*, pp. 265–272.

process of divine selection is beyond human understanding and occurs in a hidden manner.[2] The kernel of light and good is concealed in an enveloping darkness, just as the spiritual greatness of Abraham could not be foreseen in the wickedness of his idolatrous father Terach. Only in the time of Jacob was the *segulah* nature of his children revealed to all. At that time it became apparent that his entire family was a "seed blessed by God."

Why should this kernel of future good be concealed in evil and wicked people? Even negative character traits have their place in the world. Ultimately, they too will serve the greater good. In order to perfect righteous traits and straight paths, these bad traits and convoluted ways must be elevated. This occurs when the righteous are able to utilize them for their true purpose.

Isaac's Love for Esau

The process of divine selection must be free to progress according to God's design, without human intervention. Only God knows the path by which the pure will come forth out of the impure. Therefore, we should not disrupt the inheritance of the first-born according to what seems to us reasonable and logical.

Isaac felt that, despite Jacob's obvious spiritual and moral superiority, it was not up to him to decide who will carry on Abraham's spiritual legacy. Isaac assumed that the separating of the *segulah* was not yet complete. Perhaps from the cruel and brutal traits of Esau, his first-born son, would come an even greater heir, capable of utilizing and elevating those destructive traits.

Furthermore, Isaac knew that the world may be mended in different ways. It could be gently uplifted, as people stream from every corner of the earth to learn Israel's teachings of kindness and truth. Or the world could be rectified through the complete destruction of those

---

[2] *The Kuzari*, Part I, par. 95.

corrupt and violent elements from which no good will come (as we see in the obligation to destroy Amalek and the nations of Canaan). Jacob, the gentle scholar in the tents of Torah, did not possess the temperament necessary to wage wars and fight against cruel and vicious opponents. How could the *segulah* of Israel come from him? True, Jacob was righteous – but many righteous individuals lived before him whose progeny did not continue in their path.

Jacob appeared to totally lack these necessary traits of dominance and power. And Esau was anyway the firstborn, a sign that he was chosen by God. Isaac valued Esau's potential to forcibly correct the entire world. The Torah thus explains Isaac's love of his firstborn son: "Isaac loved Esau, for his hunt was in his mouth" (Gen. 25:28). Isaac appreciated Esau's ability to hunt and dominate the beasts, the trait needed to dominate bestial peoples.

The Torah contrasts the different ways in which Isaac and Rebecca loved their sons. On the one hand, it says, "Isaac will love Esau" (with the conversive *Vav* switching it to the past tense). Isaac valued Esau's future, his progeny, not his present state, that even Isaac could see was savage and violent. But for Rebecca, the Torah uses the present tense: "Rebecca loves Jacob." She loved and appreciated Jacob's current state of righteousness.

Esau under Jacob's Hand

In fact, Jacob did have a connection to his brother's traits of cruelty, but these traits were not an integral part of his soul. This is the significance of Jacob's hand holding on to Esau's heel when they were born. The heel represents instinctive nature (the Hebrew words for "foot" and "habit," *regel* and *hergel*, share the same root), while the hand indicates willed and planned action. Jacob had a hold onto Esau's heel, i.e., a connection to those savage traits that were an intrinsic part of Esau's nature. For Jacob, however, these traits were not wild and undisciplined, but under the control of his hand and mind.[3]

Jacob will be capable of performing the same brutal actions as Esau, albeit out of necessity and judicious choice. He will be distressed by the need to utilize his brother's characteristics, but will recognize their usefulness in achieving the final goal.

Acquiring Esau's Blessings

Now we understand why Isaac chose to bless Esau. But why did Jacob need to take his brother's blessing?

Jacob realized that he was the true spiritual heir, and he needed the blessings of rule and sovereignty – "nations will serve you," "you will be a like a lord over your brother." But it was important that his father think that fierce Esau was the object of the blessing. These blessings require strength and leadership. They helped Jacob utilize Esau's traits when necessary, even though they were not part of his inner nature. Therefore, his mother clothed him in Esau's garments. For the sake of the blessings of stable rule and firm reign, Jacob's outer appearance needed to be like that of ruthless Esau.

When Jacob announced to his father, "I am Esau your first-born," he did not truly lie. Jacob had truly acquired his brother's traits. He had become Esau, only in a better fashion. Most certainly, his father had spoken to him in the past about the need to acquire these negative traits for the sake of serving God. Jacob could now proudly report to his father, "I have done as you have requested." And afterwards, Isaac was able to

---

[3] We find a similar idea with regard to King David. The Midrash states that Samuel was reluctant to anoint David as king after he saw David's ruddy complexion. Samuel feared this was a sign that David would spill blood like the reddish Esau. But God responded, "He has beautiful eyes." Esau killed for his own pleasure, but David will kill according to the dictates of the Sanhedrin (the high court), which is called the "eyes of the people."

'I have eaten of all." All that I desired to taste, I have found in *'Yes, he shall be blessed."*

Vayeitzei

The Prayers of the *Avot*[1]

According to the Talmud (*Berachot* 26b), the *Avot* (forefathers) instituted the three daily prayers:

- Abraham – *Shacharit*, the morning prayer.
- Isaac – *Minchah*, the afternoon prayer.
- Jacob – *Ma'ariv*, the evening prayer.

Is there an inner connection between these prayers and their founders? Rav Kook wrote that each of these three prayers has its own special nature. This nature is a function of both the character of that time of day, and the pervading spirit of the righteous *tzaddik* who would pray at that time.

The Morning Stand

Abraham, the first Jew, established the first prayer of the day upon rising from sleep. He would pray at daybreak, standing before God:

> Abraham rose early in the morning, [returning] to
> the place where he had stood before God.
> (Gen. 19:27)

Why does the Torah call attention to the fact that Abraham would stand as he prayed? This position indicates that the function of this

---

[1] Adapted from *Ein Ayah* vol. I, p. 109, Olat Re'iyah vol. I, p. 409.

morning prayer is to make a spiritual stand. We need inner fortitude to maintain the ethical level that we have struggled to attain. The constant pressures and conflicts of day-to-day life can chip away at our spiritual foundation. To counter these negative influences, the medium of prayer can help us, by etching holy thoughts and sublime images deeply into the heart. Such a prayer at the start of the day helps protect us from the pitfalls of worldly temptations throughout the day.

This function of prayer – securing a solid ethical foothold in the soul – is reflected in the name *Amidah* ("standing prayer"). It is particularly appropriate that Abraham, who successfully withstood ten trials and tenaciously overcame all who fought against his path of truth, established the "standing" prayer of the morning.

Flowering of the Soul in the Afternoon

The second prayer, initiated by Isaac, is recited in the afternoon. This is the hour when the temporal activities of the day are finished, and we are able to clear our minds from the distractions of the world. The soul is free to express its true essence, unleashing innate feelings of holiness, pure love and awe of God.

The Torah characterizes Isaac's afternoon prayer as *sichah* (meditation): "Isaac went out to meditate in the field towards evening" (Gen. 24:64). The word *sichah* also refers to plants and bushes (*sichim*), for it expresses the spontaneous flowering of life force. This is a fitting metaphor for the afternoon prayer, when the soul is able to naturally grow and flourish.[2]

Why was it Isaac who established this prayer? Isaac exemplified the attribute of Justice (*midat hadin*), so he founded the soul's natural prayer of the afternoon. The exacting measure of law is applied to situations where one has deviated from the normal and accepted path.

---

[2] See also *Chayei Sarah*: Isaac's Afternoon Prayer.

Spontaneous Evening Revelation

And what distinguishes *Ma'ariv*, the evening prayer? Leaving his parents' home, Jacob stopped for the night in Beth-El. There he dreamed of ascending and descending angels and divine promises. Jacob awoke the following morning awestruck; he had not been aware of holiness of his encampment.

> He chanced upon the place and stayed overnight,
> for it became suddenly night. (Gen. 28:11)

The "chance meeting" – a spiritual experience beyond the level to which the soul is accustomed – that is the special quality of the evening prayer. The night is a time of quiet solitude. It is a time especially receptive to extraordinary elevations of the soul, including prophecy and levels close to it.

Unlike the other two prayers, the evening prayer is not obligatory. This does not reflect a lack of importance; on the contrary, the essence of the evening prayer is an exceptionally uplifting experience. Precisely because of its sublime nature, this prayer must not be encumbered by any aspect of rote obligation. It needs to flow spontaneously from the heart. The voluntary nature of the evening prayer is a continuation of Jacob's unexpected spiritual revelation that night in Beth-El.

Vayeitzei

The Blessing of a Scholar's Presence[1]

After working at Laban's ranch for 14 years, Jacob was anxious to return home, to the Land of Israel. Laban, however, was not eager to let his nephew go. "I have observed the signs," he told Jacob, "and God has blessed me for your sake" (Gen. 30:27).

The Talmud (*Berachot* 42a) points out that Laban's good fortune was not due only to Jacob's industriousness and hard work. "*Blessing comes in the wake of a Torah scholar,*" the Sages taught. The very presence of a saintly scholar brings with it blessings of success and wealth.

Yet, this phenomenon seems unfair. Why should a person be blessed just because he was in the proximity of a Torah scholar?

The Influence of a *Tzaddik*

To answer this question, we must understand the nature of a *tzaddik* and his profound impact on those around him. The presence of a Torah scholar will inspire even a morally corrupt individual to limit his destructive acts. As a result of this positive influence, material benefits will not be abused, and divine blessings will be utilized appropriately. Such an individual, by virtue of a refining influence, has become an appropriate recipient for God's blessings.

In addition to the case of Laban and Jacob, the Talmud notes a second example of "Blessing coming in the wake of a Torah scholar." The Torah relates that the prosperity of the Egyptian officer Potiphar was in Joseph's merit (Gen. 39:5). In some aspects, this case is more remarkable.

---

[1] Adapted from *Ein Ayah* vol. II, pp. 187–8.

Unlike Laban, Potiphar was not even aware of the source of his good fortune. Nonetheless, Joseph's presence helped raise the ethical level of the Egyptian's household, making it more suitable to receive God's blessings.

Vayishlach

Reliance on Miracles[1]

Miracles were no novelty for Rabbi Zeira. The Talmud in *Baba Metzia* 85a relates that the third-century scholar fasted for a hundred days in order to protect himself from the fires of hell. But Rabbi Zeira was not content with theoretical preparations. Once a month he would test himself by sitting down in a burning furnace, to see if he would feel the heat. He didn't. (Once his clothes were singed, but that story is for another time.)

Yet, on very windy days, Rabbi Zeira was careful not to walk among the palm-trees, lest a strong wind should knock a tree over. His caution in orchards seems bizarre. Why should a man who can sit unharmed in a burning furnace be concerned about the possibility of a falling tree?

The Talmud (*Shabbat* 32a) counsels the following attitude towards miracles:

> One should never put himself in a dangerous situation and say, "A miracle will save me." Perhaps the miracle will not come. And even if a miracle occurs, one's merits are reduced.

The Sages learned that one should not rely on miracles from Jacob. When Jacob returned home after twenty years in Laban's house, he greatly feared meeting his brother Esau. He prayed to God, "I am unworthy of all the kindness and faith that You have shown me" (Gen. 32:11). The Sages explained Jacob's prayer in this way: "I am unworthy *due*

---

[1] Adapted from *Ein Ayah* vol. III, pp. 166–168.

to all the kindness and faith that You have shown me." Your miracles and intervention have detracted from my merits.

We need to examine this concept. What is so wrong with relying on miracles? Does it not show greater faith? And why should miracles come at the expense of one's spiritual accomplishments?

The Function of Skepticism

Skepticism is a natural, healthy trait. Miracles can have a positive moral influence, but they also have a downside. Reliance on miracles can lead to a weakened or even warped sense of reality.

At certain times in history, God disrupted natural law in order to increase faith and knowledge. However, this intervention in nature was always limited as much as possible, in order that we should not belittle the importance of personal effort and initiative. This is where skepticism fulfills its purpose. Our natural inclination to doubt the occurrence of miracles helps offset these negative side effects, keeping us within the framework of the naturally-ordered world, which is the greatest good that God continually bestows to us. It is preferable that we do not rely on divine intervention, but rather say, "Perhaps a miracle will not occur."

Miracles and Nature

Ultimately, both miracles and natural events are the work of God. So how do they differ? A miracle occurs when we are unable to succeed through our own efforts. By its very nature, a miracle indicates humanity's limitations, even helplessness. When miracles occur, we are passive, on the receiving end.

Natural events are also the work of God, but they are achieved through our skill, initiative, and effort. When we are active, we spiritually advance ourselves by virtue of our actions. Our *zechuyot* (merits) are the result of the positive, ethical deeds that we have performed. We should strive for an active life of giving, not a passive one of receiving. Such an engaged, enterprising life better fulfills God's will – the attainment of the highest level of perfection for His creations.

Jacob "used up" merits when he required God's intervention to protect him from Laban and Esau. He admitted to God, "I am unworthy due to all the kindness and faith that You have shown me." But Jacob later regained spiritual greatness through his active struggle against the mysterious angel. "For you have struggled with angels and men, and have overcome them" (Gen. 32:29).

Vayishlach

Jacob Arrived Whole[1]

Having survived the trickery of his uncle Laban and the enmity of his brother Esau, Jacob finally returned to his homeland: "Jacob arrived whole (*shalem*) to the city of Shechem in the land of Canaan" (Gen. 33:18).

In what way was Jacob *shalem*? The Talmud (*Shabbat* 33b) explains that he was "*whole in body, whole in money, whole in his Torah knowledge.*"

According to the medieval commentator Rashi, these three areas are directly related to Jacob's previous ordeals. Physically – Jacob healed from the lameness the stranger had afflicted upon him in their mysterious struggle at Peniel. Financially – he did not lack money, despite the expensive gifts he had offered this brother Esau. And spiritually – he had not forgotten his Torah learning, despite the long years of intensive labor at Laban's house.

Jacob's Holistic Perspective

In truth, Jacob's wholeness was not to be found in any quantitative accomplishments. It could not be measured by how fast he could run, by the number of sheep he owned, or by the number of scholarly discussions he had memorized. Rather, Jacob's wholeness was in his holistic approach towards these diverse spheres.

People think that the pursuit of excellence in one field entails neglecting other areas. A person who seeks perfect health and physical strength will come to the realization that one needs money to attain this goal. But the pursuit of wealth can become such an all-absorbing goal that

---

[1] Adapted from *Ein Ayah* vol. III, p. 209.

it may come at the expense of one's original objective – good health. Ironically, the anxiety to acquire wealth can end up ruining one's health.

It is clear that both good health and financial security help provide the quietude needed to refine character traits and attain intellectual accomplishments. However, these different areas, instead of complementing one another, often compete with each other. We suffer spiritually when our desire to strengthen the body and cultivate social living (which requires certain financial means) are not understood in their overall context.

The perfection of Jacob – the *ish tam,* "the complete man" (Gen. 25:27) – was in his ability to live in a way that no single pursuit of excellence, whether spiritual or material, needed to contradict or detract from other personal goals. On the contrary, when they are understood properly, each aim complements and strengthens the others.

This is the profound message of the Talmudic statement. Jacob was whole in body and wealth, and from both of these together, he found the inner resources to be whole in Torah. Jacob exemplified the trait of *emet,* truth – "Give truth to Jacob" (Micah 7:20). He demonstrated how, in their inner depths, all accomplishments are united together; all reflect different facets of the same inner truth.

Vayishlach

Reuben's Sin[1]

In an enigmatic passage after the death of Rachel, the Torah harshly condemns Reuben: "Reuben went and lay down with Bilhah, his father's concubine" (Gen. 35:22).

According to Talmudic tradition, what actually transpired was far less shocking. Reuben was in fact protesting his mother's honor and place in the family. When Rachel was alive, Jacob kept his bed in Rachel's tent. After she died, Jacob moved his bed to the tent of Rachel's handmaid, Bilhah.

But Reuben, Leah's first-born, was upset. Perhaps his aunt Rachel could displace his mother as Jacob's primary wife; after all, Rachel had been the woman that Jacob intended to marry. But surely Rachel's handmaid held a lower position in the household than his mother Leah! So Reuben removed his father's bed from Bilhah's tent and placed it in the tent of his own mother, Leah.

The Talmud in *Shabbat* 55b explains that we should not think that Reuben literally slept with Bilhah; rather, he "disturbed Bilhah's sleeping arrangements." The Sages could not accept the idea that one of Jacob's sons was guilty of incest. Furthermore, the verse immediately continues, "Jacob had twelve sons." Surely we know this already! The Torah is emphasizing that, even after this disruption in Jacob's household, all twelve were still sons of the *tzaddik* Jacob; all twelve were equally righteous.

---

[1] Adapted from *Ein Ayah* vol. IV, pp. 43–44.

Still, we need to understand. If the incident in Jacob's house occurred the way the Sages described, why did the Torah not write it that way? Why does the Torah "mislead" us into thinking that Reuben had performed such a serious offense?

Two Perspectives on One Event

Rav Kook wrote that the Torah describes events in a particular way so that they will make a certain desired impression. Every detail in the Torah is carefully measured, so that the narrative will suitably affect us.

Sometimes a story, when written in a straightforward fashion, cannot be properly appreciated by those reading it, especially if they are greatly removed from the incident in time and place. From afar, we may not be properly sensitive to the moral outrage that took place. In such instances, divine wisdom dictates the precise fashion with which to clothe the story, in order that it should make the appropriate impression on the reader.

Together, the two Torahs, the Oral and the Written, paint a complete picture of what occurred. The Written Torah gives a simpler account, providing the emotional impact to which we are accustomed from our youth. The Oral Torah adds to the written account a more insightful understanding that is acquired through careful examination.

The activities of the Patriarchs deeply influenced, and continue to influence, the Jewish people. The spirit of Jacob's house lives with us to this day; the light of his family will forever illuminate our hearts. Any dimming of that light, any inner strife or moral imperfection, will also be felt by us. In fact, even more so: any minor eclipse of light from that time will reach us from afar as a serious and deeply disturbing darkness.

For us, the true extent of Reuben's offense – upsetting the delicate balance in his father's household and eroding Jacob's authority in his own home – is as if Reuben had actually committed incest with Bilhah. The literal account of the written Torah corresponds to our natural feelings of hurt and indignation.

But if we wish to accurately evaluate this offense in terms of Reuben's moral level, we must return to the Talmudic version of this event. Here the Midrashic insight reveals the event as it actually occurred: Reuben disturbed the sleeping arrangements in his father's house, in order to protect his mother's honor.

The Conflict between Joseph and Judah[1]

Having overcome the difficult challenges posed by Esau and Laban, Jacob looked forward to more peaceful times. But intense resentment among his sons shattered these wishful hopes, and led to the sale of his favorite son, Joseph, as a slave in Egypt.

How could the brothers sell Joseph, and even consider killing him? Is it possible that they were motivated by petty jealousy over a colorful coat?

Also, is there a connection between the story of Joseph and the holiday that falls out this time of the year – Chanukah?

Integration versus Separation

The root of the disagreement among the brothers was in fact ideological. There were two schools of thought in Jacob's family, one championed by Joseph, the other by Judah. Joseph stressed the mission of the Jewish people as "a light unto the nations." In order to fulfill this goal, Joseph felt that we must interact with the nations of the world and expose them to the monotheistic teachings of Judaism.

Judah, on the other hand, was concerned about the negative influences when intermingling with pagan cultures. He emphasized the separate sanctity of the Jewish people, "a nation that dwells alone" (Num. 23:9). Judah feared that Joseph's philosophy of openness and integration would endanger the future of the Jewish people. But how to safely neutralize this threat?

---

[1] Adapted from *Shemuot HaRe'iyah* 10, 5630 (1929).

Simon and Levy, who had already fought against assimilation when they decimated the city of Shechem for kidnapping Dina, planned to simply kill Joseph. Judah objected, "What profit is there if we kill our brother?" (Gen. 37:26). The true danger is not Joseph, but his school of thought. Let us put his theories to the test. We will sell Joseph to the Ishmaelites, and let him assimilate among the nations. Then all will see where his ideas lead to.

The Tabernacle and the Temple

These conflicting views are reflected by the contrast between the *Mishkan* (Tabernacle) in Shiloh and the Temple in Jerusalem. In Shiloh, offerings could be eaten outside the walls, as long as the city of Shiloh was in sight. Temple offerings, on the other hand, could only be eaten within the Temple walls. Why this difference?

For Joseph, the primary mission was to publicly demonstrate the sanctity of Israel and educate the nations. Thus, the holiness of the Shiloh Tabernacle – in Joseph's portion – spread beyond its walls. The Temple in Jerusalem, however, was located in the land of Judah and followed his view. It is necessary to build walls and restrict the dissemination of Torah, in order to protect the sanctity of the Jewish people.

The Hellenists versus the Hasmonean Priests

The holiday of Chanukah commemorates a similar struggle, the conflict between those seeking integration with the rest of the world, and those striving to preserve the distinct sanctity of the Jewish people. The Hellenistic Jews demanded adoption of Greek customs, the prevalent culture of the day. They claimed to be following Joseph's path of openness. Their slogan was, "Write on the ox horn that you have no share in the God of Israel" (*Vayikra Rabbah* 13:5). Why an ox horn? This is an allusion to Joseph, who was compared to a powerful ox (Deut. 33:17).

The Hellenists called for the people to continue in Joseph's path of openness and assimilation.

However, they ignored Joseph's underlying goal, to educate the nations. The Hellenists "broke down the walls of my towers." They breached the walls protecting Jerusalem and the Temple Mount, and allowed the idolatrous nations to defile the holy Temple.

The Hasmonean priests, *kohanim* from the tribe of Levy, naturally followed the path of Judah and Levy, that of separation. As *kohanim*, they benefited from the special sanctity of priesthood separating them from the rest of the Jewish people. The ultimate victory for the Hasmoneans was the discovery of a ritually clean jar of oil, with the seal of the High Priest intact. This jar of pure oil was a sign that the inner sanctity of Israel remained undefiled by pagan contact.

In the future, the nations will recognize the necessity for the walls of the House of Jacob that separate the Jewish people from the other nations. The nations will accept upon themselves the *mitzvot* of the Torah, while the entire Jewish people will be elevated to the level of *kohanim*. Then the Jewish people will relate to the nations of the world in a fashion analogous to the current connection of *kohanim* to the rest of the Jewish people.

Vayeishev

The Nature of Exile[1]

> They took Joseph and threw him into the pit. The
> pit was empty, without water in it. (Gen. 37:24)

When the brothers threw Joseph into the pit, the exile began – not just Joseph's personal exile from his father's house and the Land of Israel. From that dark, empty pit, began the exile of the entire Jewish people to Egypt.

Joseph's pit is a metaphor for *Galut*, for each exile of the Jewish people from their land.

Three Types of Pits

There are, of course, different kinds of pits. There are pits filled with water, wells that provide life to those living near them. One must be careful not to fall in and drown, but these are productive, useful pits.

Then there are empty pits. They serve no purpose, and are dangerous. Nonetheless, even empty pits have a positive side to them. With effort and skill, they may be filled with water and transformed into useful pits.

And there is a third type of pit. The Talmud (*Shabbat* 22a) quotes Rabbi Tanchum that Joseph's pit belonged to this third category. It was empty of water, but it contained other things – snakes and scorpions. Such a pit is of no use – neither actual nor potential – for humans.

---

[1] Adapted from *Ein Ayah* vol. II, pp. 67–8.

Some mistake the pit of Exile for a well of water. Yes, one must be careful not to drown in it; but overall, they claim, it is a positive experience. If Jews are careful to act in a manner that will not arouse anti-Semitism, they can dwell comfortably in their foreign homes.

But the true nature of Exile is like Joseph's pit, full of snakes and scorpions. It is a dangerous and deadly place for the Jewish people. Such a pit has only one redeeming quality, intrinsic to its very nature: it will never mislead the Jews into mistaking it for their permanent homeland.

Snakes and Scorpions

Rabbi Tanchum spoke of a pit containing snakes and scorpions. What is the difference between these two dangerous animals? A snake bites with its head, while a scorpion stings with its tail. The snakebite is a planned and intentional act, executed by the directives of the snake's brain. A scorpion stings from its tail instinctively, without thought.

Exile is accompanied by both of these "blessings." There are times of intentional and malevolent persecution, such as those perpetrated by the Crusaders, Chmielnicki's Cossacks, Nazi Germany, and other sinister snakes of history. These are dark hours for the Jewish people, but they are also times of shining heroism and self-sacrifice.

Worse than these intentional snakebites are the continual, unintentional scorpion stings which are an intrinsic part of Exile. Cultural dissonance, intermarriage, and assimilation take their slow, unintended toll on the Jewish people and their connection to the Torah.

The afflictions of Exile are by heavenly decree, lest we confuse a temporary resting place in the Diaspora for a permanent home for the Jewish people. The only true remedy for these snakebites and scorpion-stings is to rescue the Jews from the pit, and restore them to their proper homeland.

Interpreting Dreams[1]

The Sages made a remarkable claim regarding dreams and their interpretation: *"Dreams are fulfilled according to the interpretation"* (*Berachot* 55b). The interpreter has a key function in the realization of a dream: his analysis can determine how the dream will come to pass. The Talmud substantiated this statement with the words of the chief wine-butler: "Just as he interpreted, so [my dream] came to be" (Gen. 41:13).

Do dreams foretell the future? Does the interpreter really have the power to determine the meaning of a dream and alter the future accordingly?

The Purpose of Dreams

Clearly, not all of our dreams are prophetic. Originally, in humanity's pristine state, every dream was a true dream. But with the fall of Adam, mankind left the path of integrity. Our minds became filled with wanton desires and pointless thoughts, and our dreams became more chaff than truth.

Why did God give us the ability to dream? A true dream is a wake-up call, warning us to correct our life's direction. Our eyes are opened to a vivid vision of our future, should we not take heed to mend our ways.

To properly understand the function of dreams, we must first delve into the inner workings of divine providence in the world. How are we punished or rewarded in accordance to our actions?

---

[1] Adapted from *Midbar Shur*, pp. 222–227.

The *Zohar* (*Bo* 33a) gives the following explanation for the mechanics of providence. The soul has an inner quality that naturally brings about those situations and events that correspond to our moral level. Should we change our ways, this inner quality will reflect that change, and will lead us towards a different set of circumstances.

Dreams are part of this system of providence. They are one of the methods utilized by the soul's inner quality to bring about the appropriate outcome.

The Function of the Interpreter

But the true power of a dream is only realized once it has been interpreted. The interpretation intensifies the dream's impact. As the Sages taught, "A dream not interpreted is like a letter left unread" (*Berachot* 55b). When a dream is explained, its images become more intense and vivid. The impact on the soul is stronger, and the dreamer is more primed for the consequential outcome.

Of course, the interpreter must be insightful and perceptive. He needs to penetrate the inner message of the dream and detect the potential influences of the soul's inner qualities that are reflected in the dream.

Multiple Messages

All souls contain a mixture of good and bad traits. A dream is the nascent development of the soul's hidden traits, as they are beginning to be realized. A single dream may contain multiple meanings, since it reflects contradictory qualities within the soul.

When the interpreter gives a positive interpretation to a dream, he helps develop and realize positive traits hidden in the soul of the dreamer. A negative interpretation, on the other hand, will promote negative traits. As the *Zohar* (*Miketz* 199b) admonishes:

> A good dream should be kept in mind and not forgotten, so that it will be fulfilled.... Therefore

> Joseph mentioned his dream [to his family], so that
> it would come to pass. He would always anticipate
> its fulfillment.

It is even possible to interpret multiple aspects of a dream, all of which are potentially true. Even if they are contradictory, all may still be realized. Rabbi Bena'a related that, in his days, there were 24 dream-interpreters in Jerusalem. "Once I had a dream," he said, "and I went to all of them. No two interpretations were the same, but they all came to pass" (*Berachot* 55b).

Dreams of the Nation

These concepts are also valid on the national level. Deliverance of the Jewish people often takes place through the medium of dreams. Both Joseph and Daniel achieved power and influence through the dreams of gentile rulers. The Jewish people have a hidden inner potential for greatness and leadership. As long as this quality is unrealized, it naturally tries to bring about its own fulfillment – sometimes, by way of dreams.

When a person is brought before the Heavenly court, he is questioned, "Did you yearn for redemption?" (*Shabbat* 31a). Why is this important? By anticipating and praying for the redemption, we help develop the inner quality of the nation's soul, thus furthering its advance and the actualization of its destined mission.

Mikeitz

Joseph and the Evil Eye[1]

Rabbi Yochanan, the third century scholar, had an unusual custom. He would sometimes sit down outside the town *mikveh* (ritual bath). This way, he explained, the Jewish women will see me as they leave the bath and will have children as beautiful as me. Rabbi Yochanan's colleagues asked him: Are you not afraid of the Evil Eye?

> "I am descended from Joseph," he replied, "and the Evil Eye had no power over him."
> (Berachot 20a)

Apart from the issue of Rabbi Yochanan's beauty, this story raises some interesting questions. What is the Evil Eye? Is it just a primitive superstition? And why was Joseph, more than any other Biblical figure, immune from it?

The Talmud explains that Joseph merited protection from the Evil Eye since "his eye did not wish to benefit from that which did not belong to him." Despite Mrs. Potiphar's attempts to seduce him, Joseph remained faithful to God and his employer. Truly an act of great moral integrity – but what does this have to do with the Evil Eye?

Rav Kook explained that the Evil Eye is an example of how one soul may affect another through unseen connections between them. We are all influenced by our environment. Living among the refined and the righteous has a strong positive effect, while living among the crass and the

---

[1] Adapted from *Ein Ayah* vol. I, p. 102.

corrupt has a negative one. The Evil Eye is simply the venomous impact from malignant feelings of jealousy and envy of those around us.

A person who has hardened his inner resolve and does not allow himself to be misled from the correct path, despite outside pressures – such a person has built a "firewall" protecting his soul from external influences. The Biblical hero who most prominently demonstrated this strength of character and refusal to be led astray is Joseph. Seventeen years old, young and handsome, estranged from the protective framework of his family and culture, a slave propositioned by a powerful and attractive woman, Joseph nevertheless beat the odds and remained faithful to his ideals. Joseph determined that he would not be swayed by his surroundings, no matter how persuasive. Through his heroic stance, he merited that the Evil Eye would have no power over him and his descendants.

Vayigash

The First Exile[1]

The very first exile of the Jewish people, the exile to Egypt, began as Jacob and his family left the Land of Israel. They intended to spend a short stay in Egypt until the famine passed.

The Midrash (*Yalkut Shimoni* Hosea 528) makes a startling observation:

> Jacob should have gone down to Egypt in chains. Yet God said, "Jacob, My first-born, how could I banish him in disgrace? Rather, I will send his son to go down before him."

What did Jacob do to deserve being exiled in iron chains?

Two Purposes to Exile

We need to analyze the purpose of exile. The Jewish people have spent more years in exile than in their own land. Why was it necessary to undergo these difficult trials? Could they not be punished by other means?

In fact, the Midrash states that the Jewish people are particularly suited for exile. They are called "the daughter of exiles," since the *Avot* (forefathers) were sojourners and refugees, subjected to the whims and jealousies of local tyrants (Midrash *Eicha Petichta* 1 on Isaiah 10:30).

Exile accomplishes two goals:

1. The people of Israel were created to serve God. The nation needs a pure love of God, undiluted by materialistic goals. Clearly, people

---

[1] Adapted from *Midbar Shur*, pp. 233–241.

are more prone to become absorbed in worldly matters when affluence and prosperity are readily attainable. In order that the Jewish people should realize their true spiritual potential, God made sure that the nation would lack material success for long periods of time.

2. Exile serves to spread the belief in one God throughout the world. As the Sages wrote in *Pesachim* 87b, "The Holy One exiled Israel so that converts will join them." Similarly, we find that God explained the purpose of exile and redemption in Egypt, "so that Egypt will know that I am God" (Ex. 7:5).

The major difference between these two objectives lies in the conditions of the exile. If the purpose of exile is to avoid significant material success over a long period of time – to prepare the Jewish people for complete dedication to God and His Torah – then such an expulsion by definition must be devoid of prestige and prosperity.

If, on the other hand, the goal is to influence and uplift the nations of the world, then being honored and respected in their land of exile will not contradict the intended purpose. On the contrary, such a state of honor would promote this aim.

Jacob's Exile

Jacob had spiritually perfected himself to the extent that nothing in this world could dampen his burning love for God. His dedication was so great that he could interrupt the emotional reunion with his beloved son Joseph, after an absence of 22 years, and proclaim God's unity with the *Shema* prayer (Rashi on Gen. 46:29). Certainly, for Jacob himself, only the second goal of exile was applicable.

Jacob's descendants, however, would require the degrading aspects of exile in order to purify them and wean them from the negative influences of a materialistic lifestyle. As their father, it was fitting that Jacob be led to Egypt in iron chains. But since Jacob personally would not be adversely affected by worldly homage and wealth, he was permitted to be exiled in honor, led by his son, viceroy of Egypt.

Vayigash

The Shepherd-Philosopher[1]

Fourth-century scholar Rabbi Zeira once found his teacher Rabbi Yehudah in an unusually good mood. Realizing that it was a propitious time to ask whatever he wanted, Rabbi Zeira posed the following question: "Why is it that the goats always stride in front of the herd, to be followed by the sheep?"

Perhaps the last thing we would expect Rabbi Zeira to ask would be a mundane fact of animal husbandry. Rabbi Yehudah, however, was not fazed. Good-humoredly, he explained that this phenomenon reflects the order of creation. "It is like the creation of the universe: first there was darkness [the goats, who are usually black], and afterwards light [the white sheep]" (*Shabbat* 77b).

A treasure-trove of wisdom had opened up for Rabbi Zeira – he had the opportunity to inquire into the deepest secrets of the universe! – and instead he quizzed his master about goats and sheep?

The Shepherd-Philosopher
In fact, Rabbi Zeira's query was not so out of line. The great leaders of the Jewish people in ancient times were shepherds. As Joseph's brothers informed Pharaoh, "Like our fathers before us, we are shepherds" (Gen. 47:5). Moses and David also worked in this profession. There must be a reason that our ancestors chose to herd goats and sheep.

Shepherding is a lifestyle that allows for reflection and inner contemplation. The labor is not intensive. Unlike farming, one does not

---

[1] Adapted from *Ein Ayah* vol. IV, pp. 144–5.

need to immerse all of one's energies in physical matters. At the same time, the shepherd remains in constant contact with the real world. His reflections are sound, based on life experiences. He does not delve in artificial philosophies detached from reality. For this reason, our forefathers, the great thinkers of their time, worked as shepherds.

Development of Thought

Rabbi Zeira's observation about flocks makes a connection between the external focus of the shepherd – his goats and sheep – and his internal focus – his thoughts and ideas.

Ideas first come to us as vague thoughts, obscured by the blurry mist of our imagination. Hidden in the murky fog, however, lies a great treasure. Over time, we refine and clarify our thoughts, and from the shrouded darkness comes forth light and wisdom.

The pattern of traveling animals corresponds to the development of thought in the shepherd's mind. The image of dark goats breaking out in front of the white sheep is an apt metaphor for the inspired but hazy notions that surge forth in our thoughts. These streaks of insight are followed by a flock of clarified ideas that have been examined by our faculties of reason. In this way we develop the reasoned concepts that form the basis for our intellectual and spiritual life.

The Need for Opacity

As Rabbi Yehudah pointed out, this order is inherent to the nature of the world. The light in the universe was created out of the darkness. This phenomenon is also true on a personal level. We cannot completely dismiss the illusory aspects of our minds, for they inspire us to originality of thought. Our imagination dominates our thought processes; it is only through its fuzzy insights that we can arrive at the path of enlightened wisdom.

Vayechi

Fishy Blessings[1]

Realizing that his death was not far off, Jacob gave his grandchildren, the sons of Joseph, the following blessing:

> May [God] bless the lads, and let them carry my name, along with the name of my fathers, Abraham and Isaac. May they increase like fish in the land. (Gen. 48:16)

Yes, fish have astonishingly large families. But so do frogs and many other animals. Why were Joseph's children blessed to be like fish?

Furthermore, the phrase "increase like fish in the land" sounds like a very mixed-up metaphor. Fish do not thrive on land; they certainly do not increase there! What kind of blessing is this?

Immunity from the Evil Eye

The Talmud (*Berachot* 55b) explains that Joseph shared a special quality with fish:

> The fish in the waters are concealed by the water, and thus not susceptible to the Evil Eye. So too, the descendants of Joseph are not susceptible to the Evil Eye.

---

[1] Adapted from *Ein Ayah* vol. II, pp. 275–276.

What does it mean that Joseph was immune to the Evil Eye like the fish? We explained previously[2] that the Evil Eye is an example of hidden influences that exist between souls. An environment of jealousy and hatred can poison not only the atmosphere but also the soul against whom they are directed. This, however, is only true for weaker souls that are easily influenced. The Evil Eye can only harm those whose sense of self-worth is not fully developed, people who need to live their lives in a way that meets the approval of foreign "eyes." But if we are secure within ourselves, and our life is focused on our inner truths, then we will not be susceptible to the Evil Eye of those around us. The Evil Eye has no power over those whose robust sense of self-esteem does not let others dictate what is important and worthwhile.

Why are fish immune to the Evil Eye? Fish are not concerned with envious eyes above the water. They live in their own world below the surface, a secluded realm that determines the direction of their lives. Like the fish, Joseph remained faithful to his inner convictions, despite the external pressures and influences of his roller-coaster life. Family estrangement, a foreign land, a foreign culture, temptations, slavery and imprisonment – none of these succeeded in leading Joseph astray. Even when he needed to contend with the hardest test of all – the incredible success, wealth, and power as Egyptian viceroy – Joseph was steadfast in his beliefs and inner convictions. Joseph remained true to his own inner world, despite his active participation in a vastly different outer world. Just like a "fish in the land."

---

[2] See "*Miketz:* Joseph and the Evil Eye."

Vayechi

Jacob Did Not Die[1]

Third-century scholar Rabbi Yochanan made an astounding claim regarding Jacob:

> Rabbi Yochanan stated, "Our father Jacob did not die." Rabbi Nachman asked, "Was it in vain that they eulogized Jacob and embalmed his body and buried him?" Rabbi Yochanan responded, "I derive this from a verse: "Fear not, Jacob My servant... for I will save you from afar, and your offspring from the land of their captivity" (Jeremiah 30:10). The verse likens Jacob to his offspring: just as his offspring lives, so too, Jacob lives." (*Ta'anit* 5b)

What did Rabbi Yochanan mean that Jacob did not die? If he intended to say that Jacob's soul is still alive, that requires no verse – the souls of all righteous people are eternal. And if he meant that Jacob's body did not die, several verses explicitly state that he died.[2]

The medieval Talmudic commentary Tosafot explains that, when describing Jacob's death, the Torah only says that he "expired," not that he "died" (Gen. 50:33). We need to examine the difference between these two verbs.

---

[1] Adapted from *Midbar Shur*, pp. 242–251.
[2] For example, "Joseph's brothers realized that their father had died" (Gen. 50:15).

Also, why did Rabbi Yochanan make this claim of eternity only for Jacob, and not for Abraham and Isaac?

Two Aspects of Death

When a person dies, two things occur. First, the bodily functions (breathing, pumping of the heart, and so on) cease. This is called *geviyah* (expiring). The natural cessation of bodily functions is a sign of a virtuous, well-lived life, since an unhealthy and profligate lifestyle brings about an early demise of the body.

The second aspect of death concerns the soul. After the sin of Adam, death was decreed in order to allow the soul to purify itself from its contact with the body's physical drives and desires. Death purges the soul of those sensual influences that distance one from true closeness to God. The aspect of death that cleanses the soul is called *mitah*.

Thus, Solomon wrote that "Love is strong as death" (Song 8:6). How is love like death? Just as death purifies the soul from the body's physical wants, so too, a truly intense love for God will overwhelm any other form of desire.

The Impact of Intermediate Actions

All actions that we perform during our lifetime make a deep impression on the soul. The soul is influenced not only by our ultimate goals, but also by the intermediate actions we take to achieve those goals. Sometimes, these actions are themselves worthy means for attaining goals, and their impact on the soul is a positive one.

On other times, a specific goal is achieved via means that contradict the overall objective. This is like scaffolding that is erected when building. The scaffolding is needed to aid in the construction, but is removed once the building is complete. So too, these temporary means will be canceled after the goal is attained, and their impure influence on the soul must be purged.

Jacob's Family was Complete

Abraham, Isaac, and Jacob are called the *Avot* (forefathers), since the main objective of their lives was to father a holy nation.

Abraham and Isaac's efforts towards this goal included using means that needed to be relinquished once the objective is attained – i.e., they bore and raised Ishmael and Esau. Even though these offspring contested the true goal of the *Avot*, they were needed in order to accomplish their overall aim. Therefore, the Torah uses the word *mitah* to describe Abraham and Isaac's death. It was necessary to purge the influence of fathering and raising these non-Jewish nations on their souls, since this occupation conflicted with their soul's inner mission.

But while the souls of Abraham and Isaac required the cleansing effect of *mitah*, Jacob's "bed was complete." All of his children were included within the people of Israel. Jacob did not need to occupy himself with any transitory means; all of his efforts were eternal, in accordance with God's design for His world. Therefore the verse says, "For I, God, have not changed; and you, the children of Jacob, are not consumed" (Malachi 3:6). The eternal quality of the Jewish people is particularly related to Jacob, the forefather who "did not die."

In certain respects, Jacob did die, but this was only in personal matters, due to the baseness of the physical world and its negative influence upon the human soul. That was not the true essence of Jacob's soul. When the Torah describes Jacob's passing, it does so in terms of his life's goal, as the father of the Jewish people. The Torah does not use the word "death," since there was no need to purge his soul of its ties to its worldly occupations.

This explains why we do not find in the Torah that Jacob's sons eulogized their father. Only the Egyptians did so – "A profound mourning for Egypt" (Gen. 50:11). Jacob had assisted the Egyptians by bringing the years of famine to an early end. From the standpoint of the Egyptians, Jacob had died, and the connection of his soul to these matters was severed. Therefore, the Egyptians had reason to mourn. But Jacob's sons, who knew that Jacob was still alive with them, had no need to eulogize their father.

Sefer Shemot – The Book of Exodus

The Ongoing Process of Redemption

The redemption continues onwards. The
redemption from Egypt and the complete
redemption of the future is one, uninterrupted act.
The process of the "strong hand and the
outstretched arm"[1] that began in Egypt continues
its activity in all events. Moses and Elijah[2] work to
bring the same single redemption. One begins and
one concludes; together they complete a unit.

The spirit of Israel listens to the sounds of
redemptive activity, the result of all events, until
the full sprouting of salvation, in its fullness and
goodness.
(*Orot*, p. 44)

---

[1] Deut. 4:35. The "strong hand" indicates the actual and the current (God's
supernatural intervention in Egypt), while the "outstretched arm" indicates the
potential and the future, i.e., the ongoing process of redemption throughout the
ages. See *Bo*: The Exodus and *Tefillin*.

[2] Moses was God's emissary for the redemption in Egypt, while Elijah will be the
harbinger of the final redemption.

Shemot

Moses Hid His Face[1]

> God's angel appeared to [Moses] in the heart of a
> fire, in the midst of a thorn-bush.... Moses hid his
> face, since he was afraid to look at God."
> (Ex. 3:2, 6)

During Moses' first prophetic revelation, he covered his face, afraid to look directly at this holy sight. Was his response an appropriate display of awe and reverence? Or did it reflect a flaw in Moses' personality, a sign of unwarranted timidity?

This question is the subject of a Talmudic disagreement in *Berachot* 7a. Rabbi Yehoshua ben Korcha noted that, later on, God would inform Moses, "You shall not see My face" (Ex. 33:23). In effect, God told Moses: "When I wanted [at the burning bush], you did not want. Now that you want, I do not want." Moses had missed an extraordinary opportunity when he turned away from the burning bush. Because of his failure to strive for greater enlightenment, at Mount Sinai he would only merit a lesser prophetic vision.

Rabbi Yochanan, on the other hand, argued that Moses' action was praiseworthy. As reward for humbly hiding his face, Moses merited that his face would shine with a brilliant light as he descended from Mount Sinai (Ex. 34:29).

---

[1] Adapted from *Ein Ayah* vol. I, p. 32.

Human Perfection

Rav Kook explained that this Talmudic discussion revolves around a fundamental question regarding our principle aim in life. In what way do we fulfill our potential? How do we achieve perfection?

According to Maimonides, human perfection is attained though the faculties of reason and intellect. Our goal is to gain enlightenment and knowledge of the Divine, through the study of Torah and metaphysics. This is also the viewpoint of Rabbi Yehoshua. By hiding his face at the burning bush, Moses lost a golden opportunity to further his understanding of the spiritual realm. If our fundamental purpose in life is to seek enlightenment, Moses' demonstration of humility was out of place.

The author of *Duties of the Heart*, however, wrote that our true objective is the perfection of character traits and ethical behavior. This concurs with the opinion of Rabbi Yochanan. What Moses gained in sincere humility and genuine awe of Heaven at the burning bush outweighed any loss of knowledge. Since the overall goal is ethical perfection, Moses' action was proper, and he was justly rewarded with a radiant aura of brilliant light, a reflection of his inner nobility.

Shemot

Moses' Mistake[1]

Appearing in a burning bush, God charged Moses with the task of leading the Jewish people out of Egypt. Moses, however, had doubts about the feasibility of the mission:

> They will not believe me and they will not listen to me, because they will say, "God did not appear to you." (Ex. 4:1)

In fact, Moses was wrong. The Hebrew slaves did believe him. Why did Moses doubt God's plan? How could the "master of all prophets" so gravely misjudge his own people?

Another curiosity is the nature of the miraculous signs God provided Moses to prove his authenticity – a staff that transforms into a snake, a hand that becomes leprous, and fresh water that turns into blood. None of these are particularly auspicious omens!

Hidden Treasure of the Soul

What is faith? The wonderful trait of *emunah* (faith), in its purest form, is a hidden quality of the soul. It is unlike any other wisdom or intellectual awareness. It is an integral part of the inner soul, forming the very basis for life, its light and splendor.

However, this source of happiness and eternal life is not always discernible to the outside world. We are not even fully aware of the

---

[1] Adapted from *Ein Ayah* vol. IV pp. 241–242.

magnitude of our own resources of faith. Certainly, its true dimensions are concealed from others.

The Israelites in Egypt had sunk to the lowest levels of impurity and idolatry. Outwardly, they were indistinguishable from their Egyptian masters. The two nations were so similar that the Torah (Deut. 4:34) describes the Exodus from Egypt as "taking a nation from the midst of a nation." It was like removing a fetus encapsulated in its mother's womb.

In such a state of affairs, even the penetrating eye of Moses failed to detect the people's inner reserve of faith. Too many masks and covers concealed the holy light of their inner faith. This hidden treasure of the Jewish people, their eternal heritage, was only revealed to God. The Sages taught in *Shabbat* 97a,

> God knew that Israel would believe. He told Moses, "They are believers, the children of believers... while you will lack faith in the future." As it says (Num. 20:12) [regarding the incident at *Mei Merivah*, the Waters of Dispute], "You did not believe in Me, to sanctify Me in the presence of the Israelites."

Unquestionably, the inner fire of faith always burns in the soul. It is an intrinsic aspect of the Jewish soul, regardless of choices made and paths taken. If we judge only according to external actions, however, there may not be any outward expression of this inner spark. This was God's message to Moses: if you measure faith only by what occurs in the outer realm of deed, then even the greatest and most perfected individuals – even spiritual giants like Moses – can stumble, and fail to act upon their inner faith.

The Message of the Signs

The Sages explained that the various signs were a punishment for being unjustly suspicious of the people. The sign of leprosy was particularly appropriate for the message that God wanted to impart to Moses. Leprosy afflicts the skin, the outer layer of the body. This sign hinted to Moses: there may occur imperfections on the exterior and the external expression may not match the inner holiness, but the holy light of divine faith is always safeguarded within the inner soul.

One cannot claim that the Jewish people will not believe the word of God, even when their lives appear dark and tarnished. This discoloration is only superficial, as it is written, "Do not look upon me that I am black; for [it is only] the sun that has tanned me" (Song of Songs 1:6).

Going to Peace[1]

After agreeing to lead the Israelites out of Egypt, Moses took leave of his father-in-law. Jethro blessed Moses, "Go in peace" (Ex. 4:18). Actually, Jethro said, "Go *to* peace." The Talmud (*Berachot* 64a) picks up on this fine nuance:

> One who takes leave from his friend should not say "Go in peace" (*lech BE-shalom*), but "Go to peace" (*lech LE-shalom*). Jethro told Moses, "Go to peace" – Moses went and succeeded in his mission. David told his son Absalom, "Go in peace" – Absalom went and was hanged.
> When taking leave of the deceased, however, one should say, "Go in peace."

What is the difference between these two salutations? Why is one appropriate for the living, and the second for the dead?

Ready for the Journey
Life is full of struggles, both spiritual and physical. We are not doing our acquaintances a favor by pretending these battles do not exist. Implying that the road is easy will only lower their guard, lessening their preparation for the obstacles that lie in the way towards their ultimate destination.

Therefore, we should warn our friends at the start of their journey: know that peace and tranquility are far from us. There are many who

---

[1] Adapted from *Ein Ayah* vol. II, p. 396

strive against us, and there are many obstacles on the way that must be overcome. We tell our friends, "Go *to* peace." Proceed towards your destination, but do not expect that the path itself will be peaceful and easy. The road is full of impediments; only by overcoming them, will you reach peace and completeness.

Of course, the story is much different for souls who have already completed their journey on earth. Their material struggles are over, and these obstacles no longer exist. The soul may continue to grow in that world too, but the path is a tranquil one. Therefore, we take our leave from the dead by saying, "Go *in* peace."

With these two salutations, the Sages contrasted the nature of this world and the next. The physical world is replete with struggles and challenges which we must be prepared to face. The World to Come, on the other hand, is one of rest and peace, which we need not fear.

Va'eira

Order in Miracles[1]

Presenting his "credentials" before Pharaoh, Moses threw down his staff before the Egyptian king, and it transformed into a viper. When the magicians of Egypt did the same with their magic, "the staff of Aaron swallowed up their staffs" (Ex. 7:12).

The Sages in *Shabbat* 97a noted that the Torah does not say that Aaron's snake swallowed up the magicians' staffs. It says Aaron's *staff* did the swallowing. A double miracle, a "miracle within a miracle" occurred. The viper became a staff once again, and only then – as a staff – did it swallow up the other staffs. What is the significance of this double miracle?

Levels of Miracles

Just as there is an underlying order in the world of nature, so too there is order and structure in the realm of miracles. We may distinguish between two types of laws of the natural world: those of a fundamental nature, and those that have a detailed and specific function. The extent to which a miracle defies natural law depends on the purpose of that divine intervention.

Sometimes it is sufficient to have a minor disruption, and still remain within the overall system of natural law. For example, when the prophet Elisha advised the widow in debt how to miraculously produce oil (II Kings 4:1–7), the oil was not created *ex nihilo*. Rather, the miracle was based on an existing jar of oil. There occurred no blatant abrogation

---

[1] Adapted from *Ein Ayah* vol. IV, pp. 243–244.

of the laws of nature; they were merely "extended," as the small cruse of oil sufficed to fill up many large pots. But the basic framework of natural law was left undisturbed.

The purpose of Elisha's miracle was to help out a poor woman in need. The goal of Moses' miraculous signs in Egypt, on the other hand, was far more grandiose. These wonders were meant to demonstrate the power and greatness of the Creator, "so that you will know that I am God here on earth" (Ex. 8:18).

In Egypt, God willed to demonstrate His ability to overrule any law and limitation of the natural world. Therefore, it was necessary to have a "miracle within a miracle." This exhibited independence and autonomy at all levels of natural law, both specific and fundamental. The miracle of the staff occurred not only as a minor disruption of nature – a level at which the Egyptian magicians could also function – but also at the level of total disregard for the most basic laws of nature, so that one staff could "swallow up" other staffs.

Hamotzi – For all Times[1]

It was definitely the low point in Moses' mission to free the Hebrew slaves. Pharaoh responded to the demand for freedom by adding more oppressive measures, and the Israelites began to wish that Moses had never come. Even Moses had his doubts. In response, God commanded Moses to relay the following message to the Israelites:

> You will know that I am the Lord your God, the One who brings you out (*hamotzi*) from under the Egyptian subjugation. (Ex. 6:7)

Hamotzi – Past or Future?

The tense of the verb *hamotzi* here is unclear. The Israelites have not yet been freed. Why say, "who *brings* you out"? The future tense, "who *will bring* you out," would make more sense.

The word *hamotzi* brings to mind the blessing recited before eating bread. The Talmud (*Berachot* 38a) records a debate regarding this blessing. Rabbi Nehemiah felt the blessing should read, "Blessed are You.... Who brought forth (*motzi*) bread from the earth." But the other sages argued that the blessing should be "the One Who brings forth (*hamotzi*) bread from the earth" – as in our verse. What is the difference between *motzi* and *hamotzi*?

---

[1] Adapted from *Ein Ayah* vol. II, pp. 176–177. This article provides a fascinating example of how a Talmudic disagreement over a single letter may reveal a profound philosophical discussion.

The Talmud explains that their disagreement is based on how the verse in Exodus should be understood. According to Rabbi Nehemiah, the word *hamotzi* implies the future. The Jews were still slaves in Egypt, and God assured them that He would take them out in the future. The future tense, however, is not appropriate for the blessing over bread. We recite this blessing in recognition of the wheat that has already come out of the earth. The word *motzi*, on the other hand, refers to the past and is therefore more suitable.

Rabbi Nehemiah's colleagues felt that the word *hamotzi* implies both the past and the future. They understood the verse as follows: the Israelites will be freed (in the future), after which they will recognize God as their Liberator (in the past). Since *hamotzi* also includes past events, it is also appropriate for the blessing over bread.

What is the essence of this disagreement? Is it simply an argument over Hebrew grammar? What is the significance of the blessing over bread being in the past or the future?

Contemplating God

There are two basic ways to attain love and awe of Heaven. The first approach is to contemplate God's greatness by examining His works. Reflecting on His amazing creations allows one to appreciate God's infinite wisdom and justice, and instills a tremendous longing to know God's great Name.[2]

The second approach maintains that intellectual reflection alone is insufficient. There must also be an emotional element. We need to awaken within ourselves love and awe for the Essence that creates these spectacular works.

Rabbi Nehemiah, by preferring the word *motzi*, concurred with the first approach. Before eating bread, we need to raise our intellectual awareness of the event that occurred: this bread was baked from wheat

---

[2] Maimonides, *Mishneh Torah, Yesodei HaTorah* 2:1.

that God brought forth from the earth. The word *motzi* is a verb, referring to an event that has taken place. Rabbi Nehemiah stressed the importance of the past tense, since appreciation of God's greatness is achieved by objectively analyzing God's hand in history and past events.

The other scholars disagreed. The blessing should be *hamotzi*, "the One Who brings forth." *Hamotzi* is not a verb but a descriptive phrase. We do not only observe the event itself, but we attempt to look beyond it to the Cause of the action. This is a supra-scientific, intuitive approach, relating to God according to His actions. The scholars held that the blessing over bread is not jut a way of contemplating the process of wheat growing out of the earth. We must concentrate on the Source of this process, and form a corresponding mental image of God.

Beyond Time

Since this opinion stresses not the event but the Cause of the event, the framework of time becomes irrelevant. *Hamotzi* thus implies both past and future. This changes our understanding of God's promise to the Israelites, "You will know that I am the Lord your God, *the One who brings you out* from under the Egyptian subjugation." We now understand that the present tense is just as accurate as the past and the future. For all time, we will recognize God's attribute of *Hamotzi*, the One who liberates us from slavery.

Destroy *Chametz*, Gain Freedom[1]

> By the first day, you must clear out your homes of
> all leaven. (Ex. 12:15)

Why Clear Out *Chametz*?

Why does the Torah command us to destroy all *chametz* (leaven) found in
our homes during Passover? It is logical to eat matzah; this fast-baked
food is historically bound to the Exodus, and it recalls our hurried escape
from Egyptian slavery. But how does clearing out leaven from our homes
relate to the Passover theme of freedom and independence?

Freedom of Spirit

There are two aspects to attaining true freedom. First, one needs to be
physically independent of all foreign subjugation. But complete freedom
also requires freedom of the spirit. The soul is not free if it is subjected to
external demands that prevent it from following the path of its inner
truth.

The difference between a slave and a free person is not just a
matter of social standing. One may find an educated slave whose spirit is
free, and a free person with the mindset of a slave. What makes us truly
free? When we are able to be faithful to our inner self, to the truth of our
divine image (*tzelem Elokim*) – then we can live a fulfilled life, a life focused
on our soul's inner goals. One whose spirit is servile, on the other hand,
will never experience this sense of true self-fulfillment. His happiness will

---

[1] Adapted from *Olat Re'iyah* vol. II, p. 244.

always depend upon the approval of others who dominate him, whether this control is *de jure* or *de facto*.

The Foreign Influence of Leaven

What is *chametz*? Leaven is a foreign substance added to the dough. The leavening agent makes the dough rise; it changes its natural shape and characteristics. Destruction of all leaven in the house symbolizes the removal of all foreign influences and constraints that prevent us from realizing our spiritual aspirations.

These two levels of independence, physical and spiritual, exist on both the individual and the national level. An independent people must be free not only from external rule, but also from foreign domination in the cultural and spiritual spheres.

For the Israelites in Egypt, it was precisely at the hour of imminent redemption that the dangers of these foreign "leavening" forces were the greatest. At that time of great upheaval, true permanent emancipation was not a given. Would the Israelites succeed in freeing themselves, not only from Egyptian bondage, but also from the idolatrous culture in which they had lived for hundreds of years? To commemorate their complete liberation from Egypt, both physical and spiritual, the Passover holiday of freedom requires the removal of all foreign "leavening" agents.

Cleansing Ourselves of Foreign Influences

In our days too, an analogous era of imminent redemption, we need to purge the impure influences of alien cultures and attitudes that have entered our national spirit during our long exile among the nations.

Freedom is the fulfillment of our inner essence. We need to aspire to the lofty freedom of those who left Egypt. To the Israelites of that generation, God revealed Himself, and brought them into His service. This is truly the highest form of freedom, as the Sages taught in *Avot* (6:2):

Instead of "engraved (*charut*) on the tablets," read it as "freedom" (*cheirut*). Only one who studies Torah is truly free.

Draining Egypt[1]

> The Israelites did as Moses had said. They
> requested silver and gold articles and clothing from
> the Egyptians. God made the Egyptians respect
> the people, and they granted their request. The
> Israelites thus drained Egypt of its wealth.
> (Ex. 12:35–36)

God's command that the Hebrew slaves request gold and silver
from the Egyptians is commonly explained as reparations for hundreds of
years of slave labor. But why was it necessary to completely drain Egypt of
its wealth?

The Talmud (*Berachot* 9b) describes this "draining" of Egypt with
two different metaphors:

> Rabbi Ami said: they made Egypt like a trap
> without bait.
> Resh Lakish said: they made Egypt like a net
> without fish.

What do these metaphors mean? What is the difference between a
"trap without bait" and a "net without fish"?

Trap without Bait

We find that the Torah prohibits returning to Egypt in order to prevent
the Jews from falling once again under the spell of the idolatrous Egyptian

---

[1] Adapted from *Ein Ayah* vol. I, p. 45.

culture.[2] The Canaanites also worshipped idols, yet Egypt posed a bigger threat to the spiritual purity of the nation. Having lived there for centuries, the Jewish people were comfortable with all aspects of Egyptian life, including their idolatrous practices.

In order to neutralize the attraction of Egypt, it was necessary to impoverish the country. One of the principle reasons for migrating to another land is the possibility of increasing personal wealth. But without its gold and silver, the Egyptian economy was in shambles. It was like a *"trap without bait"* – the country held no real incentive to lure back Jews seeking to do business there.

Net without Fish

There could be, however, a second factor in the decision of certain individuals to return to Egypt. The local culture and arts, the Egyptian lifestyle, so familiar to the newly freed slaves, could also serve as a lure to draw back nostalgic former residents. Resh Lakish therefore compared Egypt to a *"net without fish."* Fish swim together, and are more likely to be drawn to a net that has already caught other fish.[3] By draining Egypt of its wealth, not only was the country devastated economically, but it also suffered from a dramatically lower standard of living and poverty of culture. The final memories of the departing Israelites would be of an impoverished land whose remaining inhabitants struggled to eke out a living. It would be a "net without fish," holding little enticement for them to return.

---

[2] Deut. 11:16. See *Sefer HaChinuch, Mitzvah* 500.

[3] Scientists explain that the instinctive behavior of fish to swim in schools is due to the "improved antipredator responses of the school resulting from increased predator confusion" (Magurran 1990, Pitcher and Parrish 1993). While useful against sharks and bigger fish, this schooling behavior works against the fish when dealing with nets. A major problem in the fishing industry is the phenomenon of small fish that refuse to leave the net.

The Exodus and *Tefillin*[1]

The Torah commands us to commemorate the Exodus from Egypt by wearing *tefillin* (phylacteries) on the arm and head.

> These words will be for a sign on your arm and a reminder between your eyes, so that God's Torah will be in your mouth; for God brought you out of Egypt with a strong arm. (Ex. 13:9)

What is the connection between *tefillin* and the Exodus? How does wearing *tefillin* ensure that the Torah will be "in our mouths"?

An Outstretched Arm

Superficially, the redemption from Egypt was a one-time historical event, forging a potent memory in the collective consciousness of the Jewish people and all of humanity. But if we listen carefully to our inner soul, we will recognize that the Exodus is truly a continuous, ongoing act. The divine miracles and signs that took place in Egypt launched the continual revelation of the hand of God, openly and publicly, on the stage of world history. The Exodus was an outburst of Divine light, potent and vibrant, in all realms of the universe, and its impact continues to resonate throughout the ages.

Before wrapping *tefillin* on the arm, we reflect that this *mitzvah* commemorates God's *zero'a netuyah*, the "outstretched arm" with which the Israelites were extracted from Egypt. What does this metaphor mean?

---

[1] Adapted from *Olat Re'iyah* vol. I, pp. 26–7, 39.

The word "arm" (*zero'a*) comes from the root *zera*, meaning "seed." The divine redemption of Israel in Egypt was a holy seed, planted at that point in time. That wondrous event initiated the dissemination of its message, unhindered and uninterrupted, over the generations. As we bind the *tefillin* to our arms, we are reminded of God's "outstretched arm," the inner Godliness that continually develops and perfects the world, until it elevates its treasures of life to the pinnacle of divine fulfillment.

A Strong Arm

The Torah uses a second metaphor to describe the Exodus – the *yad chazakah*, God's "strong arm." This phrase indicates a second, deeper connection between the *mitzvah* of *tefillin* and the Exodus. The liberation from Egyptian bondage served to combat the debasement of life, which threatened to drown humanity in the depths of its crassness and vulgarity.[2] Since the materialistic side of life is so compelling, it was necessary for God to reveal a "strong arm" to overcome our base nature, and allow the light of our inner holiness to shine from within. The holy act of fastening the *tefillin* to the arm and head helps us transform the coarse and profane aspects of life into strength and vitality, revealing an inner life beautiful in its holiness.

To triumph over humanity's coarseness, then at its peak in the contaminated culture of Egypt, required God's "strong arm." We similarly need to make a strong effort so that the Torah will remain in our minds and hearts. *Tefillin* are called a "sign" and a "reminder," for they evoke the wondrous signs and powerful miracles of our release from Egyptian slavery. We must engrave the legacy of those miracles on all aspects of life: deed, emotion, and thought. Thus we bind these memories to our hand, heart, and mind, and transform our coarse nature to a holy one.

---

2 Cf. Ezekiel 23:20, where the prophet describes the animalistic crassness that typified ancient Egyptian culture.

Then the Torah will naturally be "in your mouth," in the thoughts and reflections of the heart.

Through this powerful *mitzvah*, engaging both the arm (our actions) and the eye (our outlook and thoughts), we continue the divine process that God initiated in Egypt with a "strong arm."

Beshalach

"This is My God"[1]

The Midrash (*Shemot Rabbah* 23:15) makes a startling claim about the Israelites who witnessed the splitting of the Red Sea:

> Come and see how great were those who crossed the Sea. Moses pleaded and beseeched before God that he should merit seeing God's Divine Image, "Please, show me Your glory!" (Ex. 33:19). Yet God told him, "You may not see My face...." But every Israelite who descended into the Sea pointed with his finger and said, "This is my God and I will glorify Him" (Ex. 15:2).

Could it be that those who crossed the Red Sea saw more than Moses, about whom the Torah testifies, "No other prophet like Moses has arisen in Israel" (Deut. 34:10)? Furthermore, Moses was also there when they crossed the sea – he certainly saw what everyone else experienced!

Total Suspension of Nature

Clearly, the Midrash cannot be referring to the level of prophecy, for it is a fundamental article of faith that Moses' prophecy was unparalleled. Rather, the Midrash must be referring to some aspect of prophetic vision that was only experienced by those who participated in this miraculous crossing.

---

[1] Adapted from *Midbar Shur*, pp. 353–357.

What was so special about the splitting of the Red Sea? God performed other miracles for Israel, but those miracles did not entail the complete abrogation of the laws of nature. Nature as a whole continued on its usual path; God only temporarily changed one aspect for the benefit of His people.

But with the miraculous splitting of the Sea, God suspended the entire system of natural law. The Sages wrote that this miracle did not occur solely in the Red Sea. On that night, bodies of water all over the world were split. According to the Maharal,[2] water symbolizes the physical world, so that this miracle affected the entire physical realm of creation (*Gevurot Hashem* chap. 42). The entire rule of nature was breached.

Immediate Awareness of Divine Rule

Our world is governed by the framework of cause and effect. When the underlying rule of nature was suspended during the splitting of the Red Sea, the entire system of causality was arrested. During that time, the universe lost its cloak of natural law, and revealed itself as a pure expression of divine will.

What is the essence of prophecy? This unique gift is the ability to look at God's works and recognize in them His greatness.

As long as nature's causal structure is functioning, a prophet may attain sublime and even esoteric knowledge, but he will never achieve immediate awareness of God's directing hand. Through his physical senses and powers of reasoning, the prophet will initially recognize the natural system of cause and effect. Only afterwards does the prophet become aware that the entire universe is created and directed by an ultimate Cause.

At Mount Sinai, God told Moses, "You will only see My back." What is God's "back"? Maimonides explained that this is a metaphor for the system of natural law by which God governs the

---

[2] Rabbi Yehudah Loew of Prague (1525–1609).

universe. God granted Moses an awareness of the inner connectivity within creation. This understanding of God's true nature exceeded that of any other prophet.

When God split the Sea, all laws of nature were temporarily suspended. God took "direct control" of the universe. Those witnessing this miracle were instantly aware of God's intervention and providence, each according to his spiritual level. Certainly none reached the prophetic level of Moses. But whatever enlightenment they attained, it was perceived immediately. They did not need to first examine the natural system of causality, and from this, recognize the prime Cause of creation.

Therefore, those experiencing the miracle of the Red Sea called out spontaneously, "*This* is my God." Their comprehension was not obscured by the logical system of cause and effect; they witnessed God's revealed rule directly, without the cloak of causality.

Beshalach

Innate and Acquired Holiness[1]

Crossing the Jordan River

On the banks of the Red Sea, with Egyptian slavery behind them, the Israelites triumphantly sang *Shirat HaYam*. This beautiful "Song of the Sea" concludes with a vision of a future crossing into freedom and independence – across the Jordan River, to enter the Land of Israel.

> Until Your people have crossed, O God;
> Until the people that You acquired have crossed
> over. (Ex. 15:16)

Why the repetition – "until Your people have crossed," "until the people... have crossed over"?

The Talmud (*Berachot* 4a) explains that the Jewish people crossed the Jordan River twice. The first crossing occurred in the time of Joshua, as the Israelites conquered the Land of Israel from the Canaanite nations. This event marked the beginning of the First Temple period. The second crossing took place centuries later, when Ezra led the return from Babylonian exile, inaugurating the Second Temple period.

The verse refers to both crossings. In what way does each phrase relate to its specific historical context?

Two Forms of Holiness

Rav Kook wrote that the Jewish people possess two aspects of holiness. The first is an inner force that resides naturally in the soul. This trait is a

---

[1] Adapted from *Olat Re'iyah* vol. I, p. 236.

spiritual inheritance passed down from the patriarchs, which Rav Kook referred to as a *segulah* (innate) *holiness*. It is an intrinsic part of the Jewish soul, and is immutable.

The second aspect of holiness is based on our efforts and choices. Rav Kook called this *willed-holiness*, as it is acquired consciously, through our actions and Torah study. Innate-holiness is in fact infinitely greater than willed-holiness, but it is only revealed to the outside world according to the measure of acquired holiness. It is difficult to perceive an individual's inner sanctity when it is not expressed in external actions or character traits.

Each of the two eras in Jewish history, the First and Second Temple periods, exemplified a different type of holiness.

The First Temple period commenced with Joshua leading the people across the Jordan River. The people of Israel at that time were characterized by a high level of intrinsic holiness. The *Shechinah*, God's Divine Presence, was openly revealed in the Temple, and miracles occurred there on a constant basis. It was an era of prophecy, and books were still being added to Scripture. This period corresponds to the phrase, "until Your people have crossed, O God." The expression *"Your people"* emphasizes their inherent connection to God, i.e., the aspect of innate-holiness.

The return to Zion in the time of Ezra marked the beginning of the Second Temple period. The Second Temple did not benefit from the same miraculous phenomena as the First Temple. Prophecy ceased, and the canonization of Scripture was complete.

However, the willed-holiness of that era was very great. The Oral Law flourished, the Mishnah was compiled, and new rabbinical decrees were established. This period corresponds to the second phrase, "until the people that You *acquired*." The main thrust of their connection to God was willed-holiness, acquired through good deeds and Torah study.

The Generation Preceding the Messiah

The Rabbi of Safed, Rabbi Jacob David Willowsky (known by the acronym the *Ridbaz*), criticized Rav Kook for his congenial relations with the non-religious (and often anti-religious) pioneers who were settling the Land of Israel. Rav Kook responded to this criticism by noting the distinction between different forms of holiness.

> In our generation, there are many souls who are on a very low level with regard to their willed-holiness. Thus, they are afflicted with immoral behavior and dreadful beliefs. But their innate *segulah* light shines brightly. That is why they so dearly love the Jewish people and the Land of Israel. (*Igrot HaRe'iyah* vol. II, letter 555 (1913), pp. 187–188)

Rav Kook went on to explain that heretics and non-believers usually lose their inner *segulah* holiness, and separate themselves from the Jewish people. However, we live in special times. The *Zohar* describes the pre-Messianic generation[2] as being "good on the inside and bad on the outside." That is to say, they have powerful inner holiness, even though their external, acquired holiness is weak and undeveloped. They are the allegorical "donkey of the Messiah,"[3] as the donkey bears both external signs of impurity, but nonetheless, contains an inner sanctity, as evidenced by the fact that firstborn donkeys are sanctified as *bechorot* (Ex. 13:13).

---

[2] *Ikva deMashicha*, literally, "Footstep of the Messiah."
[3] Zechariah 9:9 describes the arrival of the Messiah as "a pauper riding on a donkey."

Beshalach

The Influence of Amalek[1]

The treacherous attack of Amalek, striking against the weak and helpless, was not a one-time enmity, a grievance from our distant past. God commanded Moses to transmit the legacy of our struggle against Amalek for all generations:

> God told Moses, "Write this as a reminder in the Book, and repeat it in Joshua's ears: I will totally obliterate the memory of Amalek from under the heavens...." God shall be at war with Amalek for all generations. (Ex. 17:14, 16)

Erasable Writing

The evil of Amalek invaded every aspect of the universe. Even holy frameworks were not immune to this defiling influence. Therefore, they too require the possibility to be repaired by erasing, if necessary.

For this reason, the Talmud (*Sotah* 17b)[2] rules that scribes should not add calcanthum (vitriol or sulfuric acid) to their ink, since calcanthum-enhanced ink cannot be erased by rubbing or washing. All writing – even holy books – must have the potential to be erased, as they may have been tainted by sparks of evil.

An extreme example of a holy object that has been totally contaminated is a Torah scroll written by a heretic. In such a case, it must

---

[1] Adapted from *Igrot HaRe'iyah* vol. III, pp. 86–7 (1917).
[2] See *Shulchan Aruch*, *Yoreh De'ah* 271:6, *Pitchei Teshuvah* ad loc 17.

be completely burned by fire.[3] Usually, however, holy objects only come in light contact with evil, and it is sufficient to ensure that the scribal ink is not permanent, so that the writing has the potential to be erased.

The Unique Torah of Rabbi Meir

However, we find one scribe who did add calcanthum to his ink: the second-century scholar Rabbi Meir. Rabbi Meir was a unique individual. The Talmud states that there was none equal to Rabbi Meir in his generation. His teachings were so extraordinary that his colleagues were unable to fully follow his reasoning. Because of Rabbi Meir's exceptional brilliance, the Sages were afraid to rule according to his opinion (*Eiruvin* 13a–b).

The Talmud further relates that Rabbi Meir's true name was not Meir. He was called Meir because "he would enlighten *(me'ir)* the eyes of the Sages in Halachah." What made Rabbi Meir's approach to Torah so unique? His teachings flowed from his aspiration to attain the future enlightenment of the Messianic Era. Because of this spiritual connection to the Messianic Era, the Jerusalem Talmud (*Kilayim* 9:3) conferred upon him the title "your messiah."

Rabbi Meir had no need to avoid using calcanthum, since his Torah belonged to the future era when Amalek's evil will be eradicated. On the contrary, he took care to enhance his ink, reflecting the eternal nature of his lofty teachings.

Rabbi Akiva, on the other hand, taught that scribes should not avail themselves of calcanthum. In the world's current state, everything must have the potential to be erased and corrected, even that which contains holy content. Only in this way will we succeed in totally obliterating Amalek and his malignant influence. Then we will halt the spread of evil traits in all peoples, the source of all private and public tragedy.

---

[3] Shabbat 116a; *Shulchan Aruch, Yoreh De'ah* 281:1.

Uniting the Oral and Written Law

The influence of Amalek had a second detrimental effect on the Torah. God commanded Moses to communicate the struggle against Amalek in two distinct channels. Moses transmitted God's message in writing – "Write this in the Book" – and orally – "Repeat it in Joshua's ears." The refraction into divergent modes of transmission indicated that the Torah had lost some of its original unity.

Consequently, the Talmud rules that a scribe may not write from memory, not even a single letter (*Megillah* 18b). Our world maintains a entrenched division between the written and spoken word. Only with the obliteration of Amalek and the redemption of the world will we merit the unified light of the Torah's oral and written sides.

Once again, we find that Rabbi Meir and his Torah belonged to the future age, when this artificial split will no longer exist. Thus, when Rabbi Meir found himself in a place with no books, he wrote down the entire book of Esther from memory.

In the time of Mordechai and Esther, when we gained an additional measure of obliterating Amalek (with the defeat of Haman, a descendant of Amalek), the Torah regained some of its original unity. That generation accepted upon itself the Oral Law, in the same way that the Written Law had been accepted at Sinai (*Shabbat* 88a).

Serving the Community[1]

> Moses sat to judge the people. They stood around
> Moses from morning to evening. (Ex. 18:13)

From the account in the Torah, it would seem that Moses spent all his time judging the people. Yet, it was clear to the Sages that this could not be the case.

Overworked Judges

The Talmud (*Shabbat* 10a) relates that two dedicated judges worked such long hours that they were overcome with fatigue. (It is unclear whether this was a physical weakness from overwork, or a psychological depression from time lost from Torah study.) When Rabbi Chiyya saw their exhaustion, he advised the two scholars to limit their hours in court:

> It says that Moses judged the people "from morning to evening." But could it be that Moses sat and judged all day? When did he have time for Torah study?
> Rather, the Torah is teaching us that a judge who judges with complete fairness, even for a single hour, is considered to be God's partner in creating the world. For the Torah uses a similar phrase to describe Creation, "It was evening and morning, one day" (Gen. 1:5).

---

[1] Adapted from *Ein Ayah* vol. III, pp. 4–5.

Rabbi Chiyya's statement requires clarification. If judging is such a wonderful occupation – one becomes a partner with God! – then why not adjudicate all day long? And in what way is the work of a judge like creating the world?

Personal Well-Being and Public Service

Great individuals aspire to serve the community and help others to the best of their abilities. The two judges felt that they could best serve their community by bringing social justice and order through the framework of the judicial system. Therefore, they invested all of their time and energy in judging the people. For these scholars, any other activity would be a lesser form of divine service. However, their dedication to public service was so intensive that it came at the expense of their own personal welfare, both physical and spiritual.

Rabbi Chiyya explained to the scholars that while their public service was truly a wonderful thing, it is not necessary to neglect all other aspects of life. If one only judges for a single hour, and spends the rest of his time improving his physical and spiritual well-being so that he can better serve in his public position, then his entire life is still directed towards his true goal. It is clear that personal growth will enhance one's community service. Better an hour of productive activity in a fresh, relaxed state of mind and body, than many hours of constant toil in a tired and frenzied state.

Two Parts of the Day

What is the connection between Moses' judging "from morning to evening" and the description of the first day of Creation, "It was evening and morning, one day"? The day is one unit, made up of two parts – daytime and night. The daytime is meant for activity and pursuing our goals, while the night is the time for rest and renewal. Together, daytime and night form a single unit, constituting a "day."

The balance of these two aspects – activity and renewal – is particularly appropriate for those who labor for the public good. The hours that we devote to physical and spiritual renewal help us in our public roles; they become an integral part of our higher aspiration to serve the community.

Yitro

The Lesson of Mount Sinai[1]

What does the name *Sinai* mean? The Talmudic interpretation is surprising – and somewhat shocking:

> What is Mount Sinai? The mountain that brought enmity (*sin'ah*) upon the nations of the world. (*Shabbat* 89b)

What is the nature of this animosity? What does it have to do with Mount Sinai?

Why Sinai?

Where would one expect that God would reveal His Torah to the Jewish people? The logical place would be on the holiest mountain in the world – Jerusalem's Mount Moriah, the site of the Binding of Isaac, Jacob's holy "gate to heaven" (Gen 28:17), the spot where both Temples stood. Why did the revelation of the Torah take place outside of the Land of Israel, in the middle of the desert?

The fact that the Torah was not given to the Jewish people in their own land, but rather in a desert, in no-man's land, is very significant. This indicates that the inner content of the Torah is relevant to all peoples. If receiving the Torah required the special holiness of the Jewish people, then the Torah should have been given in a place that reflects this

---

[1] Adapted from *Ein Ayah* vol. IV, pp. 219–220.

holiness. Revelation on Mount Sinai attests to the Torah's universal nature.

This idea is corroborated by the Talmudic tradition that "God offered the Torah to every nation and every tongue, but none accepted it, until He came to Israel, who received it" (*Avodah Zarah* 2b). This Midrash is well known, but it contains an implication that is often overlooked. How could God offer the nations something that is beyond their spiritual level? It is only because the Torah is relevant to all peoples that their refusal to accept it reflects so harshly on them.

The Torah's revelation on Mount Sinai, as a neutral location belonging to none and thus belonging to all, emphasizes the disappointment and estrangement from God that the nations brought upon themselves by rejecting the Torah and its ethical teachings. It is for this reason that Mount Sinai "brought enmity upon the nations of the world."

In the future, however, the nations will recognize this mistake and correct it:

> In those days, it shall come to pass that ten men from all the languages of the nations will take hold of every Jew by a corner of his cloak and say, "Let us go with you, for we have heard that God is with you." (Zechariah 8:23)

Yitro

Seeing Sound[1]

And all the people *saw the sounds*.... (Ex. 20:15)

The Midrash calls our attention to an amazing aspect of the revelation at Sinai: the Jewish people were able to see what is normally only heard. What does this mean?

Standing near the Source

At their source, sound and sight are united. Only in our limited, physical world, in this *alma deperuda* (disjointed world), are these phenomena disconnected and detached. It is similar to our perception of lightning and thunder, which become increasingly separated from one another as the observer is more distanced from the source.

If we are bound and limited to the present, if we can only perceive the universe through the viewpoint of the temporal and the material, then we will always be aware of the divide between sight and sound. The prophetic vision at Mount Sinai, however, granted the people a unique perspective, as if they were standing near the source of Creation. From that vantage point, they were able to witness the underlying unity of the universe. They were able to see sounds and hear sights. God's revelation at Sinai was registered by all their senses simultaneously, as a single, undivided perception.

---

[1] Adapted from *Mo'adei HaRe'iyah* p. 491.

Mishpatim

Trust in God vs. Self-Reliance[1]

The Talmud (*Berachot* 10b) tells a puzzling story about the righteous king Hezekiah. It is related that the king secreted away the medical books of his day. Why? King Hezekiah felt that the people relied too heavily on the prescriptions described in those texts, and did not pray to God to heal them.

Surprisingly, the Sages approved of King Hezekiah's action. Such an approach would appear to contradict another Talmudic ruling. The Torah says one who injures his neighbor must "provide for his complete healing" (Ex. 21:19). The Talmud (*Baba Kama* 85a) deducts from here that the Torah granted doctors permission to heal. Even with natural diseases, we do not say, "Since God made him ill, it is up to God to heal him," but do our best to heal him. Which is the correct attitude? Should we rely on doctors and medical books, or place our trust only in God and prayer?

There is in fact a larger question at stake. When are we expected to do our utmost to remedy the situation ourselves, and when should we rely on God's help?

Two Forms of *Bitachon*
Rav Kook explained that there are two forms of *bitachon*, reliance on God. There is the normative level of trust, that God will assist us in our efforts to help ourselves. And there is the simple trust in God that He will perform a miracle, when appropriate.

---

[1] Adapted from *Ein Ayah* vol. I, p. 57.

Regarding the community as a whole, we find apparent contradictions in the Torah's expectations. Sometimes we are expected to make every possible effort to succeed, as in the battle of HaAi (Joshua 8). On other occasions, human effort was considered a demonstration of lack of faith, as when God instructed Gideon not to send too many soldiers to fight, "Lest Israel should proudly say 'My own hand saved me'" (Judges 7:2). Why did God limit Gideon's military efforts, but not Joshua's in the capture of HaAi?

The answer is that the spiritual level of the people determines what level of *bitachon* is appropriate. When we are able to recognize God's hand in the natural course of events, when we are aware that God is the source of our strength and skill – "Remember the Lord your God, for it is He Who gives you strength to succeed" (Deut. 8:18) – then God is more clearly revealed when He supplies our needs within the framework of the natural world. In this situation, we are expected to utilize all of our energy and knowledge and talents, and recognize divine assistance in our efforts. This reflects the spiritual level of the people in the time of Joshua.

On the other hand, there are times when the people are incapable of seeing God's help in natural events, and they attribute any success solely to their own efforts and skills. They are likely to claim, "My own hand saved me." In this case, only miraculous intervention will enable the people to recognize God's hand – especially when the Jewish nation was young, miracles were needed to bring them to this awareness.

Educating the People

Consider the methods by which parents provide for their children. When a child is young, the parent feeds the child directly. If the child is very small, the parent will even put the food right in his mouth. As the child grows older, he learns to become more independent and take care of his own needs. Parental care at this stage is more indirect, by supplying him with the wherewithal – the knowledge, skills, and training – to provide for himself. The grown child does not wish to be forever dependent on his parent. He wants to succeed by merit of his own talents and efforts, based on the training and tools that his parents provided him.

So too, when the Jewish people was in its infancy, miracles served to instill a fundamental recognition and trust in God. In the time of Gideon, the people's faith had lapsed, and needed strengthening. Similarly, in the time of King Hezekiah, the king realized that the corrupt reign of Ahaz had caused the people to forget God and His Torah. He calculated that the spiritual gain through prayer outweighed the scientific loss due to hiding the medical texts.

But when faith and trust in God are strong, it is preferable that we utilize our own energies and talents, and recognize God's hand within the natural universe. The enlightened viewpoint calls out, "Lift up your eyes on high and see: Who created these?" (Isaiah 40:26). So it was when Joshua conquered the city of HaAi. After forty years of constant miracles in the desert, the people were already thoroughly imbued with trust in God. It was appropriate that they use their own resources of cunning and courage to ambush the fighters and destroy the city.

What about the future redemption of the Jewish people? It may occur with great miracles, like the redemption from Egypt; or it may begin with natural events, as implied by several statements of the Sages that the redemption will progress gradually.[2] It all depends on the level of our faith in God. It is certainly integral to our national pride that we take an active role in rebuilding the House of Israel.

---

2 The Jerusalem Talmud (*Berachot* 1:1) recounts that two sages were walking in the Arbel Valley when they witnessed the first rays of dawn break forth. Rabbi Chiyya told his colleague, "So is the redemption of Israel. In the beginning it starts out slowly; then, as it progresses, it becomes greater and greater."

Mishpatim

Slavery in the Torah[1]

> If a man strikes his male or female slave with a
> rod, and the slave dies under his hand, the death
> must be avenged [the master is punished by death].
> However, if the slave survives for a day or two, his
> death shall not be avenged, since he is his master's
> property. (Ex. 21:20–21)

The Torah portion of *Mishpatim* deals primarily with laws
governing society – personal damages, lending money and articles,
manslaughter, kidnapping, and so on. Overall, they fit in well with a
modern sense of justice. The laws dealing with slaves, however, are
difficult for us to digest. Why does the Torah distinguish between a
mortally wounded slave who dies immediately, and one who lingers for a
day or two? Is a slave truly "his master's property"? In general, does the
Torah look favorably on the institution of slavery?

His Master's Property
Slavery, Rav Kook explained, is like any other natural phenomenon. It can
be used properly and responsibly, or it can be abused. As long as some
people are wealthy and powerful, while others are poor and weak, the
wealthy will hire out the poor to do their labor and will control them. This
is the basis of natural servitude, which exists even if slavery as a formal
institution is outlawed.

---

[1] Adapted from *Igrot HaRe'iyah* vol. I, pp. 95–98.

For example, coal miners are *de facto* slaves to their employer, and in some ways worse off than legal slaves. The mine owner often cares more about his profits than his workers. He allows his miners to work without proper light and ventilation, in poorly built mines. The owner is not perturbed that his workers' lives are shortened due to their abysmal working conditions. He is not overly troubled that the mine may collapse, burying alive thousands of miners – he can always hire more.

Yet, if these miners were his legal slaves for whom he paid good money, then the owner would look out for their lives and welfare just as he watches over his machines, animals, and the rest of his property. For this reason, the Torah emphasizes that a slave is his master's property. When it is in the master's self-interest to look after his slave's welfare, the servant can expect a better, more secure future.

Why does the Torah distinguish between a slave who dies immediately after being struck by his master, and one who lingers for a day? The verse specifically mentions that the master struck with a rod, an indication that his intention was not to harm the slave, but to discipline him. If the slave dies due to mistreatment at the hands of his master, we take into account the natural concern that all people have for their possessions. The Torah rules that no death penalty is incurred, "since he is his master's property." In these circumstances, intentional murder becomes improbable, and the Torah looks for an additional factor – a non-immediate death – to indicate that the death was accidental. The Torah stresses that the goal is to serve justice, not to avenge. Thus the unusual phrasing, "his death shall not be avenged."

The Institution of Slavery

The legalized slavery of the Torah only comes to correct certain potential pitfalls of the natural phenomenon of slavery. As long as slavery exists, the Torah legislated laws to protect slaves from abuse and mistreatment.

If an owner knocked out his slave's tooth, the slave went free.[2] An owner who killed his slave was executed, like any other murderer.

Since the destruction of the Temple, however, the Torah's positive influence upon general society has greatly weakened. The darkness of the Middle Ages severely corrupted natural forms of life, transforming slavery into a monstrous institution. Instead of protecting the weak by giving them the security of property, slavery became such a horror that humanity decided it needed to be permanently outlawed.

The Torah's form of servitude must be set aside, until the era when, once again, "Torah will go forth from Zion." At that time, servitude will provide not only financial security, but also moral and spiritual mentorship.

When the heart has once again become a sensitive vessel of integrity and compassion, it is fitting that the morally deficient should be taken under the wings of those righteous and wise.

---

[2] The Torah (Ex. 21:26–27) only specifically mentions the loss of an eye or a tooth, but the Talmud (*Kiddushin* 24a) teaches that this law applies to all external limbs, including fingers, toes, ears, and nose.

Revealing Our Inner Essence[1]

The ultimate moment of glory for the Jewish people – their greatest hour – occurred as God revealed His Torah to them at Mount Sinai. The Israelites made an amazing proclamation: *Na'aseh VeNishma* – "We will do and we will listen to all that God has declared" (Ex. 24:7).

They promised two things: to do, and to listen. The order is crucial. They promised to keep the Torah, even before knowing why. The Midrash (*Shabbat* 88a) says that, in merit of this pledge of loyalty, the angels rewarded each Jew with two crowns. And a Heavenly Voice exclaimed, "Who revealed to My children this secret that is used by the angels?"

What was so special about this vow, "we will do and we will listen"? On the contrary, would not fulfilling *mitzvot* with understanding and enlightenment be a higher level of Torah observance? And why is this form of unquestioning allegiance a "secret used by the angels"?

Intuitive Knowledge

While wisdom is usually acquired through study and reflection, there exists in nature an intuitive knowledge that requires no formal education. The bee, for example, naturally knows the optimal geometric shape for building honeycomb cells. No bee has ever needed to register for engineering courses at MIT.

Intuitive knowledge also exists in the spiritual realm. Angels are sublime spiritual entities who do not need Torah studies in order to know

[1] Adapted from *Mo'adei HaRe'iyah*, p. 486.

how to serve God. Their holiness is ingrained in their very nature. It is only human beings, prone to being confused by pseudo-scientific indoctrination, who need to struggle in order to return to their pristine spiritual selves.

For the Jews who stood at Mount Sinai, it was not only Torah and *mitzvot* that were revealed. They also discovered their own true, inner essence. They attained a sublime level of natural purity, and intuitively proclaimed, "we will do." We will follow our natural essence, unhindered by any spurious, artificial mores.

Terumah

Betzalel's Wisdom[1]

The Torah reading of *Terumah* begins the section dealing with building the *Mishkan* (Tabernacle) and making the priestly clothes. These chapters are among the few in which the Torah places great emphasis on external beauty – art, craftsmanship, and aesthetics.

Of particular interest is the protagonist of this unique construction: the master craftsman, Betzalel. The Midrash weaves many stories about Betzalel's wisdom and skill. In particular, the Sages noted the significance of his name, which means, *"in God's shadow"*:

> Betzalel's name reflected his wisdom. God told Moses, "Tell Betzalel to make the tabernacle, the ark, and the vessels." When Moses relayed the message to Betzalel, however, Moses changed the order, mentioning first the ark, then the vessels, and lastly, the tabernacle.
> Betzalel turned to Moses. "Moses, our teacher, usually one first builds the house, and then places the furniture inside. Yet you said to make the vessels and then the tabernacle. These vessels that I will make – where shall I put them? Perhaps God told you, 'tabernacle, ark and vessels'?" Moses replied in amazement, "You must have been in God's shadow and overheard!" (*Berachot* 55a)

Betzalel was certainly sharp to be able to reconstruct the original divine message. Why did Moses change the order that God had told him?

---

[1] Adapted from *Ein Ayah* vol. II, p. 263.

The Scholar and the Artist

One way in which we can distinguish between the scribbles of a five-year-old and a masterpiece by Rembrandt is the degree to which the work of art reflects reality. A true artist is acutely sensitive to the finest details of nature. He must be an expert in shading, color, texture, and composition. A great artist will be disturbed by the smallest deviations, just as a great musician is perturbed by a note that is not exactly right in pitch, length, and emphasis.

There is a difference between the natural order of the world as perceived through the trained eye of an artist, and the proper order as understood through the wisdom of a scholar. The artist always compares the subject at hand to reality. The scholar, on the other hand, organizes topics according to their ethical and spiritual significance.

When Moses heard God command that Betzalel build the "tabernacle, ark, and vessels," he did not know whether the order was significant. Since the tabernacle was in effect just the outer building containing the ark and the other vessels, Moses knew that the ark and vessels were holier. Therefore, when relaying the command to Betzalel, he mentioned them in order of importance, starting with the most sacred.[2]

Why then did God put the tabernacle first? Moses decided that the original command started with the general description – the Tabernacle, the overall goal – and then continued with the details, the ark and vessels.

Betzalel, an artist with a finely tuned sensitivity to physical reality, noticed the slight discrepancy in Moses' description. He realized that the word *tabernacle* did not refer to the overall construction, but to the outer building. As such, it should have come first, just as in the building of any home. The order was not from the general to the detailed, nor from the less holy to the holier, but from the outside to the inside.

---

[2] Ordering according to relative holiness has a legal basis. The Talmud (*Zevachim* 89a) rules that the holier should come first.

Moses then comprehended the significance of Betzalel's name, "in God's shade." Why *shade*? Wisdom may be compared to light, while artistic talent is like shade. Light is certainly greater and brighter then shade; but if we want to perceive an object completely, we need to see all of its aspects, both light and shade. In order that the Tabernacle could achieve its purpose, it required the special artistic insight of Betzalel.

Terumah

Tachash Skins in the Tabernacle[1]

The uppermost covering of the *Mishkan*, the mobile Tabernacle of the desert, was made from the colorful skins of the *tachash*. The exact nature of this unusual animal is not clear. The Sages (*Shabbat* 28b) were not even sure whether the *tachash* was a kosher animal. According to Rabbi Meir, it was a unique, multi-colored creature, with a single horn in its forehead. After the *tachash* made its appearance in the time of Moses, it disappeared from sight.

How could the holy Tabernacle be constructed from an impure animal? What purpose would this serve?

The difference between pure and impure is similar to the difference between good and evil. These distinctions are true and valid, and it is necessary for our moral development to recognize and emulate good, while abhorring evil and corruption. However, these distinctions are really only by way of comparison. Good and evil are in fact relative terms. On a very fundamental level we recognize – at least intellectually – that everything has some ultimate purpose and value. Nothing can exist, nothing was created, which is absolute evil. Everything must relate, on some level, to the underlying good of the universe.

This abstract recognition of the hidden value of evil has no practical application, since morality is based upon the strongest possible feelings of hatred for evil and love for good. Therefore, when it comes to fulfilling *mitzvot*, which are practical ethical guidelines, it is not appropriate to use impure objects.

---

[1] Adapted from *Ein Ayah* vol. III, pp. 105–107.

The Tabernacle, however, may have been an exception to this rule.

The generation of Jews who lived in the desert for forty years was a special generation. Their spiritual achievements were for all times. They encompassed the essence of all future generations, so that the covenant they made with God – and the Torah which they accepted upon themselves – obligated not only their generation, but all future ones as well.

Like the special generation of the desert, the *Mishkan* embodied timeless aspects of the universe. The holy sanctuary of the desert was not a matter of specific morality for a particular era, but encompassed the expanse of all times and all things. It reflected the beautiful harmony of the entire universal order, and the divine aim of elevating all of creation. It was therefore possible that its outermost covering was made from an impure animal. The *tachash*, with its many hues and colors, represented the ultimate value of the many forces in the world, in all their variations. Its inclusion in the Tabernacle, albeit in its outermost layer, enabled an expression of our intellectual recognition of God's essential unity, that nothing exists outside of Him and that all was created in His Glory.

Terumah

Rising Above Ten Handbreadths[1]

What is so important about the construction of the Tabernacle that the Torah describes in such loving detail its measurements and furnishings? Was it not just an interim precursor to the Temple? What eternal message does this temporary structure have to impart?

The Tabernacle enabled the Jewish people to express their devotion and love of God. But the Tabernacle was more than just a hallowed place to serve God. By examining its structure and parts, we may reveal the paths by which the human soul draws close to its Maker.

The *Mishkan*, the Altar, and the Ark

The two largest objects of the Tabernacle were the *mishkan* structure, composed of upright wooden beams, and the copper altar that stood in the courtyard. These parts of the Tabernacle symbolize the path of contemplation and reflection. The design of the *mishkan* reflects the overall structure of the universe. Careful examination of its dimensions and details, like contemplation of the universe in which we live, leads us to recognize the world's spiritual foundations. Through His creative acts, we gain awareness of the Creator.

The altar is a continuation of this path of reflection. The soul's meditation on the inner nature of the universe awakens within us love and awe for God and the desire to serve Him. This was the function of the altar, the focal point for serving God in the realms of emotion and deed.

---

[1] Adapted from *Ein Ayah* vol. IV, pp. 232–233.

Together, the *mishkan* and the altar formed a complete framework of Divine service. Thus, Talmudic tradition (*Shabbat* 92a) connects them with a *hekesh*, teaching that both reached full stature: "Just as the *mishkan* was ten cubits tall, so too the altar was ten cubits tall."

The third major furnishing of the Tabernacle was the *aron*, the gold-plated ark encasing the stone tablets from Sinai. The ark represents the path of Torah, enlightenment through God's word that transcends the limitations of the human mind.

Carrying with Poles

The copper altar was not lifted directly, but via wooden poles. So too, our reflection on the inner nature of the universe does not come naturally, without effort. The service of God as represented by the altar is performed by using the analytic and contemplative faculties of the soul.

The ark containing the tablets was also carried with poles, indicating that we approach the Torah with our physical senses and intellect. However, these paths go beyond the overt abilities of the soul. The Sages taught that "anything carried by poles, one third is above [the porter's height] and two thirds are below." Two thirds are within the realm of our revealed faculties, the senses and the intellect. One third, however, rises above the human mind. It comes from the hidden recesses of the soul; we are able to connect to the Torah only through spiritual gifts.

Above Ten Handbreadths

The Sages taught that the furnishings of the Tabernacle were carried ten handbreadths (about 90 cm.) above the ground. What is the significance of this height? Ten handbreadths designate an individual's place and legal domain (*reshut*). This measurement signifies our binds to the physical realm. Our ties to the material world are so powerful that even Moses and

Elijah were unable to escape the constraints of ten handbreadths (*Sukkah* 5a).

Rabbi Elazar taught that, in general, people carry their loads above ten handbreadths, like the Levites who were charged with transporting the Tabernacle furnishings (*Shabbat* 92a). By extension, we may say that the calling of every individual is like the mission of the Levites; our purpose in life is to carry our load above ten handbreadths. We must aspire to transcend the physical forces that bind us to the earth, going beyond our material needs. Just as the Levites carried the altar and the ark above ten handbreadths, we too should utilize these two paths – contemplation of the universe, with its resultant emotional and practical service, and the study of Torah, God's elevated word – to transcend the material binds of our physical nature.

The High Priest's Clothes and the Convert[1]

The Talmud (*Shabbat* 31a) tells the story of three Gentiles who wished to convert. In each case, they were initially rejected by the scholar Shamai, known for his strictness, but they were later accepted and converted by the famously modest Hillel.

The Convert Who Wanted to be High Priest

In one case, a Gentile was walking near a synagogue when he heard the Torah being read and translated: "These are the clothes that you should make: the jeweled breast-plate, the ephod-apron..." (Ex. 28:4).

His interest was piqued. "For whom are these fancy clothes?" he asked. "They are special garments for the *Kohen Gadol*, the High Priest." The Gentile was excited. "For this, it is worth becoming a Jew. I'll go convert and become the next High Priest!"

The Gentile made the mistake of approaching Shamai. "I want you to convert me," he told Shamai, "but only on condition that you appoint me High Priest." Shamai rebuffed the man, pushing him away with a builder's measuring rod.

Then he went to Hillel with the same proposition. Amazingly, Hillel agreed to convert him. Hillel, however, gave the man some advice. "If you wanted to be king, you would need to learn the ways and customs of the royal court. Since you aspire to be the High Priest, go study the appropriate laws."

---

[1] Adapted from *Ein Ayah* vol. III, pp. 144–147.

So the new convert began studying Torah. One day, he came across the verse, "Any non-priest who participates [in the holy service] shall die" (Num. 3:10). "To whom does this refer?" he asked. Even King David, he was told. Even David, king of Israel, was not allowed to serve in the holy Temple, as he was not a descendant of Aaron the *kohen*.

The convert was amazed. Even those born Jewish, and who are referred to as God's children, are not allowed to serve in the Temple! Certainly, a convert who has just arrived with his staff and pack may not perform this holy service. Recognizing his mistake, he returned to Hillel, saying, "May blessings fall on your head, humble Hillel, for drawing me under the wings of the Divine Presence."

Shamai's Rejection and Hillel's Perspective

A fascinating story, but one that requires to be examined. Why did Shamai use a builder's measuring rod to send away the potential convert? What did Hillel see in the Gentile that convinced him to perform the conversion?

Shamai felt that the man lacked a sincere motivation to convert. By chance, he had overheard the recitation of the High Priest's special garments. The garments, beautiful though they may be, represent only an external honor. His aspirations were shallow and superficial, like clothing that is worn on the surface.

Furthermore, the chance incident did not even awaken within the Gentile a realistic goal. How could conversion to Judaism, with all of the Torah's obligations, be based on such a crazy, impossible fancy – being appointed High Priest? The foundations of such a conversion were just too shaky. Shamai pushed him away with a builder's measuring rod, indicating that he needed to base his goals on solid, measured objectives.

Hillel, however, looked at the situation differently. In his eyes, the very fact that this man passed by the synagogue just when this verse was being read, and that this incident should inspire him to such a lofty goal –

converting to Judaism – this person must have a sincere yearning for truth planted deeply in his heart. He was not seeking the honor accorded to the rich and powerful, but rather the respect granted to those who serve God at the highest level. The seed of genuine love of God was there, just obscured by false ambitions, the result of profound ignorance. Hillel was confident that as he advanced in Torah study, the convert would discover the beauty and honor of divine service that he so desired through the sincere observance of the Torah's laws, even without being the High Priest.

Both Traits Needed

Once, the three converts who were initially rejected by Shamai and later accepted by Hillel, met together. They all agreed: "The strictness of Shamai almost made us lose our [spiritual] world; but the humility of Hillel brought us under the wings of God's Presence."

Rav Kook noted that the converts did not talk about Shamai and Hillel. Rather, they spoke of the *strictness of Shamai* and the *humility of Hillel.* These are two distinct character traits, each one necessary in certain situations. In order to maintain spiritual attainments, we need the traits of firmness and strictness. On the other hand, in order to grow spiritually, or to draw close those who are far away, we need the traits of humility and tolerance. The three converts recognized that it was Hillel's quality of humility that helped bring them "under the wings of God's Presence."

Tetzaveh

Beyond the Holy[1]

One Line or Two?

One of the most impressive of the special vestments worn by the High Priest was the *tzitz*, a pure gold plate placed across the forehead. Engraved on the *tzitz* was the phrase, "Holy to God."

According to Talmudic tradition, these words were split into two lines. God's name appeared on the top line, and underneath was written, "Holy to." In contradiction to this tradition, however, Rabbi Eliezer testified that he had seen the *tzitz* among the plundered Temple articles in Rome – and the engraving was made on a single line (*Shabbat* 63b).

Why should the phrase "Holy to God" be split into two lines? And if that was the way the inscription was supposed to be engraved, why did the actual *tzitz* used in the Temple bear the entire phrase on one line?

The Realm of *Kodesh Kodashim*

We are accustomed to viewing the world as being divided into two realms: *kodesh* and *chol*, the holy and the profane. We are deeply aware of this dichotomy, and the friction between them, in all levels of existence: in our actions, feelings, thoughts, areas of study, and so on. The conflict between sacred and secular exists both in our private lives and in the public sphere.

There is, however, a third realm, even higher than *kodesh*. This is the level of *kodesh kodashim*, the "holy of holies." This is the very source of holiness, and it is based on both *kodesh* and *chol*. While the realms of *kodesh* and *chol* appear to us as competing and contradictory, in fact, each one

---

[1] Adapted from *Ein Ayah* vol. IV, p. 114; *Ma'amerei HaRe'iyah*, pp. 400–407.

complements and supports the other. The holy gives meaning to the profane; without it, the world of *chol* is lost, without direction or purpose. And the profane gives strength and substance to the holy. Without it, the *kodesh* has nothing to refine and elevate.

The lofty realm of *kodesh kodashim* is attained by the complementary interactions of *kodesh* and *chol*. This level reveals the common source of elevated holiness that resides in both *kodesh* and *chol*. In fact, *kodesh kodashim* is so much higher than the other two realms, that, when viewed from such heights, the differences between the holy and the profane disappear.

The Oral Tradition states that God's name was engraved on a separate line above the words, "Holy to." In other words, God's name belongs to the exalted world of *kodesh kodashim*. Since it reflects a vision far beyond the apparent contradictions of holy and profane, it could not be written on the same line as "Holy to."

Distinguishing Between *Kodesh* and *Chol*

This elevated outlook is, however, only theoretical. In our world, it is crucial that we distinguish between *kodesh* and *chol*. Humanity's moral development depends on *havdalah*, a clear awareness and distinction between what is sacred and what is not.

Furthermore, if we do not separate these two areas, and ensure that each one maintains its independence, both *kodesh* and *chol* will suffer. Lack of clear boundaries between them greatly hinders human advance. For example, cold academic analysis and dissection of Torah subjects can leave them lifeless and dismembered. Religious encroachment on secular areas of study, on the other hand, can obstruct scientific progress (consider Galileo's struggles with the Church). Therefore, in practice it was necessary to lower God's name on the *tzitz* to share the same level as "Holy to." In this way, the holy is set apart from the profane.

Still, the potential to perceive the inner unity of *kodesh* and *chol* was – at least theoretically – engraved on the High Priest's forehead-plate, raising his thoughts to the unified reality of *kodesh kodashim*, where God's name is inscribed above and beyond the *kodesh*.

Ki Tissa

Wisdom for the Wise[1]

When appointing Betzalel and other craftsmen to construct the Tabernacle, God declared, "In the heart of all wise-hearted, I have placed wisdom" (Ex. 31:6). Why should God give wisdom to the wise – it is the fools who need it!

A person who wishes to increase his physical strength will not achieve his goal by developing his intellectual powers. He needs to concentrate on building up his body, with physical exercise, healthy food, and proper sleep.

But the opposite can also be true. When we strengthen the body, we enable the mind to reach its full potential. This is nature's rule of "A healthy mind in a healthy body."

Beyond the objective of strengthening the intellect and broadening one's knowledge lies an even higher goal: the pursuit of divine inspiration (*ruach hakodesh*) and prophecy. The relationship between the body and the mind parallels the relationship between "natural wisdom" (the arts and sciences) and "divinely-emanated wisdom." We may aspire to prophetic enlightenment, but we must first gain proficiency in the natural sciences. Maimonides mentions this requisite intellectual preparation for prophecy in the *Mishneh Torah, Yesodei HaTorah* 7:1:

> Prophecy is only bestowed to a sage who is great in wisdom, of strong character... and he must possess an extremely expansive and accurate worldview.

---

[1] Adapted from *Orot HaKodesh* vol. I, pp. 66–67.

We need to expand all of the mind's intellectual capabilities in order to fulfill the rule of "a healthy mind in a healthy body" on a spiritual level. Then an enriched prophetic inspiration will emerge within the broadened framework of a penetrating, enlightened mind.

Ki Tissa

A Lesson in Leadership[1]

Moses was on top of Mount Sinai, experiencing divine revelation on a level beyond the grasp of ordinary prophets. At the foot of the mountain, however, the people began to worry. Not knowing why Moses was taking so long, not understanding how he could live without food and water for forty days, they felt abandoned and leaderless. They demanded that Aaron make them a golden calf, and they worshipped it.

God's response was immediate – He banished Moses from Mount Sinai.

> Leave! Go down! The people whom you brought
> out of Egypt have become corrupt. (Ex. 32:7)

It seems unfair. The people sin, and Moses is kicked off the mountain?

A Suitable Leader

In order for a leader to succeed, he must be appreciated and valued by his followers. The leader may possess a soul greatly elevated above the people, but it is crucial that the people should be able to relate to and learn from their leader.

At Mount Sinai, the Jewish people were on a lofty spiritual level. As a result, Moses was able to attain a supreme level of prophecy and revelation on top of the mountain. But after they sinned with the golden

---

[1] Adapted from *Ein Ayah* vol. I, pp. 142–143.

calf, Moses would no longer be a suitable leader were he to retain his spiritual attainments. It was necessary for Moses to "step down," to lower himself, in order to continue serving as their guide and leader.

This idea is clearly expressed by the Talmud (*Berachot* 32a):

> What does it mean, "Go down"? God told Moses, "Go down from your greatness. I only gave you pre-eminence for the sake of the Jewish people. Now they have sinned – why should you be elevated?" Immediately, Moses' [spiritual] strength left him.

Ki Tissa

When Bad Things Happen to Good People[1]

After Moses succeeded in petitioning God to forgive the Jewish people for the sin of the golden calf, he made an additional request from God: "If You are indeed pleased with me, allow me to know Your ways" (Ex. 33:12).

What exactly did Moses desire to know? The Talmud (*Berachot* 7a) explains that Moses wanted to understand the age-old problem of reward and punishment in this world:

> "Master of the Universe, why is it that some righteous people prosper, while others suffer? Why do some wicked people prosper, and others suffer?"

According to Rabbi Yossi, God fulfilled Moses' request. The Talmud initially explains that anomalies in divine justice in this world are the result of ancestral merit. A righteous person whose parents were wicked may undergo suffering in this world, while a wicked person whose parents were righteous may be rewarded.

However, the Sages were not satisfied with this explanation. Why should a righteous person who rejected his parents' evil ways be punished? He should be rewarded doubly! The Sages concludes that if there are righteous who suffer, it must be because they are not fully righteous. (This is usually understood that they are punished in this world to atone for their sins so that their reward in the next world will be

---

[1] Adapted from *Ein Ayah* vol. I, p. 32.

complete.) Similarly, the wicked who prosper must not be totally evil. They receive reward in this world for the few merits they do possess.[2]

Upon inspection, we discover that these two mitigating factors – ancestral merit and incompleteness of righteousness or wickedness – are interrelated. All actions may be broken up into two categories. Some actions are performed purposely, by choice; while others – the majority – are done without thought, but by habit or training. For a righteous person from a righteous family, good deeds come naturally. He does not need suffering in order to refine his soul. The righteous individual born in a wicked family, on the other hand, must work harder. His good deeds are a conscious effort, going against his education and natural bent. He therefore needs the refinement that comes from suffering in order to perfect his character traits.

The wicked person who hails from a righteous family is naturally helpful to others, and may have inherited many other positive character traits. Therefore, his portion in life is good, as he contributes to the world. But the wicked who comes from a wicked family is usually an utterly evil person. His lot in life is made difficult and unstable, in order to limit the damage that he may cause in the world.

The Talmud records a second opinion, Rabbi Meir, who disagreed with Rabbi Yossi. According to Rabbi Meir, God did not fulfill Moses' request to explain the mechanics of suffering and reward in this world. The complex calculations of how much of our actions is a function of free will, and how much is due to society, education, and family background – belong to the Creator alone. The knowledge needed in order to understand divine justice in this world is beyond the grasp of all humans – even the master of all prophets, Moses.

---

[2] The Talmud also mentions an additional factor, called "Afflictions of Love." Even a perfectly righteous individual may suffer in this world in order to gain additional reward in the afterlife.

Vayakheil

Technology and the Sabbath[1]

Do not ignite fire in any of your dwellings on the
Sabbath. (Ex. 35:3)

The Torah forbids 39 different categories of activity on the
Sabbath. Yet only one – lighting fire – is explicitly prohibited in the Torah.
Why? Why does the Torah qualify the prohibition of lighting fire with the
phrase, "in any of your dwellings"? Is it not forbidden to start a fire in any
location?

The control and use of fire is unique to humanity. It is the basis
for our advances in science and innovations in technology. Even now, fuel
sources for burning, coal and oil, are what power modern societies. In
short, fire is a metaphor for our power and control over nature, the fruit
of our God-given intelligence.

What is the central message of the Sabbath? When we refrain
from working on the seventh day, we acknowledge that God is the
Creator of the world.

One might think that only the pristine natural world is truly the
work of God. Human technology, on the other hand, is artificial and
perhaps alien to the true purpose of the universe. Therefore, the Torah
specifically prohibits lighting fire on the Sabbath, emphasizing that our
progress in science and technology is also part of creation. Everything is
included in the ultimate design of the universe. Our advances and
inventions contribute towards the goal of creation in accordance with
God's sublime wisdom.

---

[1] Adapted from *Ein Ayah* vol. III, p. 53.

Along with the recognition that all of our accomplishments are in essence the work of God, we must also be aware that we have tremendous power to change and improve the world. This change will be for a blessing if we are wise enough to utilize our technology within the guidelines of integrity and holiness.

Fire in the Temple

This caveat leads to the second question we asked: why does the Torah limit the prohibition of lighting fire on the Sabbath to "your dwellings"? The Talmud (*Shabbat* 20a) explains that lighting fire is only forbidden in private dwellings, but in the Temple, it is permitted to burn offerings on the Sabbath. Why should fire be permitted in the Temple?

The holy Temple was a focal point of prophecy and divine revelation. It was the ultimate source of enlightenment, for both the individual and the nation. The fire used in the Temple is a metaphor for our mission to improve the world through advances in science and technology. We need to internalize the message that it is up to us to develop and advance the world, until the entire universe is renewed with a new heart and soul, with understanding and harmony. Permitting the technological innovation of fire in Temple on the Sabbath indicates that God wants us to utilize our intellectual gifts to innovate and improve, in a fashion similar to God's own creative acts.

We need to be constantly aware of our extraordinary potential when we follow the path that our Maker designated for us. At this spiritual level, we should not think that we are incapable of accomplishing new things. As the Talmud declares, "If they desire, the righteous can create worlds" (*Sanhedrin* 65b). When humanity attains ethical perfection, justice will then guide all of our actions, and scientific advances and inventions will draw their inspiration from the source of divine morality, the holy Temple.

Vayakheil

Choosing a Leader[1]

Betzalel's Appointment

God informed Moses of Betzalel's appointment to oversee the construction of the Tabernacle, and Moses subsequently apprised the people. According to the Midrash (*Berachot* 55a), however, this was not just a perfunctory notification.

> God asked, "Moses, is Betzalel acceptable to you?"
> "Master of the universe," exclaimed Moses, "if he is acceptable to You, then certainly he is acceptable to me!"
> "Nevertheless, I want you to speak with the people."
> So Moses went to the people, and asked them, "Is Betzalel acceptable to you?"
> "If he is acceptable to God and to you," responded the people, "then certainly he is acceptable to us!"

The Sages learned from this story a lesson in public appointments: one should seek the people's approval before assigning a leader. Still, it seems superfluous for God Himself to consult with Moses and the people. Certainly God knows who is best qualified to organize the Tabernacle construction; why bother consulting with Moses and the people? Was this just a formality, out of politeness?

---

[1] Adapted from *Ein Ayah* vol. II, p. 262.

Three Qualifications for a Leader

A great leader must possess three qualities. These qualities vary in importance and the ease by which they may be recognized.

The first trait of leadership is integrity and purity of soul. This is an inner quality, only fully revealed to the One Who examines innermost thoughts and feelings. It is also the key trait of true leadership.

The second quality sought in a leader is the wisdom needed to successfully guide the people. This quality is recognizable to people – but not to all people. Only the astute can accurately gauge a leader's sagacity. While not as crucial as the trait of personal integrity, an administrator cannot successfully lead the people without good judgment and political acumen.

The final quality that marks a successful leader consists of external talents apparent to all, such as charisma and eloquence. While these qualities are less important than the previous two, they certainly contribute to a leader's popularity and effectiveness.

The order is, of course, important. Candidates who excel only in the superficial qualifications make poor and even corrupt leaders. Good leadership is based on honesty and integrity. Upon these traits, the other two levels, political acumen and charisma, are built.

The Midrash about Betzalel reflects this prioritization. First, God affirmed Betzalel's qualifications in terms of those inner qualities that only God can truly know. While critical, these traits of integrity and purity are not sufficient. Therefore, He consulted with a wise leader – Moses – whether Betzalel also qualified in terms of the political wisdom necessary for the position. And finally, the people were consulted whether Betzalel met the qualifications that they sought in a popular leader.

Vayakheil

Stars in the Tabernacle[1]

There is an interesting tradition concerning the beautiful tapestries covering the Tabernacle. The covering was comprised of ten large tapestries with patterns of cherubs woven into them. These colorful tapestries were sewn together in two sets of five, and the two sections were then fastened together with fifty gold fasteners.

We know that the structure of the Tabernacle corresponded to the entire universe. What did these metal fasteners represent?

Like the Stars

The Talmud (*Shabbat* 99a) tells us that from inside the Tabernacle, the gold fasteners would sparkle against the background of the rich tapestries like stars twinkling in the sky.

This analogy of fasteners to the stars requires further examination. Stars and constellations represent powerful natural forces in the universe, influencing and controlling our world.[2] The Tabernacle fasteners, however, indicate a second function of the stars. The fasteners held the tapestries together. In fact, they emphasized the overall unity of the Tabernacle. By securing the two sets of tapestries together, they would "make the Tabernacle one" (Ex. 36:13).

---

[1] Adapted from *Ein Ayah* vol. IV, p. 245.
[2] "Good are the luminaries that our God has created.... He granted them strength and power, to be dominant within the world" (from the Sabbath morning prayers).

Holding the Universe Together

In general, the design of the Tabernacle reflected the structure of the universe and its underlying unity. For example, the Tabernacle building consisted of wooden beams with pegs that slid into silver sockets, called *adanim*. The precise interlocking of the Tabernacle's supporting base of *adanim* with the upright beams symbolizes the harmonious synchronization of the universe's foundations with the diversified forces and mechanisms that regulate and develop the world. When we reflect on the beautiful harmony of the different parts of the Tabernacle, we begin to be aware of the fundamental unity of the universe and all of its forces. This insight allows us to recognize that everything is the work of the Creator, Who unites all aspects of creation in His sublime Oneness.

For all of their grandeur and apparent autonomy, the true function of the stars is to act like the Tabernacle fasteners. They hold together the great canopy of the cosmos, in accordance with the Divine plan of creation. Like the sparkling fasteners, the stars "are filled with luster and radiate brightness" on their own accord, but their true function is to bind together the forces of the world, making the universe one.

Sefer Vayikra – The Book of Leviticus

Beyond our Imagination

When the Temple stands in its place, and the people of Israel reside in their homes; when God's *Shechinah*... is revealed in the Temple with strength and beauty; when the nation's children are learned in God; when the nation's select are true and righteous prophets, in whom the spirit of God speaks... ; when the burning fire of love for God, the God of Israel, enlightens the hearts of the nation... – then, the holy Temple, with all of its holy and wonderful service, "*Kohanim* in their service, Levites on their platforms, and Israel in their delegations," reveals, with flowing waves of vibrant life, the majesty of the nation's inner life, the cleaving of the nation's soul to its God, its extolled love, its holy connection to serving Him, with all of the passion of life, and with all the emotions of heart, soul and spirit....

But after the great destruction that we suffered; after our beloved House was burnt down, and the honor of our lives was lost; after our bones were scattered at the entrance of *Sheol;* after the voice of our inner life, strong and brave with the power of divine might and eternity, was laid low and silenced – it became impossible for us even to imagine the greatness and the power, the beauty and the purity... of the holy Temple service.
(*Olat Re'iyah* vol. I, pp. 117–118)

Vayikra

Animal Sacrifices in the Third Temple?[1]

What will the rebuilt Temple be like? Will we really offer animal sacrifices once again?

Protecting Animals

Some people object to the idea of sacrifices out of concern for the welfare of animals. However, this objection contains a measure of hypocrisy. Why should compassion for animals only be expressed with regard to humanity's spiritual needs? If our opposition to animal slaughter is based not on weakness of character, but on recognition of the issue's fundamental morality, then our first step should be to outlaw the killing of animals for food, clothing, and other material benefits.

In the world's present state, the human race is weak, both physically and morally. The hour to protect animal life has not yet arrived. We still need to slaughter animals for our physical needs, and human morality requires that we maintain clear boundaries to distinguish between the relative value of human and animal life.

At this point in time, to advocate the protection of animals in our service of God is disingenuous. Is it moral to permit cruelty towards animals for our physical needs, yet forbid their use for our spiritual service, in sincere recognition and gratitude for God's kindness? If our

---

[1] Rav Kook's views on the Temple service are sometimes misconstrued. A superficial reading of a passage in *Olat Re'iyah* (vol. I, p. 292) indicates that only grain offerings will be offered in the reinstated Temple service. To properly understand Rav Kook's approach, it is necessary to read a related essay from *Otzerot HaRe'iyah* vol. II, pp. 101–103.

dedication and love for God can be expressed – at its highest level – with our willingness to surrender our own lives and die *al kiddush Hashem*, sanctifying God's name, then certainly we should be willing to forgo the life of animals for this sublime goal.

The Return of Prophecy

Currently, however, we are not ready for an immediate restoration of the sacrificial service. Only with the return of prophecy will it be possible to restore the Temple order. In a letter penned in 1919,[2] Rav Kook explained:

> With regard to sacrifices, it is more correct to believe that all aspects will be restored to their place.... We should not be overly troubled by the views of European culture. In the future, God's word to His people will elevate all the foundations of culture to a level above that attainable by human reason.
>
> It is inappropriate to think that sacrifices only reflect the primitive idea of a worship of flesh. This service possesses a holy inner nature that cannot be revealed in its beauty without the illumination of God's light to His people[3] and a renewal of holiness to Israel. And this will be recognized by all peoples. But I agree with your honor that we should not approach the practical aspects of sacrifices without the advent of revealed divine inspiration in Israel.

The Future World

In the writings of the Kabbalists, we find a remarkable description of how the universe will look in the future, a world vastly changed from our

---

[2] *Igrot HaRe'iyah* vol. IV, p. 24.
[3] i.e., the return of prophecy to the Jewish people.

current reality. All aspects of the universe will be elevated. Even the animals in that future era will be different; they will advance to the level of people nowadays (*Sha'ar Hamitzvot* of the Ari z"l[4]). Obviously, no sacrifice could be offered from such humanlike animals. At that time, there will no longer be strife and conflict between the species. Human beings will no longer need to take the lives of animals for their physical, moral, and spiritual needs.

It is about this distant time that the Midrash (*Tanchuma Emor* 19; *Vayikra Rabbah* 9:7) makes the startling prediction, "All sacrifices will be annulled in the future." The prophet Malachi (3:4) similarly foretold of a lofty world in which the Temple service will only consist of grain offerings, in place of the animal sacrifices of old:

> Then the grain-offering of Judah and Jerusalem will be pleasing to God as in the days of old, and as in ancient years.

Hints to the Future

Even in the current reality, we may feel uncomfortable about killing animals. This does not mean that the time for full animal rights has already arrived. Rather, these feelings come from a hidden anticipation of the future that is already ingrained in our souls, like many other spiritual aspirations.

Hints of these future changes may be found in the text of the Torah itself. Thus, it says that offerings are slaughtered on the northern side of the altar. Why this side? The north traditionally represents that which is incomplete and lacking, as it is written, "Out of the north, the evil shall break forth" (Jeremiah 1:14). In other words, the need to slaughter animals is a temporary concession to life in an incomplete world.

---

[4] Rabbi Isaac Luria Ashkenazi (1534–1572) of Safed, founder of Lurian Kabbalah.

Furthermore, the Torah stipulates that sacrifices must be slaughtered *lir'tzonchem* – "willingly" (Lev. 19:5). The Temple service must correspond to our needs and wants. As the Talmud in *Erchin* 21a explains, one must be able to say, "I want to bring this offering." When the slaughter of animals is no longer generally acceptable to society, this condition will not be fulfilled.

Finally, the Torah describes a person offering an animal sacrifice as *adam* (Lev. 1:2). This word indicates our current state of moral decline, a result of the unresolved sin of Adam, the first man. An individual who brings a grain offering, on the other hand, is called *nefesh*, or "soul" (Lev. 2:1). The word *nefesh* implies a deeper, more essential level of humanity, independent of any temporary failings.

Vayikra

Sacrifices vs. Fasting[1]

When the fourth-century scholar Rabbi Sheshet fasted, he would add the following request to his *Amidah* (Standing) prayer:

> Master of the Universe! You know that when the Temple stood, a person who sinned would bring a sacrifice. Although only the fats and blood would be offered on the altar, the person would be granted atonement.
>
> Now I have fasted, and my fat and my blood have diminished. May it be Your Will that the decrease in my fat and my blood should be considered as if I offered them on the altar, and my offering was accepted. (*Berachot* 17a)

Rabbi Sheshet's prayer is inspiring, but it makes one wonder: Why should one go to the trouble of bringing a sacrifice if the same atonement may be achieved through fasting?

His prayer draws our attention to a second issue. Why were only the fats and blood of sin sacrifices (*chatat* and *asham*) offered on the altar?

Two Types of Sin

Regarding the offering of fats and blood, Rav Kook explained that there are two major inducements to sin. Some sins are the result of overindulgence in sensual pleasures and excessive luxuries. These wrongdoings are appropriately atoned by offering the *fats*.

---

[1] Adapted from *Ein Ayah* vol. I, p. 82.

The second category of transgressions is motivated by actual need: hunger and poverty. Great pressures can tempt one to lie, steal, even murder. The corresponding atonement for these sins is through the *blood* of the offering.

The Disadvantage of Fasting

By fasting, we can attain atonement in a way similar to the sacrifice of fats and blood in the Temple service. However, there is an important distinction between fasts and sacrifices. Offering a sacrifice in the holy Temple instilled the powerful message that it should really be the offender's blood spilled and body burned, were it not for God's kindness in accepting a substitute and a ransom. This visceral experience was a humbling encounter, subduing one's negative traits and desires.

Fasting, on the other hand, weakens all forces of the body. Just as chemotherapy treatment poisons other parts of the body as it fights the cancer, so too, fasting saps both our positive and negative energies. Fasting has the unwanted side effect of weakening our strength and energy to help others, perform *mitzvot*, and study Torah.

Therefore, Rabbi Sheshet added a special prayer when he fasted. He prayed that his fasting would achieve the same atonement as an offering in the Temple, without the undesirable effect of sapping positive energies.

Vayikra

Black Fire on White Fire[1]

With the construction of the Tabernacle complete, the holy structure began to fulfill its primary purpose: a conduit for communication between God and Moses. "I will commune with you there, speaking to you above the ark-cover" (Ex. 25:22). Before each actual communication, God would first summon Moses to the tent, with a Voice that only Moses could hear: "God called to Moses, speaking to him from the Communion Tent" (Lev. 1:1). What was the nature of this divine call?

The Miniature *Aleph* and the Four-Pronged *Shin*

The word *Vayikra* ("He called") is written in an unusual fashion. The last letter, the *aleph*, is written in miniature in the Torah. Did God command Moses to write it that way? Or was this an expression of Moses' extraordinary humility – an attempt to "hide" the *aleph*, so to speak, so that it would appear that God only "happened" (*vayikar*) to speak with Moses, similar to the chance prophetic experiences of evil Balaam?

We find a second unusual letter in the *tefillin* (phylacteries) worn on the head. Usually, the letter *shin* is written with three upward strokes, but the *shin* embossed on the left side of the *tefillin* has four. Some commentaries connect this peculiar *shin* to the Midrashic description of the Torah's transmission to Israel via black fire engraved on white fire. What does this mean? What are these black and white fires?

---

[1] Adapted from *Shemuot HaRe'iyah* IV.

Black Ink on White Parchment

When we think about a Torah scroll, we usually only consider the letters themselves, written in black ink. Yet, the Talmud (*Menachot* 29a) rules that every letter in a Torah scroll must be completely surrounded by parchment. This requirement is called *mukaf gevil*. In other words, the white parchment around the letters is an integral part of the Torah; without it, the Torah scroll is disqualified. In fact, the white space is a higher form of Torah. It is analogous to the white fire of Sinai – a sublime, hidden Torah that cannot be read in the usual manner.

There is a delicate balance between black and white in the Torah. The *shirot*, the poetic portions in the Torah, are written in a special fashion, like a wall constructed from layers of black and white bricks. These poetic sections are the loftiest parts of the Torah. Consequently, they have more white space, as they contain a greater measure of the esoteric white fire. If a scribe were to write other sections of the Torah in this special layout, the Torah scroll would be rendered invalid. After the Torah was revealed and restricted to our limited world, it must be written with the appropriate ratio of black to white.

What about the four-pronged *shin* on *tefillin*? The *mitzvah* of *tefillin* is closely connected to the manifestation of Torah after its revelation into the finite world. "All of the peoples of the land shall see that the name of God is called upon you, and they shall be in awe of you" (Deut. 28:10; see *Menachot* 35b). Thus, *tefillin* correspond to the lower realm of black fire, and are marked with a *shin* bearing an extra measure of black.

We can deepen our understanding of the white and black fires by considering another example of white space in the Torah. Extra space is left blank to separate sections of the Torah. The Sages explained that these separations allowed Moses to reflect upon and absorb the previous lesson. In other words, the white fire corresponds to the loftier realm of thought and contemplation. The black fire of the letters, on the other hand, is the revelation of intellect into the realm of language – a contraction and limitation of abstract thought into the more concrete level of speech.

The Divine Call before Revelation

The distinction between white and black fire also sheds light on God's call to Moses before speaking with him. The Voice summoning Moses to enter the tent was in fact the divine call from Sinai, an infinite call that never ceased (Deut. 5:19). The summons would reach Moses as he stood outside the tent, before being constrained within the four walls of the Tabernacle. This Voice was not a revelation of Torah, but an overture to its revelation. It belonged to the esoteric white fire of Torah, before its constriction and revelation into the physical world.

This is the reason that Moses made the *aleph* of the divine call smaller. Since it belonged to the realm of white fire, the summons required an extra measure of white space over black ink. Superficially, Moses' miniature *aleph* humbly implies a diminished state of the revealed Torah of black fire, but on a deeper level, it reflects an increase in the esoteric Torah of white fire.

Tzav

The *Olah* Offering and Prophecy[1]

The ultimate objective of the Temple service is *hashra'at Shechinah*, bringing the Divine Presence into our physical world. This goal is clearly connected to the unique phenomena of divine inspiration and prophecy. God's Presence in the Temple parallels on the national level the dwelling of prophecy in the mind of the prophet.

In particular, the *Olah* offering, completely burnt on the altar, corresponds to the highest level of communication between us and God, a sublime level in which the material world is of no consequence. Just as the altar fire utterly consumed the physical aspect of the offering, so too, this type of spiritual encounter completely transcends our physical existence. By examining the *Olah* service, we can gain insight into the prophetic experience.

Beyond the Physical Realm
The daily *Tamid* offering was completely consumed by fire on the altar during the night. What was done with the ashes? The following day, a *kohen* placed one shovelful of ashes next to the altar. To dispose of the rest, he changed into less important clothes, and transported the ashes to a ritually clean spot outside the camp.

Thus, we see that the *Olah* service involved three different locations, with descending sanctity:

- The fire on top of the altar.

---

[1] Adapted from *Olat Re'iyah* vol. I, pp. 122–124.

- Next to the altar, where a shovelful of ashes was placed.
- A ritually clean place outside the camp for the remaining ashes.

Three Stages

The prophetic experience is a blaze of sacred flames inside the human soul, a divine interaction that transcends ordinary life. This extraordinary event corresponds to the first stage, the nighttime burning of the offering in the fire of the holy altar.

However, the prophet wants to extend the impact of this lofty experience so that it can make its mark on his character traits and inner life. This effort corresponds to the placement of some of the ashes, transformed by the altar's flames, next to the altar. This is a secondary level of holiness, analogous to those aspects of life that are close to the holy itself, where impressions of the sacred vision may be stored in a pure state.

The lowest expression of the prophetic vision is in its public revelation. Informing the people of the content of God's message, and thereby infusing life and human morality with divine light – this takes place at a more peripheral level. Outside the inner camp, bordering on the domain of secular life, the *kohen* publicly brings out the remaining ashes. Even this area, however, must be ritually pure, so that the penetrating influence of the holy service can make its impact. For the sake of his public message, the *kohen*-prophet needs to descend somewhat from his former state of holiness, and change into lesser clothes. In the metaphoric language of the Sages, "The clothes worn by a servant while cooking for his master should not be used when serving his master wine" (*Shabbat* 114a).

The Constant Altar Fire

The Torah concludes its description of the *Olah* service by warning that the altar fire should be kept burning continuously: "The *kohen* will kindle wood on it each morning" (Lev. 6:5). Why mention this now?

Precisely at this juncture, after the *kohen*-prophet has left the inner nucleus of holiness in order to attend to life's temporal affairs, he must be aware of the constant fire on the altar. Despite his involvement with the practical and mundane aspects of life, the holy fire continues to burn inside the heart. This is the unique characteristic of the altar fire: from afar, it can warm and uplift every soul of the Jewish people. This sacred fire is a powerful, holy love that cannot be extinguished, as it says, "Mighty waters cannot extinguish the love; neither can rivers wash it away" (Song of Songs 8:7).

Yet, it is not enough for the holy fire to burn only in the inner depths of the heart. How can we ensure that its flames reach all aspects of life, and survive the "mighty waters" of mundane life?

The Torah's concluding instructions present the solution to this problem: "The *kohen* will kindle wood on it each morning." What is the purpose of this daily arrangement of kindling wood? New logs of wood nourish the altar's holy flames. We find a similar expression of daily spiritual replenishment in Isaiah 50:4: "*Each morning* He awakens my ear to hear according to the teachings." Just as renewal of the altar's hearth each day revives the holy fire, so too, daily contemplation of God's wonders and renewed study of His Torah rejuvenates the soul. This renewal energizes the soul, giving strength for new deeds and aspirations, and awakening a new spirit of life from the soul's inner fire.

Tzav

The Prohibition of *Cheilev*[1]

Do not eat any of the hard fat (*cheilev*) in an ox,
sheep, or goat. (Lev. 7:23)

Some commentaries[2] explain that the Torah prohibits eating these
fats for health reasons. Yet, if this were true, why is only the *cheilev* of
these three animals forbidden?

Curiously, we find that the *mitzvah* of *kisuy hadam*, covering the
blood after slaughtering, only applies to non-domesticated animals and
fowl. Why does the Torah not require *kisuy hadam* also for cattle, sheep,
and goats? Why do these two *mitzvot*, both of which pertain to the
preparation of kosher meat, apply to two mutually exclusive groups of
animals?

Domesticated and Wild Animals
If we analyze the degree of sensitivity one should have when taking the
life of an animal for food, we should differentiate between two categories
of animals. The first category consists of animals that we do not feed and
raise. These are wild animals that are hunted and killed. All birds are
included in this category, as they usually need to be trapped.[3] We should
feel embarrassment when we must stoop to such ignoble and cruel
behavior. Therefore, when stalking and killing untamed animals and birds,

---

[1] Adapted from *Otzerot HaRe'iyah* vol. II, p. 95.
[2] Maimonides, *Guide for the Perplexed*, III: 48; *Sefer HaChinuch, mitzvah* 147.
[3] Of course, this was more applicable in the days when chickens and other
poultry were allowed to roam freely, not cooped up in small cages.

the Torah commands us to cover the blood, a sign of our inner shame at this merciless act. "If any man... traps a wild animal or bird that may be eaten and sheds its blood, he must cover the blood with earth" (Lev. 17:13).

The second category of animals is comprised of domesticated beasts: cattle, sheep, and goats. We raise and feed them for their milk, wool, and labor. Not to kill these animals for food after they approach old age and are much less productive, requires a higher and more refined sense of ethical sensitivity. Regarding this category of animals, who become a burden to their owner in old age, the Torah does not require that their blood be covered after their slaughter. We need not feel the same extent of embarrassment as when taking the life of a wild animal.

Nonetheless, the Torah created for domesticated animals a special prohibition to remind us that we should only take their lives for our essential needs. This is the purpose of the prohibition of *cheilev*. We are permitted to slaughter these animals for their meat, to give us energy and strength, but they should not be killed for the sake of their fats. We should not kill them merely for the pleasure of eating their fatty meat, so pleasurable to the palate of the gastronome. The prohibition of *cheilev* emphasizes that we should only take their lives out of genuine necessity.

Why does the Torah not prohibit eating the fats of birds and wild animals? We should feel ashamed at this cruel act, regardless of whether our intent is for pure enjoyment or true need. If the Torah distinguished between their meat and their fats, this would only obscure the moral impact of covering their blood, a sign of our profound embarrassment over spilling the blood of a free animal, no matter what the circumstances.

Shemini

The Priestly Benediction[1]

The Tabernacle inauguration concluded with a blessing from the High Priest:

> Aaron lifted his hands towards the people and blessed them. He then descended from preparing the sin offering, the burnt offering, and the peace offerings. (Lev. 9:22)

When Was the Blessing Recited?

From the Torah's account, it would seem that Aaron blessed the people before he completed the service in the newly dedicated Tabernacle. The Sages, however, explained that the actual order was different. First, Aaron completed the offerings and descended from the altar. Only afterwards did he bless the people (*Torat Kohanim; Megillah* 18a).

If the priestly benediction was performed at the end of the Temple service (which nowadays is recited at the end of the *Amidah* prayer), why does the Torah imply a different order?

The True Honor of *Kohanim*

When discussing the contribution of the *kohanim* to the Jewish people, and the corresponding honor they receive, we must distinguish between their current state and their future potential.

---

[1] Adapted from *Olat Re'iyah* vol. I, pp. 284–285; *Otzerot HaRe'iyah* vol. II, pp. 211–212.

We may respect an individual *kohen* for his scholarship and piety, but the true honor we bestow to *kohanim* is in recognition of their holy influence over the entire nation. We honor them primarily for their future potential, for what a *kohen* should and can be – "for he is an emissary of God of the hosts" (Malachi 2:7). Even if the *kohen* is undeserving of such honor in his present state, "You must strive to keep him holy... he *will be* holy for you, since I am holy" (Lev. 21:8). His holiness is due to his potential benefit to the nation, as a member of the sanctified family.[2]

Two Roles of the Priesthood

The function of the *kohanim* is not only to serve in the Temple. The *kohanim* are also expected to teach and elevate the people, as it says, "From the *kohen*'s lips they will guard knowledge, and they will seek Torah from his mouth" (Malachi 2:7). These two roles are interrelated, since the source for their spiritual influence on the people originates in the holiness of their service in the Temple.

There is one duty of the *kohanim* that combines both of these roles: the priestly blessing. This blessing is part of the Temple service, and at the same time, reflects their interaction with the people. The *kohanim* recite the blessing with outstretched arms, a sign that their efforts to uplift the people are an extension and continuation of their holy service in the Temple.

Bridging the Past and the Future

The blessing also forms a bridge over time, connecting the past with the future and the actualized with the potential.

---

[2] This, by the way, is similar to the honor we give to rabbis and teachers. We respect them for their erudition and also as representatives of the institution of the rabbinate. This honor is in recognition of the overall contribution of the rabbinate to the welfare of the people. The rabbi on his part should realize that he is primarily honored for what he ought to be, and should do his best to fulfill this expectation.

The *kohanim* can best fulfill their mission to uplift the people after they have participated in the Temple service and experienced the unique elevation of soul gained through this holy public service. Their blessing will then reflect the highest level of influence and inspiration the *kohen* is able to impart. Thus, the blessing indicates the present state of the *kohen*, while being based on his past service, and extending – like his outstretched arms – to his future potential influence.

Now we can resolve the apparent contradiction between the Torah's account and actual practice. The text implies that the *kohanim* complete their service after blessing the people. The service referred to here is not their service in the Temple, but their role in uplifting the people, which is truly their primary mission. In practice, however, the priestly blessing needs to be based on the holy services that they have already performed. Therefore, it is recited only after they have completed their service in the Temple.

The Impact of Prayer

A similar phenomenon is found at the end of the *Amidah* prayer, when we say, "May the words of my mouth and the thoughts of my heart be acceptable before You" (Psalms 19:15). It would appear more logical to recite this plea before praying. In fact, the verse does not refer to the prayer about to be recited, but to our heartfelt aspiration that we should be able to apply the influence of this prayer on the coming day. Like the priestly benediction, this request forms a bridge between two states. It is based on the prayer service just performed, but it looks forward to the future influence of this spiritual elevation on our lives.

Shemini

Immersion in Water[1]

If any of these dead [animals] falls on a vessel, it will become unclean.... That article must be immersed in a *mikveh*. (Lev. 11:32)

The topic of ritual impurity is a difficult one. This impurity is not a tangible quality that may be seen or felt. It is a spiritual contamination, the result of association with death. To purify ourselves from this contamination, we must immerse ourselves in a natural spring or a ritual bath (*mikveh*) filled with rainwater.

Why Immersion in Water?

The story is told of a wealthy American Jew who decided to visit one of the leading Torah scholars of his generation. Upon arriving at the rabbi's home, the visitor was shocked to discover that the renowned scholar lived in a simple house, with a dirt floor and shabby wood furnishings. Anxious to help the rabbi improve his living conditions, the guest suggested that it would be more becoming for such an eminent scholar to have more respectable furnishings, and he would be more than happy to pay for all expenses.

The rabbi turned to his guest. "And tell me, where is your furniture?"

"My furniture?" responded the American Jew, baffled. "Why, I am only a visitor here. I don't travel with all my belongings."

---

[1] Adapted from *Ein Ayah* vol. I, p. 74.

"So with me," the rabbi replied. "I am only a visitor here in this world...."

A Lesson in Estrangement

The very act of immersing ourselves in water contains a profound psychological lesson. All immoral deeds, flawed character traits, and erroneous opinions stem from the same fundamental mistake: not recognizing that life in this world is transitory. Here, we are only visitors. Whatever we find here should be utilized for its eternal value.

When we immerse ourselves in water, we are forced to recognize our existential estrangement from the physical universe. How long can we survive under water? The experience of submerging drives home the realization that our existence in this world is transient, and we should strive towards more lasting goals.

Tents and Natural Springs

The Sages (*Berachot* 16a) hinted to this insight when they compared the results of Torah study to that of a purifying spring:

> Why did Balaam (Num. 24:6) compare the tents of Israel to streams? This teaches us that just as a spring raises one from impurity to purity, so too, the tents [of Torah learning] raise one from a state of culpability to a state of merit.

In what way is learning Torah like submerging in a natural spring? Torah study and immersion in water have a similar beneficial effect. Instead of focusing only on the material matters of this world, learning the wisdom of Torah raises our sights to eternal values and aspirations. For this reason, the Sages used the expression, "tents of Torah." Why tents? A tent is the most transient of homes. This phrase emphasizes the quality of Torah that, like a purifying *mikveh* or a natural spring, makes us aware of the transitory nature of the physical world.

191

A Return to Ritual Purity[1]

These Torah readings discuss at length topics that are among the most challenging for us to relate to. What relevance do the laws of ritual purity and impurity – after childbirth, for lepers and for various types of male and female discharges – hold for us? Why does the Torah place such emphasis on these matters? Why do we feel so far removed from them?

The *Taharah* Axiom

In his book *Orot*, Rav Kook posited the following principle: *The degree of purity required is a function of the comprehensiveness of the spiritual framework.* The more inclusive a framework is, encompassing more aspects of life, the more rigorous are the requirements for *taharah*, ritual purity.

The Temple and its service are a classic example. The Temple projected an ethical and holy influence on a wide range of life's aspects – from the noble heights of divine inspiration and prophecy, through the powers of imagination and the emotions (the outbursts of joy and awe in the Temple service), all the way down to the physical level of flesh and blood (the actual sacrifices). Because its impact reached even the lowest levels of physical existence – which are nonetheless integrally connected to all other aspects of life in an organic whole – the Temple and its service required an exact and precise purity.

By contrast, a spiritual and moral influence that is directed only towards the intellect does not require such a refined degree of physical purity. Thus, the Sages taught, Torah may be studied even when impure.

---

[1] Adapted from *Orot*, p. 81 (*Orot HaTechiyah*, section 35).

"Is not My word like fire? says the Lord" (Jer. 23:29) – "Just as fire does not become impure, so too words of Torah cannot become impure" (*Berachot* 22a).

Changes throughout History

As the Jewish people returned from exile in Babylonia and rebuilt the Temple, it was necessary to revive the Temple's strict requirements of *taharah*. For this reason, Ezra enacted a series of enactments stressing the need for greater ritual purity during this period.

The long exile that followed the Second Temple period, however, greatly weakened the emotive and imaginative abilities of the people. The intensity and aesthetic quality of spiritual life became impoverished, and the corresponding need for a rigorous degree of purity was accordingly diminished. Thus we find that one of the six orders of the Mishnah (compiled in the Land of Israel) is *Taharot*, dealing exclusively with matters of ritual purity. Of the 37 tractates of the Talmud (composed in the Babylonian exile), however, only one belongs to this order. Similarly, the Talmud repealed Ezra's decree obligating immersion before Torah study.

What remained for the Jewish people in exile? Only the Torah and its intellectual influence. It still involved the physical realm through the practical observance of *mitzvot*, but the intermediate stages of imagination and feeling were bypassed. In exile, we lament, "Nothing remains but this Torah" (from the *Selichot* prayers).

In the long centuries of exile, meticulousness in matters of ritual purity lost its obligatory nature. It became associated with idealistic longings, the province of the pious few.

A Return to *Taharah*

The Hasidic movement of the 1700's aspired to restore the concepts of physical purity to the masses. Hasidism places a greater emphasis on the imaginative and emotional faculties – particularly through prayer and song

– than the intellectual. As a result, it awakened a greater need for personal and physical purity. This objective certainly contains a healthy kernel, although it needs additional direction and refinement.

Especially now, with the national renascence of the Jewish people in the Land of Israel, these aspirations for physical *taharah* should be renewed and expanded. Our national renewal complements the renewed yearning for spirituality; and the healthy desire to restore the nation and heal its national soul applies to all aspects of life, including physical purity.

It is precisely in the camps of the Jewish army that the Torah demands a high level of purity:

> For the Lord your God makes His presence known in your camp, so as to deliver you and grant you victory over your enemy. Your camp must therefore be holy. (Deut. 23:15)

Together with the renewal of our national strength and vitality, there must be a corresponding reinforcement of emotive and physical purity. This will help prepare the basis for an integrated national life that encompasses a complete rebirth of the people: from the highest intellectual pursuits, to the simple joy in life and living.

Purifying Time and Soul[1]

The Torah discusses various types of *tum'ah* (ritual impurity), the most prominent being *tzara'at*, a skin affliction similar to leprosy. Purification from these forms of impurity includes immersion in a *mikveh* (ritual bath) or natural spring. Immersion alone, however, is not sufficient; even after immersing, the individual remains impure until the start of the evening.

> The sun sets, and then he is ritually clean. He may then eat the sacred offerings that are his portion. (Lev. 22:7)

Waiting until the Day is "Clean"

Curiously, the Talmud (*Berachot* 2) interprets this verse in a forced fashion: "The sun sets, and then it – the day – is clean [i.e., finished]." The Sages explained that the day must be completely over before the individual may partake of his offering.

Why not understand the verse literally: when the sun sets, the person is ritually clean? Why emphasize that the day must be "clean"?

According to Maimonides,[2] different forms of *tum'ah* correspond to various flawed character traits, erroneous beliefs, and impure acts. The Sages wrote that *tzara'at*, for example, is the result of slander and haughtiness. It is logical, then, that the various stages of purification – immersion in a spring or *mikveh*, waiting until nighttime, and bringing an offering – will be connected to the correction of these faults.

---

[1] Adapted from *Ein Ayah* vol. I, pp. 2–3.
[2] *Guide for the Perplexed* III: 47.

Two Aspects to Repair

The Talmud refers to two levels of purification: purifying the day (*tehar yoma*), and purifying the individual (*tehar gavra*). What is the difference between the two?

Our goal in life should be to grow spiritually and become closer to our Creator. When we sin, we stray from our overall objective. We have also misused time that could have been utilized for spiritual growth. A full life is one in which all of the days have been employed towards one's principle objective. Abraham, the Torah tells us, was *ba bayamim*, "well advanced in days" (Gen. 24:1). His days and years were full and complete, wholly occupied with spiritual pursuits.

When we stray from our spiritual aspirations, we need to make two distinct efforts in order to return to our original path. If I were to upset a friend, I would first need to correct my hurtful behavior. However, that alone would be insufficient to restore the friendship to its former state. The relationship will remain fragile until I have made an additional effort to rebuild the ties of friendship and affection.

The first stage – correcting the faulty behavior or flawed character trait – is analogous to the cleansing action of immersion in water. We immerse ourselves in the *mikveh*, leaving behind negative traits and flawed deeds. As we immerse ourselves in spiritual repair, we restore to the dimension of time its original purity. The day has not been lost to sin. With the setting of the sun, we begin a new day and a new start. This is the first level of purification, what the Sages called *tehar yoma*. The day has been purified; we have rectified the dimension of time.

Yet, we have not completely regained our previous state of purity. We still need to restore our former closeness to God. This is achieved through the final stage of purification: "he may then eat the sacred offerings." With renewed desire to be close to God, we bring an offering. The offering (*korban*, from the root *karav*, "to draw near") enables us to draw closer to our Maker with awe and love. At this point, we repair our

196

relationship with God. Not only has the element of time been rectified, we too have become cleansed and renewed. This is the level of *tehar gavra*, when the individual is fully purified, and his errors are transformed into merits.

Acharei Mot

The Ox and the Goat[1]

There are many unique aspects to the Temple service on Yom Kippur, the Day of Atonement. One special feature of Yom Kippur concerns the *chatat* sin-offerings. On all other holidays, a single sin-offering was brought, from a goat. On Yom Kippur, however, there were two sin-offerings: an ox and a goat. What is the significance of these two animals, the ox and the goat?

Forgiveness for All Actions
The ox is a symbol of great strength. Oxen were traditionally used for construction and cultivating land. The ox's strength was harnessed to till the earth, to transport goods, and other constructive purposes.

The goat is also a symbol of power – but of a corrosive, destructive nature. The Hebrew word for goat (*sa'ir*) means to storm and rage. The foraging goat devours the very roots of the plants. Overgrazing by goats leads to land-erosion and destruction of pasture.

Both of these forms of power – constructive and destructive – may be used for positive goals, and both may be utilized for evil purposes. Each has its proper place and time. We use constructive forces to build and advance, and we need destructive forces when dismantling existing structures in order to rebuild and improve. Both types of forces, however, may be abused, causing much sorrow and grief.

---

[1] Adapted from *Olat Re'iyah*, vol. I, p. 167.

The most common need for atonement is when we accidentally hurt or damage. For this reason, the standard *chatat* offering is the goat, a symbol of blight and destruction.

On Yom Kippur, however, we seek forgiveness for the misuse of all forms of power. Therefore, we offer a second *chatat* from an ox, the classic beast of labor. With this offering, we express our regret if, inadvertently, our constructive deeds may have been inappropriate or harmful.

Acharei Mot

The Goat for Azazel[1]

Perhaps the most unusual of all the Temple services was the Yom Kippur ceremony of *Azazel*, sending off a goat into the wilderness, symbolically carrying away the sins of Israel. No other Temple offering was performed in such a fashion. Even more surprising, immediately after describing the Yom Kippur service, the Torah warns, "The Israelites will then stop sacrificing to the demons who tempt them" (Lev. 17:7). The text implies that the goat sent to *Azazel* is the sole exception to this rule, in apparent contradiction to the fundamental principles of the Temple service. Was this unusual ritual a "sacrifice to the demons"?

The Highest Form of Forgiveness
In order to understand the meaning of the *Azazel* service, we must appreciate the nature of the forgiveness and atonement of Yom Kippur.

The highest level of forgiveness emanates from the very source of divine *chesed*. It comes from an infinite greatness that can embrace both the most comprehensive overview and the most detailed scrutiny. This level knows the holy and the good with all of their benefits, as well as the profane and the evil with all of their harm. It recognizes that all is measured on the exacting scale of divine justice, and that the tendencies towards evil and destruction also serve a purpose in the universe. Such an elevated level of forgiveness understands how, in the overall picture, everything fits together.

---

[1] Adapted from *Olat Re'iyah* vol. II, p. 357; *Shemoneh Kevatzim* IV:91, V:193.

This recognition creates a complicated dialectic. There is a clear distinction between good and evil, truth and falsehood, nobility and debasement. Absolute truth demands that we confront the paths of idolatry and evil, in deed and thought; it opposes all repulsiveness, impurity and sin. Still, in its greatness, it finds a place for all. Only an elevated understanding can absorb this concept: how to combine together all aspects of the universe, how to arrange each force, how to extend a measured hand to all opposites, while properly demarcating their boundaries.

The forgiveness of Yom Kippur aspires to this lofty outlook, as expressed in the *Azazel* offering. *Azazel* is the worship of demons – the demonic wildness and unrestrained barbarity to be found in human nature. For this reason, the offering was sent to a desolate cliff in the untamed wilderness. The elevated service of Yom Kippur is able to attain a level that confers a limited recognition even to the demonic evil of *Azazel*. At this level, all flaws are transformed and rectified.

Sent Away to the Wilderness

The abstract knowledge that evil also has a purpose in the world must be acknowledged in some fashion in our service of God. This acknowledgment occurs in the elevated service of Yom Kippur. In practical ethics, however, there is no place for this knowledge. Heaven forbid that evil should be considered good, or that the wicked should be considered righteous. Therefore, the goat for *Azazel* was sent to a desolate, barren place – a place uninhabited by people. Human society must be based on a just way of life, led by aspirations of holiness and purity.

Kedoshim

Sha'atnez – A Glimpse into the Future[1]

While first introduced here in Lev. 19:19, the prohibition of *sha'atnez* is more clearly defined later on in the Torah: "Do not wear *sha'atnez* – wool and linen together" (Deut. 22:11). Why does the Torah prohibit using wool and linen in the same article of clothing? Also, the special garments of High Priest contained both wool and linen. Why was he allowed to wear *sha'atnez*?

Chok – for the Future

These two materials – linen, from the flax plant, and wool, shorn from sheep – were the two major fibers available to ancient civilizations. According to one opinion in the Talmud (*Shabbat* 26b), whenever the Torah speaks of garments without specifying the material, it only refers to garments of wool or linen.

The Torah's prohibition of wearing linen and wool together is a prime example of a *chok*, a decree for which we do not know the reason. As Rashi wrote, the nations of the world and the evil inclination taunt us, saying, "What is this command? What logic is there to it?"

According to Rav Kook, it is not that a *chok* has no reason, or no reason that we are capable of grasping. Rather, this category of *mitzvot* belongs to a future reality that is different from our own. At that future time, the purpose of these decrees will become clear.

In other words, these *mitzvot* serve to morally prepare us for the future.

---

[1] Adapted from *Igrot HaRe'iyah* vol. I, p. 104.

One intriguing view of the future is the idea expressed by the Kabbalists that the future elevation of the universe will also include a radical change in the animals. Animals will develop into a state similar to the current level of human beings. This belief plays a central role in Rav Kook's writings in many areas: vegetarianism, Temple sacrifices,[2] and understanding decrees such as *sha'atnez* and not eating milk and meat together.

The use of linen from the flax plant does not raise any moral dilemmas. But the use of wool necessitates a mild censure from the standpoint of absolute morality:

> Man, in his boundless egocentricity, approaches the poor cow and sheep. From one he seizes its milk, and from the other, its fleece.... There would be no impropriety in taking the wool were the sheep burdened by its load; but we remove the wool when its natural owner needs it. Intellectually, we recognize that this is a form of theft – oppression of the weak at the hands of the strong. (*Otzerot HaRe'iyah* vol. II, p. 97)

Of course, the moral offense applies primarily with regard to the future state of sheep.

In order to distinguish between the use of wool and linen, and instill a sensitivity towards animal welfare that we will need in future times, the Torah decreed that these two fibers should not be worn together. Utilization of the flax plant and manipulation of sheep are not – in absolute terms – morally equivalent.

All of this is true when the wool is used for private consumption. But if the wool is designated for divine service – as in the clothes of the High Priest – then the principle of *bechol me'odecha*, serving God with all of our possessions, takes force. Here it is appropriate that, out of their own

---

[2] See "*Vayikra*: Animal Sacrifices in the Third Temple?"

free will, the animals will contribute their part for the sake of the universe's spiritual elevation.

Why Only Linen?

A student once asked Rav Kook why, according to this explanation, the Torah only forbids linen together with wool, but not other fibers (such as cotton) together with wool.

Rav Kook answered that *mitzvot* are like words. Through these words, we can discern the Torah's fundamental teachings. If one word is sufficient to convey the message, there is no need for another word to teach the very same concept.

However, the word chosen should be the best and most lucid. The message of concern for animal welfare needs to be ingrained in the minds of society's leaders. Therefore, the Torah chose to express this message through linen, the fiber favored for respectable and elegant clothing in olden times. Fibers such as cotton are used for purely utilitarian purposes. Linen best symbolizes our desire to clothe ourselves in dignity and honor; thus, it is the best medium to express the need for human sensitivity towards animals.

Kedoshim

First Impressions[1]

Eating before Prayer

Together with various other forbidden practices, the Torah admonishes, "Do not eat the blood" (Lev. 19:26). Literally, the verse reads, "Do not eat over the blood." What does it mean to "eat over blood"?

The Talmud offers several explanations, including the warning, "Do not eat before you have prayed over your blood [i.e., for the sake of your soul]" (*Berachot* 10b). Why is it so important to refrain from eating before reciting the morning prayers?

Refining the *Nefesh*

We find that the Torah equates blood to the *nefesh* (the soul), as it says, "The blood is the *nefesh*" (Deut. 12:23). What is the *nefesh*? This is the lowest part of the soul, the basic life-force that is common to both humans and animals. The desires of the *nefesh* naturally relate to our physical needs. However, the human intellect can guide and direct these desires. In fact, this is the function of prayer: to refine and elevate the emotional and imaginative parts of the soul. Through prayer, we bind our feelings and desires to pure and holy aims.

On this basic level, what we do in the beginning of the day sets the tone for the entire day. Our initial feelings and impressions accompany us throughout the day.

---

[1] Adapted from *Olat Re'iyah* vol. I, p. 248; Ein Ayah vol. I, p. 61.

If we start the day by eating, then we have already weighed down our souls with the burden of satisfying physical wants. This establishes the desires of the *nefesh* as base and animalistic.

But if the very first act of the day is prayer, then we have ensured that the initial impressions on the soul will be pure, directed towards higher and holier aspirations. While the day is fresh and the soul has not been burdened with lowly images, prayer can make its impact, impressing upon the soul the sublime goal of drawing close to our Creator.

Emor

Kohanim and the Illusion of Death[1]

> God told Moses, "Speak to the *kohanim*, the
> descendants of Aaron. Let no [*kohen*] defile himself
> [by contact] with a dead soul among his
> people. (Lev. 21:1)

Why are *kohanim* not allowed to come in contact with a dead
body? Why does the Torah refer to the dead person as a "dead soul"?
After all, it is the body that dies, not the soul!

The Parable of Twin Brothers

In his book on Jewish mourning practices, *Gesher Hachaim*, Rabbi
Tukachinsky used the following parable to explain the Jewish view on life
after death:

Twin brothers, fetuses in their mother's womb, enjoyed a carefree
life. Their world was dark and warm and protected. These twins were alike
in all aspects but one. One brother was a "believer": he believed in an
afterlife, in a future reality much different from their current, miniature
universe.

The second brother, however, was a skeptic. All he knew was the
familiar world of the womb. Anything besides what he could feel and
sense was only an illusion. The skeptic tried to talk some sense into his
brother. He warned him to be realistic, but to no avail. His naive brother
insisted on believing in an extraordinary world that exists after life in the

---

[1] Adapted from *Orot HaKodesh* vol. II, p. 380.

womb, a world so immense and fantastic that it transcends their wildest dreams.

The months passed, and the fatal moment arrived. Labor began. The fetuses became aware of tremendous contractions and shifting in their little world. The freethinker recognized that "this is it." His short but pleasant life was about to end. He felt the forces pressuring him to go down, but fought against them. He knew that outside the womb, a cruel death awaited, with no protective sack and no umbilical cord. Suddenly, he realized that his naive brother was giving in to the forces around them. His brother was sinking lower!

"Don't give up!" he cried, but his twin took no heed. "Where are you, my dear brother?" He shuddered as he heard the screams from outside the womb. His poor brother had met his cruel fate. How naive he had been, with his foolish belief in a bigger, better world!

Then the skeptic felt the uterine muscles pushing him out, against his will, into the abyss. He screamed out...

"*Mazal Tov!*" called out the doctor. "Two healthy baby boys!"

The Illusion of Death

Rav Kook wrote:

> Death is a false illusion; its defilement is due to its deceptive nature. What people call "death" is in fact the intensification of life. Because man wallows in pettiness, he pictures this increase of life in a pained, black fashion, which he calls "death."

The *kohanim* in their holiness are able to rise above this falsehood. Yet, falsehood and deception rule over the world. In order to overcome the illusion of death, the *kohanim* must limit their exposure to death. They need to protect themselves from those images that impress the soul with deceiving messages.

The word "soul" in the verse does not refer to soul of the dead person. It refers to the soul of the *kohen*. This is how the verse should be understood: "For the sake of the soul, the *kohen* shall not defile himself among his people" – for the sake of the *kohen*'s soul, he must distance and protect himself from death and its illusions.

Eating before Yom Kippur[1]

The Ninth of Tishrei

While there are several rabbinically-ordained fasts throughout the year, only one day of fasting is mentioned in the Torah:

> It is a sabbath of sabbaths to you, when you must fast. Keep this holiday on the ninth of the month in the evening, from evening until [the next] evening. (Lev. 23:32)

This refers to the fast of Yom Kippur. The verse, however, appears to contain a rather obvious "mistake": Yom Kippur falls out on the tenth of Tishrei, not the ninth!

The Talmud (*Berachot* 8b) explains that the day before Yom Kippur is also part of the atonement process, even though there is no fasting: "This teaches that one who eats and drinks on the ninth is credited as if he fasted on both the ninth and tenth."

Still, we need to understand: Why is there a *mitzvah* to eat on the day before Yom Kippur? In what way does this eating count as a day of fasting?

Two Forms of *Teshuvah*

The theme of Yom Kippur is, of course, *teshuvah* – repentance, the soul's return to its natural purity. There are two major aspects to *teshuvah*. The first is the need to restore the spiritual sensitivity of the soul, dulled by

---

[1] Adapted from *Ein Ayah* vol. I, p. 42.

over-indulgence in physical pleasures. This refinement is achieved by temporarily rejecting physical enjoyment, and substituting life's hectic pace with prayer and reflection. The Torah gave us one day a year, the fast of Yom Kippur, to concentrate exclusively on refining our spirits and redefining our goals.

However, the aim of Judaism is not asceticism. As Maimonides wrote (*Mishneh Torah*, *Hilchot Dei'ot* 3:1):

> One might say, since jealousy, lust and arrogance are bad traits, driving a person out of the world, I shall go to the opposite extreme. I will not eat meat, drink wine, marry, live in a pleasant house, or wear nice clothing... like the idolatrous monks. This is wrong, and it is forbidden to do so. One who follows this path is called a sinner.... Therefore, the Sages instructed that we should only restrict ourselves from that which the Torah forbids.... It is improper to constantly fast.

The second aspect of *teshuvah* is more practical and down-to-earth. We need to become accustomed to acting properly and avoid the pitfalls of material desires that violate the Torah's teachings. This type of *teshuvah* is not attained by fasts and prayer, but by preserving our spiritual integrity while we are involved in worldly matters.

The true goal of Yom Kippur is achieved when we can remain faithful to our spiritual essence while remaining active participants in the physical world. When do we accomplish this aspect of *teshuvah*? When we eat on the ninth of Tishrei. Then we demonstrate that, despite our occupation with mundane activities, we can remain faithful to the Torah's values and ideals. Thus, our eating on the day before Yom Kippur is connected to our fasting on Yom Kippur itself. Together, these two days correspond to the two corrective aspects of the *teshuvah* process.

By preceding the fast with eating and drinking, we ensure that the reflection and spiritual refinement of Yom Kippur are not isolated to that one day, but have an influence on the entire year's involvement in worldly activities. The inner, meditative *teshuvah* of the tenth of Tishrei is thus complemented by the practical *teshuvah* of the ninth.

Behar

Jubilee – National Reconciliation[1]

In 1751, the Pennsylvania Assembly ordered a special bell be cast, commemorating the 50th anniversary of William Penn's "Charter of Privileges." The Speaker of the Assembly was entrusted with finding an appropriate inscription for what later became famous as the Liberty Bell. The best expression of freedom and equality that the speaker could find was the Biblical verse describing the Jubilee year:

> You will blow the shofar on the tenth day of the seventh month; on Yom Kippur you will blow the shofar in all your land. You shall sanctify the fiftieth year, proclaiming freedom to all its inhabitants. (Lev. 25:9–10)

The triumphant announcement of the Jubilee year, with blasts of the shofar, takes place on the tenth of Tishrei. This date is Yom Kippur, the Day of Atonement. Yet, this is a curious date to announce the new year. The Jubilee year, like any other year, begins on the first of Tishrei, on Rosh Hashanah. Why was the formal proclamation of the Jubilee year postponed until Yom Kippur, ten days later?

National Sabbath Rest
The Jubilee year is a super-Sabbatical year. Like the seventh year, agricultural labor is prohibited, and landowners forego all claims on produce grown during that year. The Jubilee also contains two additional

---

[1] Adapted from the Forward to *Shabbat Ha'Aretz*, p. 9.

aspects of social justice: the emancipation of slaves and the restoration of land to its original owner.

Just as the Sabbath day allows the individual to rest, so too the Sabbatical and Jubilee years provide rest for the nation. The entire nation is able to take a break from competition and economic struggle. The Sages noted that the phrase "Sabbath to God" appears both in the context of the weekly Sabbath and the Sabbatical year. Both are designed to direct us towards spiritual growth: the Sabbath on the individual level, and the Sabbatical year on the national level.

Healing Rifts in Society

The Talmud in *Rosh Hashanah* 8b relates that during the first ten days of the Jubilee year, the slaves were not sent home. Nor did they work. They would feast and drink, celebrating their freedom "with crowns upon their heads." Only after the court blew the shofar on Yom Kippur would the newly freed slaves return home.

The freeing of slaves in the Jubilee year serves as an important safeguard for social order. Societies that rely on slave labor usually suffer from slave revolts and violent acts of vengeance by the underclass.[2] Instead of attaining social justice through bloody revolt and violent upheaval, the Jubilee emancipation allows for peaceful and harmonious social change. The restoration of rights for the poor and disadvantaged becomes an inherent part of the societal and economic order.

Most significantly, during their final days of servitude, the freed slaves celebrate together with their former masters. The Torah also obligates the master to send off his servants with generous presents (*ha'anakah*). These conciliatory acts help heal the social and psychological wounds caused by socio-economic divisions and class estrangement. The

---

[2] Slave revolts were common in ancient Rome. In the United States, the emancipation of black slaves was only achieved after a horrific civil war.

national reconciliation reaches its peak on Yom Kippur, when the shofar exuberantly proclaimed freedom and equality.

Atonement for the Nation

Thus, the formal announcement of the Jubilee year is integrally connected to Yom Kippur. On that year, the Day of Atonement becomes a time of forgiveness and absolution, not only for the sins of the individual, but also for the sins of society.

Behar

Shemitah – Window to the Future[1]

Like the Garden of Eden

Ask any farmer – agricultural labor is hard work. Plowing, planting, weeding, pruning, harvesting, and so on. That, however, is not how it was supposed to be. The world was originally designed to be like life in the Garden of Eden. Agricultural labor was only cursed after Adam's sin – "By the sweat of your brow you will eat bread" (Gen. 3:19).

As humanity advances morally, however, the earth responds in like measure with sublime blessing. The Talmud in *Ketubot* 111b foretells that, in the future, cakes and fine clothing will sprout directly from the ground. At that time, even physical labor will take on a nobler, more refined character.

We are granted a glimpse of this future world through the *mitzvah* of *Shemitah*, the Sabbatical year. During this year of cessation from all agricultural labor, we are content to partake of the land's natural produce. Like the tranquil world of the Garden of Eden, we are able to enjoy the earth's God-given bounty, without toil and labor.

Other aspects of the Garden of Eden are temporarily restored during the sabbatical year. With the prohibition of buying and selling *Shemitah* produce, economic competition is reduced. Even more: the heart is refined to recognize the common brotherhood of all creatures. We may eat of the earth's produce only for as long as it is also available to the animals in the field. The Sabbatical and Jubilee years are a taste of a future

---

[1] Adapted from *Orot HaKodesh*, vol. II, pp. 563–564.

utopia. They herald the coming of a sublime new world that is the result of a loftier spirituality.

Elevating Agriculture

Until then, it is our obligation to elevate agricultural labor from its lowly state. This is accomplished through the holy light found in technology and science. In the future, the Sages tell us, all artisans will leave their crafts and work the land (*Yevamot* 63a). This does not mean that they will no longer work in their respective professions, but that all crafts and sciences will be used to redeem the earth and its toil from its primordial curse.

This progress in agriculture, however, only redeems mankind. It is only a preparatory stage in the redemption of the entire world. In the final redemption, working the land will not be an obligation, but a privilege and a pleasure. We will pleasantly tour in the Garden of Eden (*Eden* meaning "pleasure"), working and guarding it.

There are future levels even beyond the Garden of Eden. Going past the garden to Eden itself, however, is beyond all prophetic vision; Eden is a realm that transcends all forms of labor and guarding.

Why Exile?[1]

The Torah warns us that if we fail to listen to God and keep His *mitzvot*, we will be punished with famine, war, and ultimately, exile.

> I will scatter you among the nations, and keep the sword drawn against you. Your land will remain desolate, and your cities in ruins. (Lev. 26:33)

The Purpose of Israel in their Land

Why should the Jewish people be punished with exile? To answer this question, we must first understand the true significance of residing in the Land of Israel. If the goal of the Jewish people is to bring ethical monotheism to the world, would their mission not be more effectively fulfilled when they are scattered among the nations?

There is, however, a unique reason for the Jewish people to live in the Land of Israel. They need to dwell together in the Land so that there will be a nation in the world upon whom God's honor rests; a nation for whom divine providence is revealed in its history and circumstances; a nation that will be a source for all peoples to absorb knowledge of God and His ways. Their goal is to demonstrate that divine morality can fill an entire nation – a morality that enlightens not only the private lives of individuals, but also guides the public paths of nations.

For the Jewish people to fulfill their national destiny, God's seal must be placed on the people as a whole. The nation must recognize its special mission as God's people living in His land. When the Jewish

---

[1] Adapted from *Ein Ayah* vol. IV, p. 2.

people as a whole abandoned God, even though many individuals still kept some of the *mitzvot*, the nation had lost their distinctive mark. The land was no longer recognizable as God's land, and the nation was no longer recognizable as God's nation. They saw themselves as a people like all others.

At that point, the Jewish people required exile. They needed to wander among the nations, stripped of all national assets. During this exile, they discovered that they are different and distinct from all other peoples. They realized that the essence of their nationhood contains a special quality; and that special quality is God's Name that is associated with them.

Staying in Babylonia

We find in the Talmud (*Shabbat* 41a) a startling opinion regarding the nature of exile. When fourth-century scholar Rabbi Zeira wished to ascend to the Land of Israel, he needed to evade his teacher, Rabbi Yehudah. For Rabbi Yehudah taught that anyone leaving Babylonia for the Land of Israel transgresses the positive command, "They will be carried to Babylon, and there they shall stay, until the day that I remember them" (Jeremiah 27:22).[2] Why did Rabbi Yehudah think that moving to the Land of Israel was so improper?

Babylonia at that time was the world center of Torah study. Great academies were established in Neharde'a, Sura and Pumbeditha. Jewish life in Babylonia was centered around the holiness of Torah. This great revival of Torah learning instilled a profound recognition of the true essence of the Jewish people. As such, Babylonia was the key to the redemption of Israel and their return to their land. Only when the Jewish people fully assimilate this lesson will the exile have fulfilled its purpose, and the Jewish people will be able to return to their land.

---

[2] Rabbi Zeira, however, disagreed with this interpretation. He held that the prophecy only referred to vessels of the holy Temple.

Rabbi Yehudah felt that individuals, even if they have already prepared themselves sufficiently for the holiness of the Land of Israel, should nonetheless remain in Babylonia. Why? The object of exile is not to correct the individual, but to correct the nation. The true significance of the Jewish people living in the Land of Israel – as an entire nation bearing the banner of the Rock of Israel – must not be obscured by the return of righteous individuals to the Land.

For Rabbi Yehudah, each individual Jew is like a Temple vessel. A vessel cannot fulfill its true purpose by itself, without the overall framework of a functioning Temple. So too, an individual can only join in the renascence of Israel in their Holy Land when the entire nation has been restored in its Land, via divine redemption.[3]

---

[3] Maimonides ruled that "Just as one may not leave the Land of Israel, so too one may not leave Babylonia" (*Hilchot Melachim* 5:12). It is not clear, however, whether the prohibition to leave Babylonia included ascending to the Land of Israel or not (see *Kessef Mishneh* ad. loc, *Pe'at Hashulchan*, *Eretz Hemdah* pp. 30–34). With the gradual decline of Babylonia as the center of Jewish scholarship during the Middle Ages, this prohibition became irrelevant, and is not mentioned in the *Shulchan Aruch*. See also *Pitchei Teshuvah* (*Even Ha'Ezer* 75:6), who ruled that the *mitzvah* of ascending to the Land of Israel applies to all times.

Bechukotai

Prophetic Letters[1]

Five Double Letters

Of the 22 letters in the Hebrew alphabet, five are called "double letters," as they take on a different form when appearing at the end of a word. The five letters are *Mem, Nun, Tzadi, Pay,* and *Chaf.* When placed together as one word, they spell, *M-N-Tz-P-Ch.*

According to Talmudic tradition (*Shabbat* 104a), the dual form of these letters goes back to the prophets. The abbreviation *M-N-Tz-P-Ch* can be read as *Min Tzophim* – "from the prophets."

From the Prophets

This claim – that the special form of these letters originated with the prophets – needs clarification. The Torah of Moses is complete and whole in itself. Even a prophet is not allowed to add or invent a new *mitzvah*. The Torah explicitly states, "These are the decrees, laws and codes that God set between Himself and Israel at Mount Sinai, through the hand of Moses" (Lev. 26:46). The phrase *"These* are the decrees" indicates that only the decrees that Moses set down in the Torah are in fact between God and Israel. How could the prophets change the Torah by adding new shapes of letters?

The Talmud explains that the prophets did not actually introduce anything new. There always existed two ways to write these five letters. With the passage of time, however, it was forgotten which shape belongs at the end of the word, and which at the beginning and middle. The

---

[1] Adapted from *Rosh Millin* pp. 35–36; *Ein Ayah* vol. IV, pp. 247–249.

prophets did not devise the two forms; they merely recovered the lost knowledge of which letterform belongs at the end of the word.

Why Two Forms?

Still, we need to understand: why do these letters have dual forms? What is the significance of their relative position in the word? And why were the *prophets* (and not the sages or the grammarians) the ones who restored this knowledge?

Letters are more than just elements of speech. They are the building blocks of creation. The Sages taught, "The universe was created with ten utterances" (*Avot* 5:1). Each letter in the alphabet represents a fundamental force in the world.

Rav Kook explained that the "final forms" – the shape that these letters take at the end of words – are the holiest. The final forms most accurately portray the sublime essence of each letter, fully expressing its ultimate purpose. To better understand this statement, we must analyze the morphological differences between the two forms of these letters.

With four of the letters – *Nun, Tzadi, Pay, Chaf* – the regular form (כ,פ,צ,נ) is smaller and more cramped. The "leg" of the letter is constrained and bent upwards. The form appearing at the end of the word (ך,ף,ץ,ן), on the other hand, allows the "leg" to stretch and extend itself fully. It is the final form that truly expresses the full content and power of these letters.

The two shapes of the letter *Mem* are distinguished in a different fashion. The regular *Mem* (מ) has a small opening at the bottom. It is called the *Mem Petuchah*, the Open *Mem*. It is open and revealed to all.

The final *Mem* (ם) is closed off on all sides. It is called the *Mem Setumah*, the Sealed *Mem*. Or perhaps – the Esoteric *Mem*. This form of *Mem* is more sublime than the regular Open *Mem*. Thus, the holiest written object, the stone tablets engraved with the Ten Commandments, contained only Sealed *Mems*, with the center part of the *Mem* hanging miraculously in place. The final *Mem* is closed off and concealed. It guards its inner secret, which due to its profound holiness may not be revealed to all.

Why is the more elevated form used at the end of the word? A hidden light appears at the ultimate vision of every noble matter. The hidden light of the *M-N-Tz-P-Ch* letters belongs to the end. The beginning and middle appearances of these letters are open and revealed. Their light steadily increases, until it brings us to the final, sublime conclusion.

The prophets are called *tzofim*, visionaries, as they were blessed with prophetic vision. Their greatness was that they could perceive the final outcome while still living in a flawed present. Understandably, it was these *tzofim* who sensed that the more elevated letterforms belong at the end.

Sefer Bamidbar – The Book of Numbers

Locked in the Temporal

The desert encompassed the transitory sanctity for the people of Israel, serving as a foundation and a source for the eternal sanctity for future generations.[1]

But when the eternal sanctity was impaired, the desert was no longer a preparation and a passageway from the desert to the Land, from the temporary to the permanent; it became set as an immobile station. [One is then] locked in the temporal, confined to a realm that is incapable of reaching across the generations.[2]
(*Ein Ayah* vol. IV, p. 238)

---

[1] The forty years that the Israelites sojourned in the desert were a preparatory stage for their conquest and settlement of their permanent homeland (see Maimonides, *Guide for the Perplexed* III: 32). Unlike the permanent sanctity of the Land of Israel and the city of Jerusalem, the sanctity of Mount Sinai was temporary, only for the hour of the Torah's revelation. The Tabernacle in the desert similarly reflected a transient holiness; it was a precursor to the permanent abode for God's divine Presence in the Temple in Jerusalem.

[2] Thus Tzelofchad, who desecrated the permanent sanctity of the Sabbath, lost out on a permanent inheritance in the Land of Israel. He died in the desert, never to leave the realm of the transitory. See "*Shelach*: The Sin of Tzelofchad."

Bamidbar

Flags of Love in the Desert[1]

Throughout their travels in the desert, the Israelites were commanded to set up their tents around tribal flags:

> The Israelites shall encamp with each person near the banner carrying his paternal family's insignia. They shall encamp at a distance around the Communion Tent. (Num. 2:2)

What is the significance of these banners? The Midrash (*Bamidbar Rabbah* 2:3) says that the inspiration for the banners came from Mount Sinai. Twenty-two thousand chariots of angels, each one decked out with flags, attended the Revelation of the Torah. The Israelites immediately desired to have flags just like the angels, and God agreed. This request for flags, the Midrash teaches, is described in the Song of Songs (2:4): "He brought me to the wine-house, and *His banner* over me is love."

From the Midrash we understand that banners relate to some inherent characteristic of angels, though not of people. But we are left with many questions. Why do angels bear flags? Why does the verse refer to Sinai as a "wine-house"? And what is the connection between banners and love?

The Specialized Service of Angels

According to the *Zohar*, the banners of the four major encampments (in each direction: north, south, east and west) corresponded to the four sides

[1] Adapted from *Midbar Shur*, pp. 24–25.

or "faces" of the supernal *merkavah* (chariot) in Ezekiel's mystical vision. Since these four "faces" represent fundamental divine attributes, each encampment related to a particular divine quality.

Before we can explain the meaning of the flags and their connection to angels, we must first understand what an angel is. The Hebrew word *mal'ach* literally means "messenger." An angel is essentially a divine messenger meant to fulfill a specific mission. An angel cannot perform a task, important though it may be, other than the specific mission for which it was designated.

Now we can better understand the function of the angels' flags. A banner proclaims a distinctive function or trait. Each angel, limited to a very specific area of divine service, carries its own distinguishing flag. These flags may be compared to military uniforms, where the dress and insignia indicate a soldier's unit and assignment.

Human beings, on the other hand, are not limited to serving God in one particular manner. Our divine image encompasses all spiritual spheres (see *Nefesh Hachaim* 1:10). For us, a banner is too restricting; it does not reflect our true spiritual essence.

Nonetheless, the Jewish people saw in the angelic banners of Sinai an inspiring sight that appealed to them, albeit in a non-obligatory way. Every person has special talents and interests, based on individual character traits and his soul's inner root. We are not limited in serving God in this particular way, but we are certainly more inclined towards those activities for which we have a natural proclivity. For example, a kind-hearted person may concentrate on serving God with acts of compassion and *chesed*; a strong-willed individual, with acts of courage and self-sacrifice; and so on.

The Jewish people desired flags like those the angels bore at Sinai. They wanted every individual to be able to choose an aspect of divine service that suits his personality, just as each angel executes a specific function, as defined by his flag.

The Wine-House

It is now clear why the verse refers to Mount Sinai as a "wine-house." Drinking wine releases our inhibitions, revealing our inner character. In the words of the Talmud (*Eiruvin* 65a), "Wine enters, secrets emerge." The Israelites envied the beauty and joy they witnessed in divine service of the angels. The root of this pleasantness lies in the innate affinity the angels feel towards their service. Each angel naturally identifies with its particular mission. The Jewish people sought to uncover and emphasize every individual's personal strengths, in the same way that wine liberates and highlights one's inner characteristics.

This individualized worship, however, only applies to the service of the heart and the character traits. The banners reflect our feelings of love and joy when serving God – "His banner over me is *love*" – but the banners are not directly connected to the service itself. Within the framework of Torah study and practical *mitzvot*, there is no need for distinctive forms of service. Therefore, no banners flew over the central Communion Tent where the *luchot* (the stone tablets with the Ten Commandments) were stored, since the Torah and its *mitzvot* relate equally to all souls.

Bamidbar

Jacob's Signs[1]

Ancestral Signs

During their sojourn in the Sinai desert, the Jewish people were instructed to encamp according to tribe:

> The Israelites shall encamp with each person near the banner carrying his paternal family's signs. (Num. 2:2)

What were these ancestral signs? The Midrash (*Bamidbar Rabbah* 2:8) explains that this deployment of twelve tribes surrounding the Tabernacle was in fact a 200-year-old family tradition. Once before, the Jewish people had marched through the wilderness, from Egypt to the Land of Israel. This took place when Jacob died in Egypt. Each of Jacob's twelve sons took his place around the coffin, as they brought their father to burial in Hebron.

Before his death, Jacob informed his sons where each one would stand around his coffin. The arrangement that Jacob established was the "paternal family's signs" that would later determine the position of each tribe around the Tabernacle, as they traveled in the wilderness.

Why did the tribes need separate encampments? Would not an integrated camp bring about greater national unity? And why was it Jacob who determined the tribal formations in the wilderness?

---

[1] Adapted from *Midbar Shur*, pp. 26–7.

Jacob and Moses

We find that the Torah is associated with both Jacob and Moses, as it says (Deut. 33:4), "Moses prescribed the Torah to us, an inheritance of the congregation of Jacob." Yet, the relationship of these two great personalities to the Torah was not identical. The *Zohar* states that Jacob's connection to the Torah was "from the outside," while Moses' connection was "from within." What does this mean?

In any field of study, there are two ways in which the student connects to the subject material. First, there is the student's innate interest and aptitude for that particular topic. And secondly, there is the bond that is created through the study of the subject matter.

So too, our relationship to Torah contains two aspects. The first is an innate readiness and inclination to assume the "yoke" of Torah study. We inherited this readiness to accept the Torah from Jacob – "an inheritance of the congregation of Jacob." Through his profound holiness, Jacob was able to transmit to his descendants a natural receptiveness to Torah.

This quality of the soul is like a pot-handle, enabling us to better grasp the Torah. But when compared to the Torah itself, the soul's predisposition towards Torah is like an outer garment. Therefore, the *Zohar* refers to our spiritual inheritance from Jacob as being external, "from the outside."

Moses, on the other hand, exemplifies a connection to the Torah itself. The Torah is called the "Torah of Moses" (Malachi 3:22). In the formulation of the *Zohar*, the connection through Moses is internal, "from the inside."

Uniformity and Plurality

The Torah itself is unified. "There shall be one Torah and one law for you" (Num. 15:16). Within the Torah itself, there are no divisions, no room for divergent paths. The Torah reflects the inner soul, which is indivisible. Thus, in the center of the encampment in the wilderness, there stood a single Communion Tent, a focal point for God's instructions to His people.

The soul's natural receptiveness to the Torah, on the other hand, is a function of individual character and personality traits. Here, there exist numerous paths. In these external aspects, in the ways we choose to approach the Torah and fulfill its *mitzvot*, in the *kavanot* and intentions by which we focus our minds, it is natural that there will be diversity.

When Jacob's twelve sons brought their father back to the Land of Israel, each son found his own place around the coffin. Each son positioned himself in accordance to his soul's natural disposition. Jacob's holiness imprinted upon each of his children a special connection to the Torah according to his individual nature. That holy procession determined the future arrangement of the tribes of Israel, as they marched to Mount Sinai to receive the Torah. Each tribe had its own special flag and unique place within the encampment of Israel.

Naso

Tithes and the *Sotah*[1]

The Suspected Adulteress

The first ten chapters of the book of Numbers discuss the organization of the Israelites in the desert. The census, the placement of camps according to tribe, the duties of the Levites, the dedication of the Tabernacle, the inauguration of the Levites – all of these topics pertain to the preparatory arrangements needed to organize the journey of millions in the wilderness.

Yet, in the middle of all of these rather technical subjects, the Torah discusses the *Sotah*, the suspected adulteress. What does this unfortunate story of distrust and jealousy have to do with organizing the Israelites in the desert? This topic would more naturally belong in the section on forbidden relations in *Acharei Mot* (Lev. chapter 18).

This anomaly did not escape the Talmudic sages. Rabbi Yochanan noted that the verses immediate preceding the section on *Sotah* discuss the tithes given to the *kohanim*.

> Why does the subject of the suspected adulteress immediately follow the laws of offerings and tithes for the *kohanim*? To teach that whoever does not hand over his tithes to the *kohen*, will in the end require the *kohen's* services to deal with his wife. (*Berachot* 63a)

What is the connection between withholding tithes and a wife's suspected infidelity?

---

[1] Adapted from *Ein Ayah* vol. II, pp. 381–382.

Alienation from the *Kohanim*

It is vital that the masses maintain a strong connection with those dedicated to the service of God and the study of Torah, like the *kohanim*, about whom it is written (Malachi 2:7), "From the *kohen*'s lips they will guard knowledge, and they will seek Torah from his mouth." This bond is crucial for the ethical instruction of the people, enabling the Torah's teachings to reach the entire nation. Scholars are uplifted as they study Torah and analyze its wisdom, and the rest of the people are influenced through their relationship with those who study and disseminate Torah and its ethical teachings. What is the vehicle for ensuring this connection between the people and the spiritual elite? It is through the various gifts and tithes that the Torah designated to the *kohanim*.

An individual who cuts himself off from the spiritual leadership is likely to undergo a deterioration in his moral values and spiritual sensitivity. As a result of his overriding occupation with the material world and estrangement from Torah and all that is holy, the moral level of his household will decline to such an extent that even the most basic human values – modesty and fidelity – will be seriously undermined. This spiritual collapse will necessitate the assistance of the *kohen* because of his wife's suspect behavior. When the moral decline is so great that even his simple soul is appalled by the shocking decadence in his family-life, he will realize how wrong he was to distance himself from the *kohanim* and Torah scholars.

A Nation Gone Astray

This deplorable phenomenon may also occur on the national level. When the pursuit of material pleasures causes large sectors to cast off the Torah and its teachings, they will distance themselves from Torah scholars and deem them superfluous. They may even come to despise and ridicule them.

At this point, a plague of immorality and corruption will spread among the people. The situation will continue to deteriorate, until those individuals who still retain some spark of humanity and a feeling for the light of Torah will weep with broken hearts. They will painfully recognize that their lives have become debased and bleak by rejecting the ways of Torah. Their separation from Torah brought about such a wild, unbridled national spirit, that the nation is derided and mocked by other peoples.

They brought this affliction upon themselves, however, with their scorn for Torah scholars and contempt for all that is holy. The people, once famous for integrity and modesty, will require the services of the holy *kohanim* in order to repair the collapse of fidelity and trust.

Naso

Divine Favoritism?[1]

The Complaint of the Angels

The last blessing of *Birkat Kohanim*, the priestly benediction, is a request that God should be lenient when judging us: "May God lift His countenance to you" (Num. 6:26). "Lifting one's face" is a Hebrew idiom for showing special consideration, especially by a judge. Is it fair that the Jewish people should be judged leniently, more than other nations?

In fact, the Talmud (*Berachot* 20b) relates that the angels raised this very question.

> The ministering angles asked the Holy One, "Master of the Universe, it is written in Your Torah (Deut. 10:17) that You 'do not show favor or take bribes.' And yet, You show Israel special consideration, as it is written, 'May God lift His countenance to you'!"
> God replied to them, "How can I not favor Israel? For I commanded them, 'When you eat and are satisfied, you must bless the Lord, your God' (Deut. 8:10), and they are punctilious [to say grace] over an olive-sized piece of bread [even though they are not satiated]."

What is the significance of this stringency that the Jewish people accepted upon themselves, to recite the grace after meals (*Birkat Hamazon*) even for a small piece of bread? Why should this earn them special treatment?

---

[1] Adapted from *Ein Ayah* vol. I, pp. 102–103.

When is Leniency Appropriate?

While leniency sounds like a good thing, this is not necessarily the case. We are punished for wrongdoings, not out of divine retribution or revenge, but in order to direct us to the proper path. Even if an individual is bursting with merits and good deeds, he will not gain from a reprieve, even for the slightest of errors. Without the appropriate measure of divine justice, we do not learn to mend our ways and strive towards ever-greater perfection.

There is, however, a situation when the absence of divine justice will not have an adverse effect. This case involves an individual who will continue to strive towards self-improvement even without the divine wake-up call to introspection and moral accounting.

Such a person must have acquired the quality of *hakarat hatov*, sincere appreciation. When applied to God and His kindness, this trait is the height of morality. Our sense of gratitude is intensified when we feel that we are the recipient of undeserved kindness and compassion. And the only way we can return this favor is through spiritual and ethical growth, thus fulfilling God's will.[2]

The appreciative individual recognizes that God's generosity is not commensurate to his actions. Not only will this divine leniency not cause him to become lax in his conduct, but it will inspire him to work even harder to improve himself, since he has an additional reason to be appreciative of God's ways.

Now we can understand God's response to the angels. The explanation that the Jewish people deserve special consideration because they recite blessings even on olive-sized pieces of bread is not just some form of divine tit-for-tat. Rather, their behavior is indicative of a refined appreciation of God's kindness for their physical sustenance, even keener than that which the Torah requires.

---

[2] See *Chovat HaLevavot*, introduction to *Sha'ar Avodat Elokim*.

The Appreciation Test

There is an additional factor at play here. When misdeeds go unpunished, two contradictory processes occur. On the one hand, undeserved leniency bolsters our feelings of gratitude. On the other hand, we may be ensnared by a sense that our actions are not accounted for – so why bother laboring over ethical improvement and spiritual growth?

Which feeling will prevail? An individual blessed with strong character traits will think: I am indebted to God's compassion; therefore, I must redouble my efforts to improve. A weaker person, on the other hand, will be misled by the mistaken sense that God does not fully monitor our actions.

How can we determine which way of thinking will triumph? Here is a simple test. If a person recognizes God's kindness even when all of his needs have not been met, this is a sure sign that he is blessed with a robust trait of appreciation. Such a person has a correct understanding of God's relationship to His creations, and recognizes that God does everything for the good. In this case, we can be assured that, in a conflict between these two feelings – appreciation for God's leniency, and a deluded impression of limited divine providence – the true feeling of appreciation will prevail.

Thus, one feels the need to express gratitude for even a small measure – even an olive-sized piece of bread – despite the fact that he is still hungry and his needs have not been fully met; it is clear that his natural sense of appreciation is strong and healthy. The Jewish people, who recite *Birkat Hamazon* even when they are not satiated, demonstrate their innate mind-set of *hakarat hatov*, and will always interpret God's leniency and special consideration in the correct way.

The Seven Lamps of the Menorah[1]

Speak to Aaron and tell him, "When you light the
lamps, the seven lamps should shine towards the
center of the Menorah." (Num. 8:2)

Why does the Torah emphasize this particular detail – that the
seven lamps should face the center of the Menorah? Why not begin with
the overall *mitzvah* – to light the Menorah each evening? Also, what is the
significance of the Menorah's seven branches?

Different Paths of Wisdom

The Sages wrote that the Menorah represents wisdom and enlightenment
(*Baba Batra* 25b). All wisdom has a common source, but there exist
different approaches to wisdom. Every individual pursues those spheres
of knowledge to which he is naturally drawn.

The Midrash (*Bamidbar Rabbah* 15:7) compares the seven lamps of
the Menorah to the seven planets in the solar system, illuminating the
nighttime sky. What is the meaning of this symbolism?

Many of the ancients understood that the planets and
constellations influence our nature and personality traits. A person under
the influence of Mars, for example, will have different traits then one
under the influence of Jupiter (see *Shabbat* 165a). In other words, God
created each of us with a unique character in order that we should perfect
ourselves in the particular path that suits us. In this way, all of creation is

---

[1] Adapted from *Midbar Shur*, pp. 53–55.

completed; through the aggregation of all individual perfections, the universe attains overall perfection.

Just as each planet symbolizes a distinct character trait, each branch of the Menorah is a metaphor for a specific category of intellectual pursuits. God prepared a path for each individual to attain wisdom according to his own character and interests.

Towards the Center

However, we should be careful not to follow our natural intellectual inclinations exclusively. The Torah stresses that "when you light the lamps" – when we work towards that individual enlightenment that suits our particular character – we should take care that this wisdom will "shine towards the center of the Menorah." What is the center of the Menorah? This is the wisdom of the Torah itself. We need to draw specifically from the light of Torah, whose source is the underlying unity of all wisdom.

In truth, the seven branches of the Menorah are not truly distinct, separate paths. All seven receive light from the unified wisdom with which God enlightens His world. For this reason, the Menorah was fashioned from a single piece of gold, *mikshah zahav*. The special manner in which the Menorah was formed reveals the underlying unity of all forms of wisdom.

Beha'alotecha

A Tale of Two Prayers[1]

A Short Prayer for Miriam

When Miriam was stricken with leprosy, Moses beseeched God to heal his sister, saying a remarkably brief prayer: "Please God, please heal her" (Num. 12:13). The Talmud (*Berachot* 34a) took note of the unusual brevity of this prayer in the following story:

> Once, a student led the prayers in Rabbi Eliezer's house of study, and his prayers were unusually lengthy. The other students complained, "Master, how slow this fellow is!" Rabbi Eliezer responded to them, "He is no slower than Moses, who pleaded on behalf of the Jewish people [after the sin of the golden calf] for forty days and forty nights."
>
> On another occasion, a different student led the prayers. This student recited the prayers quickly. The other students complained, "How hasty this fellow is!" This time Rabbi Eliezer replied, "He is no hastier than Moses, who pleaded for his sister's recovery with a few short words."

What determined the length of Moses' prayers? Why did his own sister merit only a brief, one-line prayer?

---

[1] Adapted from *Ein Ayah* vol. I, p. 163.

Two Types of Prayer

Prayer serves two functions. The first function is to refine character traits and deepen awareness – either for the person praying, or for the one being prayed for. This type of prayer requires tenacity and perseverance, since correction of flawed traits requires extended effort, and usually occurs gradually over time.

For this reason, Moses needed to pray extensively when he prayed for the Jewish people after the calamitous sin of the golden calf. Why forty days? This period is the time it takes for an embryo to develop limbs and become recognizable as a human fetus. The forty days of Moses' prayer indicated a rebirth of the Jewish people, with a new heart and spirit.

There is, however, a second function of prayer. Sometimes the inner emotions and character traits have already been refined and purified. Prayer only comes to put in words that which already exists in the inner soul. In such cases, an extended prayer is unnecessary; even a brief prayer may express many holy feelings. In the case of Miriam, she had already conceded her mistake.[2] Her healing, both physical and spiritual, required only a short, simple prayer.

---

[2] As Aaron pleaded to Moses for Miriam's sake, "Do not hold against us the sin that we foolishly committed" (Num, 12:11).

242

Shelach

The Sin of Tzelofchad[1]

> Our father died in the desert.... He died because of
> his own sin, and he had no sons. (Num. 27:3)

So begins the request of the daughters of Tzelofchad. Since there were no sons in the family, the daughters wanted to know: may we inherit his portion in the Land of Israel? Their question stumped Moses, and was referred to God Himself.

The Torah does not tell us, but we are curious nonetheless: what was the sin for which Tzelofchad deserved to die? The text seems to imply that his transgression was an unusual one – "He died because of his own sin."

In the reading of *Shelach* it says:

> The Israelites were in the desert, and they found a
> man collecting wood on the Sabbath. (Num. 15:32)

Interesting. Again, we find the phrase, "in the desert." (And quite superfluous, considering that the entire book takes place in the desert.) Once again, Moses is stumped, and needs to ask God what is the appropriate punishment. Who was this unidentified man, the wood-gatherer who desecrated the Sabbath?

It was Rabbi Akiva who made the connection between the man with the unknown sin, and the sin of the unknown man. Tzelofchad was

---

[1] Adapted from *Ein Ayah* vol. IV, p. 238.

the Sabbath wood-gatherer. That was his personal transgression, for which he was punished (*Shabbat* 96b).

Is there a connection between Tzelofchad's desecration of the Sabbath, and the fact that he died without sons, thus jeopardizing his inheritance in the Land of Israel? Also, why does the Torah emphasize that his sin took place "in the desert"?

Trapped in the Desert

The desert represents transience. A desert is not a place that can be settled and cultivated. We only pass through the desert as we make our way to a permanent location, to our true destination. Life in the desert is transient; it is only a preparation and a means towards a desired objective.

Even the holiness in the desert was temporary. Mount Sinai was sanctified solely for the sake of the Torah's revelation; afterwards, the mountain reverted to its previous state. Permanent holiness only exists in the Land of Israel and the city of Jerusalem.

Sanctity within the dimension of *time* – as in space – may also have varying degrees of permanence. The most eternal holiness in time is the holiness of the Sabbath. "The Israelites will observe the Sabbath, making it a day of rest *for all generations*, an eternal covenant" (Ex. 31:16).

Unlike the Sabbath, which falls out every seventh day, the holidays are dependent upon the calendar, as set by the high court. The sanctity of the holidays is thus of a less eternal nature. Additionally, the holidays relate to historical events: the Exodus from Egypt, the journey in the desert, the Revelation of the Torah. The Sabbath, on the other hand, transcends the realm of mankind. It celebrates the very essence of creation.

Tzelofchad's sin took place in the desert, and he died in the desert. When Tzelofchad desecrated the eternal sanctity of the Sabbath, he transformed the desert from a passageway into a dead-end. He became disconnected from eternal holiness, both in time and space. He lacked permanence and continuity in the dimension of time – the Sabbath day, and in the dimension of space – his inheritance in the Land of Israel.

We should learn from Tzelofchad's mistake, and avoid being locked within the temporal realm of the desert. We need to stay focused on that which is enduring and eternal, and not confuse the way-station for the final destination.

Shelach

Garments of the Soul[1]

> Speak to the Israelites and tell them to make tassels
> (*tzitzit*) on the corners of their garments for all
> generations. They shall include a thread of sky-blue
> [wool] in the corner tassels. (Num. 15:38)

Three Levels of the Soul

How is the human soul recognizable to the outside world? We may speak
of a hierarchy of three levels:

- The soul itself.
- Its character traits – compassion, generosity,
  tolerance, humility, and so on.
- Its actions and conduct.

The innermost level, the soul itself, is in fact hidden from the
outside world. The soul can only be observed through the outer two
levels, its traits and actions. Character traits are like the soul's "clothing."
Through its distinctive characteristics, the soul reveals itself to the outside
world. This is similar to the way we present ourselves to others through
our garments. We are judged by the style and quality of our clothes. Yet,
we are not our clothes; we may change them at will. So too, we are judged
by our character traits, but they are external to the soul itself, and may be
changed.

---

[1] Adapted from *Olat Re'iyah* vol. I, pp. 4–5.

The Symbolism of *Tzitzit*

The ultimate manifestation of the soul in the outside world is in its day-to-day deportment. If our character traits constitute a metaphoric garment that clothes the soul, then our deeds are tassels that emanate from the corners of the garment. Each trait of the soul is revealed in a variety of actions, since different situations require specific responses. These varied actions are like the many *tzitziot* (tassels), extending naturally from the corners of the garment.

To summarize the analogy:

- The inner soul is represented by the body itself.
- Personality traits are clothes covering the body.
- Actions are the tassels extending from the garment.

The Thread of *Techelet*

We are accustomed to the tassels being white, but the actual *Halachic* requirement is that they be the same color as the garment.[2] Sharing the same color indicates that our actions derive their power and direction from the garment, i.e., our character traits.

One thread, however, is not the color of the garment. The Torah instructs us to tie an additional thread, dyed sky-blue *techelet*. This color reminds us of hidden, sublime matters: the sea, the sky, and God's Holy Throne (*Sotah* 17a). Sky-blue is the background color of the universe. The *techelet* thread connects us to the very Source of life, from whom all forces flow. Together with the other threads, which correspond to the color of the garment and represent the diverse range of human activity, the *techelet* thread complements and completes the function of the tassels.

---

[2] Maimonides, *Hilchot Tzitzit* 2:8; *Shulchan Aruch Orach Chaim* 9:5. The Ashkenazic tradition, however, is to always use white *tzitzit* (Rama ad loc).

The Torah teaches that the *mitzvah* of wearing *tzitzit* corresponds to all 613 *mitzvot*: "When you see [the tassels], you will remember all of God's commandments and you will observe them" (Num. 15:39). By wearing a garment with these special tassels, we envelop our souls in the Torah's magnificent fabric of values and deeds.

Shelach

The Third Passage of *Shema*[1]

Every evening and morning, we say the *Shema*, Judaism's supreme declaration of monotheistic faith. In the first passage, we accept upon ourselves the yoke of God's sovereignty. And in the second, we accept God's commandments. Interestingly, the Sages added a third paragraph to the *Shema* – the passage commanding us to wear *tzitzit* (tassels) on the corners of our garments (Num. 15:37–41). Why did they decide to add this particular paragraph, out of the entire Torah, to the central prayer of Judaism?

Six Themes
The Talmud in *Berachot* 12b explains that the passage of *tzitzit* contains not one, but six major themes:

1. The *mitzvah* of wearing *tzitzit* on our garments.
2. The Exodus ("I am the Lord your God, who brought you out of Egypt").
3. Accepting the *mitzvot* ("You will thus remember and keep all of My commandments").
4. Resisting heresy ("You will not stray after your hearts").
5. Refraining from immoral and sinful thoughts ("and after your eyes").
6. Eschewing idolatry ("which have led you astray").

---

[1] Adapted from *Ein Ayah* vol. I, pp. 70–71.

Is there a common motif to these six themes? Most are indeed fundamental concepts of Judaism, but what is so special about the *mitzvah* of *tzitzit*, more than the other 612 commandments?

Spiritual Focus

This *mitzvah* in fact does contain a fundamental message. It touches on the basic issues of life: how do we realize our spiritual potential? How can we truly fulfill ourselves as human beings?

As Maimonides wryly noted, the philosophers composed numerous volumes and entire libraries trying to answer these questions. Despite their efforts, they failed to exhaust the topic. The Talmudic sages, on the other hand, succeeded in encompassing the subject by revealing its essence in one pithy statement: "Let all your deeds be for the sake of Heaven" (*Avot* 2:12).

Human perfection is attained by establishing a worthwhile spiritual goal for all of our efforts and activities in life. Once we have set our spiritual focus, we need to direct all of our aspirations, wants and actions according to that objective. Then we will be complete in all aspects and levels of our existence.

This is the message of *tzitzit*. The sky-blue *techelet* thread reminds us of the heavens and the Throne of Glory. The soul's external expressions – character traits, emotions and actions – are like a garment worn on the outside, over the body. We need to connect all of these outer manifestations to our inner spiritual goal, our *tachlit*, in the same way that we tie our outer clothes with the special thread of *techelet*.

The Exodus from Egyptian bondage expands on this theme. We are no longer slaves, subjected to physical and moral repression. A slave cannot set goals for his life and actions – they are not under his control. But we were liberated from slavery, are we are free to elevate ourselves and aspire towards our spiritual calling.

The acceptance of practical *mitzvot* perpetuates the same message. All of our detailed actions should connect with our overall objective. Thus, we attain completion in all aspects of our existence: our intellect, emotions and conduct.

Avoiding the Pitfalls

While the first three themes in the passage of *tzitzit* teach us how to fulfill the maxim, "Let all of your deeds be for the sake of Heaven," the last three themes deal with avoiding three obstacles to this guideline.

The first pitfall is heresy. The fear of all-inclusive commitment, the desire to avoid moral responsibilities, can lead to denial of God or His Oneness. The path of heresy means abandoning elevated goals and rejecting ethical aspirations. Without a comprehensive objective and direction, the soul naturally seeks some other occupation. Lacking an overriding goal, the soul is tossed and flung like flotsam in the ocean, pulled by any internal or external lure. This leads to the second pitfall: attraction to base and corrupt actions.

In the end, however, a self-indulgent lifestyle leaves the soul with feelings of horrible emptiness. The soul recognizes that a life without meaning is a contradiction to its very essence. But since it has already lost its rational beacon by rejecting the light of truth, the soul seeks purpose and meaning in foreign cultures. It tries to find spiritual sustenance in broken cisterns, in idolatrous worship.

Thus, we see that this short passage includes the fundamental themes of Judaism. It describes that which gives our lives meaning and direction, and the major obstacles that can lead the soul astray. It is a fitting conclusion to our acceptance of God's kingship in the *Shema* prayer.

Korach

Inclusion and Selection[1]

> Korach was a clever fellow – what did he see to get
> involved in this folly? His mind's eye fooled him.
> He saw by prophetic vision that a line of great men
> would descend from him, including the prophet
> Samuel, who was the equal of Moses and Aaron
> together. (*Midrash Tanchuma* 5)

While the Midrash appears to belittle Korach's dispute as foolish, the argument that Korach put forth – "All of the congregation is holy, and God is in their midst" (Num. 16:3) – does not seem silly at all. Is not Korach simply restating what God told the entire nation, "You shall be holy, for I, the Lord your God, am holy" (Lev. 19:2)? What was so wrong with his claim? Why did Moses insist that only Aaron and his descendants could serve as priests?

Korach's mistake is rooted in the dialectic between two distinct forms of divine providence: inclusion (*kirvah*), and selection (*bechirah*). During certain periods, the service of God was inclusive, available to all. At other times, God chose certain persons or places to bear a higher level of sanctity, in order to elevate the rest of the world through them.

The Temple and the *Bamot*
One example of the historical give-and-take between these two conflicting

---

[1] Adapted from *Shemuot HaRe'iyah, Korach* (1931).

approaches is the status of *bamot*, private altars for bringing offerings to God.

Until the Tabernacle was set up in Shiloh, individuals were permitted to offer sacrifices on private altars throughout the country. During the 369 years that the Tabernacle stood in Shiloh, these *bamot* were prohibited, and all offerings had to be brought to the central service in Shiloh. After the destruction of the Shiloh Tabernacle, the *bamot* were again permitted. With the selection of the city of Jerusalem and the building of the Temple on Mount Moriah, however, the *bamot* were banned forever.

When permitted, these private altars could be established in any location. They allowed all to approach God; even non-priests could offer sacrifices. The periods when *bamot* were permitted reflect an inclusive form of divine worship, enabling all to approach God and serve Him.

For the service in the Tabernacle and the Temple, on the other hand, only the descendants of Aaron were allowed to serve. When Shiloh and later Jerusalem were chosen to host the Holy Ark, the divine service was limited to the boundaries of those cities and their holy structures. Unlike the *bamot*, which were accessible to all, the Tabernacle and the Temple were enclosed buildings, set apart by walls and barriers. The various levels of holiness were spatially restricted. Thus, the Talmud (*Yoma* 54a) teaches that the *Shechinah* (Divine Presence) was confined to the space between the two poles of the Holy Ark.

Pillar Service

A second example of the contrast between these two approaches may be seen in the use of a single pillar (*matzeivah*) to serve God. The pillar was an open form of worship, attracting people to gather around it, without walls or restrictions. This form of divine service was appropriate for the time of Abraham, who tried to spread the concept of monotheism throughout the world.

In Moses' day, however, serving God though pillars became forbidden (Deut. 16:22). After the election of the Jewish people, it became necessary to first elevate the people of Israel. Only afterwards will the rest of the world attain recognition of God. Divine service thereafter required boundaries – the walls of the Tabernacle and Temple – in order to cultivate the holiness within.

Prophecy Only in Israel

A similar process took place regarding prophecy. Until the Sinaitic revelation, the phenomenon of prophecy existed in all nations. At Sinai, however, Moses requested that God's Divine Presence only dwell within the people of Israel: "[If You accompany us,] I and Your people will be distinguished from every nation on the face of the earth" (Ex. 33:16; see *Berachot* 7a).

While the boundaries created by the selection of Jerusalem and the Jewish people will always exist, the exclusive distinction of Aaron's descendants as *kohanim* is not permanent. In the future, all of Israel will be elevated to the level of priests. God's declaration to Israel, "You will be a kingdom of priests and a holy nation to Me" (Ex. 19:6), refers to this future era.

Korach's Vision

As the Midrash explains, Korach was misled by his prophetic vision. He discerned the essential truth, "All of the congregation is holy, and God is in their midst." Yet the time for this vision belongs to the distant future. Korach only saw a private vision of *ruach hakodesh*, not a universal prophecy meant to be publicized and acted upon.

Moses alluded to the future nature of Korach's vision when he dictated the type of test to be used. The dedications of the *kohanim* and the Tabernacle involved sin-offerings and burnt-offerings, so it would have been logical to suggest that Korach's men attempt to offer similar offerings. Moses, however, suggested that they offer *incense*. He hinted that Korach's vision reflected an underlying truth, but one for the distant future, when sin-offerings will no longer be needed to atone for our wrongdoing.

Korach

The Secret of the Incense[1]

> Aaron took [the fire-pan] as Moses had told him....
> He put the incense in it, and it atoned for the
> people. He stood between the dead and the living,
> and the plague was checked. (Num. 17:12–3)

From where did Moses learn the secret power of incense to arrest plagues?

The Gift of the Angel of Death

According to the Midrash (*Shabbat* 89a), when Moses went up to accept the Torah, the angels bestowed him with various presents. "You ascended on high, taking a captive [the Torah], receiving gifts among men" (Psalms 68:19). Even the Angel of Death presented Moses with a gift: the secret of the incense.

What is special about incense that it has the power to stay death? And why not take advantage of this capability to permanently rescind death?

Binding Together All Forces

All forces in the world, even the forces of death and destruction, contribute to the development and perfection of the universe. When all the realms and their forces, both spiritual and physical, draw together, each one provides a unique function. From this standpoint, the force of death also serves as a force of life.

---

[1] Adapted from *Ein Ayah* vol. IV, p. 213.

The unique character of the incense reflects this message of harmony and inter-connectivity. The Hebrew word for incense, *ketoret*, is related to the word *kesher*, meaning a "bind" or "knot." The incense unites together the core essence of all forces – life, matter, and spirit – according to the extraordinary recipe that God prescribed in the Torah.

The ability to overcome destructive forces, at a time when they rule freely and have not yet been converted into constructive and preserving forces, was an exceptional phenomenon. This hidden knowledge was granted only to Moses. This gift from the Angel of Death demonstrated the surrender of the forces of death to the pure splendor illuminating that faithful messenger, as he revealed the light of the Torah of life.

What is the root of the incense's secret power? The *ketoret* also encompasses the forces of destruction, so that they may contribute to building and perfecting the universe. Thus, we find that the *ketoret* bound together many fragrances, including galbanum (*chelbenah*), which was an essential ingredient, despite its pungent, unpleasant odor. In this way, these forces fulfill their ultimate purpose, to build and complete. True realization of this transformation, however, will only occur in the distant future, as the path for sweetening the bitterness of the universe is hidden deeply within the divine secrets of Creation.

Only as a temporary measure for the need of that hour, the harmonious quality of the incense was able to stay the power of death. The secret given to Moses demonstrated the comprehensiveness of the Torah, and the unique splendor of those who study Torah – the source of peace, life, and rectification for all worlds and their myriad inhabitants.

Korach

Holiness in the Midst of the Community[1]

The Need for a *Minyan*

Judaism has an interesting concept called a *minyan*, a prayer quorum. Special prayers sanctifying God's name (such as the *kedushah* and *kaddish* prayers) may only be said when ten men are present. An individual may pray in solitude, but without a *minyan*, certain parts of the liturgy must be omitted.

The Talmud derives the requirement for a prayer quorum from God's declaration, "I will be sanctified in the midst of the Israelites" (Lev. 22:32). What exactly does the word "midst" mean?

We find the word "midst" used again when God warned the people living nearby the dissenters in Korach's rebellion: "Separate yourselves from the *midst* of this *eidah* [community]" (Num. 16:20). From here, the Sages learned that God is sanctified within an *eidah*.

And what is the definition of *eidah*? The Torah refers to the ten spies who brought a negative report of the Land of Israel as an *eidah ra'ah*, an evil community (Num. 14:26). So we see that God is sanctified in a community of at least ten members.

The requirement for a prayer quorum, and the way it is derived, raises two issues that need to be addressed:

Prayer appears to be a private matter between the soul and its Maker. Why should we need a *minyan* of ten participants in order to pray the complete service?

---

[1] Adapted from *Ein Ayah* vol. I, p. 104.

Why is the requirement for a *minyan* derived precisely from two classic examples of rebellion and infamy – the spies and Korach?

Perfecting the Community

Holiness is based on our natural aspirations for spiritual growth and perfection. However, the desire to perfect ourselves – even spiritually – is not true holiness. Our goal should not be the fulfillment of our own personal needs, but rather to honor and sanctify our Maker. Genuine holiness is an altruistic striving for good for its own sake, not out of self-interest.

The core of an elevated service of God is when we fulfill His will by helping and uplifting society. Therefore, the *kedushah* (sanctification) prayer may not be said in private. Without a community to benefit and elevate, the individual cannot truly attain higher levels of holiness.

This special connection between the individual and society is signified by the number ten. Ten is the first number that is also a group, a collection of units forming a new unit. Therefore, the minimum number of members for a quorum is ten.

Learning from Villains

Why do we learn this lesson from the wicked? It is precisely the punishment of the wicked that sheds light on the reward of the righteous. If the only result of evil was that the wicked corrupt themselves, it would be unnecessary for the law to be so severe with one who is only hurting himself. However, it is part of human nature that we influence others and are influenced by our surroundings. Unfortunately, evil people have a negative influence on the entire community, and it is for this reason that they are punished so severely.

Understanding why the wicked are punished clarifies why the righteous are rewarded. Just as the former are punished principally due to their negative influence on the community, so too, the reward of the righteous is due primarily to their positive influence. Now it becomes clear that true holiness is in the context of the organic whole. And the *kedushah* prayer sanctifying God's Name may only be recited in a *minyan*, with a representative community of ten members.

Chukat

Total Dedication to Torah[1]

> This is the Torah: when a person dies in a tent…. (Num. 19:14).

While the topic of this passage is the ritual impurity (*tum'ah*) that comes from contact with the dead, the Talmud (*Berachot* 63b) gives a homiletic interpretation about those who toil in the study of Torah:

> From where do we learn that Torah study is only truly absorbed by one who "kills himself" over it? As it says, "This is the Torah – when a person dies in the tent [of Torah learning]."

Why does Torah study require such a high degree of self-sacrifice and commitment?

The purpose of society is to provide reasonable living conditions, without excessive hardships, for its citizens. In order to achieve this goal, however, there must be some individuals who are willing to serve the community beyond the ordinary call of duty. For example, firefighters, soldiers, police officers and other security personnel must be prepared to work long and irregular hours, and accept the dangers inherent in their jobs. Without their willingness to accept these hardships, the entire populace would suffer from untended fires, violence, crime, war, and other threats to the community's stability and safety.

---

[1] Adapted from *Ein Ayah* vol. II, p. 390.

Guarding the Spirit of the Nation

In a similar fashion, those individuals who are willing to dedicate their lives to Torah study are guardians for the entire Jewish people. Just as a soldier cannot properly perform his service to the nation without a willingness for self-sacrifice, so too, Torah scholars must totally dedicate themselves to their mission. Only with this spirit of commitment will they succeed in nurturing the spiritual light of Israel and enriching the authentic inner life of the nation.

The breadth and depth of knowledge required for true Torah scholarship necessitates long and intensive hours of study. This must come at the expense of pleasures and leisure activities that are acceptable for the general population. Only by overcoming the desire for creature comforts and "the easy life" – by demonstrating their willingness to "kill themselves" in the tents of Torah – do these scholars prove their worthiness to lead the nation in attaining its spiritual aspirations.

Chukat

The Death of a *Tzaddik*[1]

As the Israelites neared the end of their forty-year trek in the wilderness, they lost two great leaders, Miriam and Aaron. While a tremendous loss for the nation, their passing had a hidden spiritual benefit.

The Torah informs us of Miriam's death immediately after enumerating the laws of the *Parah Adumah*, the red heifer whose ashes were used for purification. The Talmudic sages already wondered what connection there might be between Miriam's death and the *Parah Adumah:*

> Why is the death of Miriam juxtaposed to the laws
> of the *Parah Adumah?* This teaches that just as the
> *Parah Adumah* brings atonement, so too, the death
> of the righteous brings atonement.
> (*Mo'ed Katan* 28a)

While this connection between Miriam and the *Parah Adumah* is well-known, the continuation of the same Talmudic statement, concerning the death of Aaron, is less so.

> And why is the death of Aaron juxtaposed to [the
> mention of] the priestly clothes? This teaches that
> just as the priestly clothes bring atonement, so too,
> the death of the righteous brings atonement.

---

[1] Adapted from *Midbar Shur* pp. 346–347.

In what way does the death of *tzaddikim* atone for the people? And why does the Talmud infer this lesson from both the *Parah Adumah* and the priestly clothes?

Larger Than Life

The principal benefit that comes from the death of *tzaddikim* is the spiritual and moral awakening that takes place after they pass away. When a *tzaddik* is alive, his acts of kindness and generosity are not always public knowledge. True *tzaddikim* do not promote themselves. On the contrary, they often take great pains to conceal their virtues and charitable deeds. It is not uncommon that we become aware of their true greatness and nobility of spirit only after they are no longer with us. Only then do we hear reports of their selfless deeds and extraordinary sensitivity, and we are inspired to emulate their ways. In this way, the positive impact of the righteous as inspiring role models increases after their death.

While stories of their fine traits and good deeds stir us to follow in their path, certain aspects of great *tzaddikim* – extraordinary erudition and scholarship, for example – are beyond the capabilities of most people to emulate. In such matters, the best we can do is to take upon ourselves to promote these qualities in our spiritual leadership, such as supporting the Torah study of young, promising scholars.

Two Forms of Emulation

In short, the death of *tzaddikim* inspires us to imitate their personal conduct – if possible, in our own actions, and if not, by ensuring that there will be others who will fill this spiritual void.

These two methods of emulation parallel the different forms of atonement through the *Parah Adumah* and the priestly clothes. Ritual purification using *Parah Adumah* ashes was only effective when they were sprinkled on the body of the impure person; no one else could be purified in his place. This is comparable to those aspects of the *tzaddik* that are accessible to, and incumbent upon, all to emulate.

The priestly garments, on the other hand, were only worn by the *kohanim*. It was through the service of these holy emissaries that the entire nation was forgiven. This is like those extraordinary traits of the *tzaddik* that are beyond the capabilities of most people. These qualities can be carried on only by a select few, with the support of the entire nation.

Chukat

The Book of God's Wars[1]

The Torah reading concludes with an obscure reference to the "Book of God's Wars," describing the Arnon canyon near the border between the Land of Israel and Moab. The verses are cryptic, and the Talmud (*Berachot* 54a–b) fills in the details with the following story:

> Just before the Israelites were to enter the Land of Israel, the Amorites (one of the Canaanite nations) laid a trap for them. They chipped away at the rock, creating hiding places along a narrow pass in the Arnon canyon. There the Amorite soldiers hid, waiting for the Israelites to pass through, when they could attack them with great advantage.
>
> What the Amorites did not know was that the Holy Ark would smooth the way for the Jewish people in their travels through the desert. When the Ark arrived at the Arnon Pass, the mountains on each side crushed together, killing the Amorite soldiers. The Israelites traveled through the pass, blissfully unaware of their deliverance. But at the end of the Jewish camp were two lepers, named Et and Vehav. The last ones to cross through, it was they who noticed the riverbed turned crimson from the crushed enemy soldiers. They realized that a miracle had taken place, and reported it to the rest of the Israelites. The entire nation sang a song of thanks, namely, the poetic verses that the Torah quotes from the "Book of God's Wars."

---

[1] Adapted from *Ein Ayah* vol. II, p. 246.

Battles of the Torah

The Talmud clearly understands that this was a historical event, and even prescribes a blessing to be recited upon seeing the Arnon Pass. Rav Kook, however, interpreted the story in an allegorical fashion. What are "God's Wars"? These are the ideological battles of the Torah against paganism and other nefarious views. Sometimes the battle is out in the open, a clear conflict between opposing cultures and lifestyles. And sometimes the danger lurks in crevices, waiting for the opportune moment to emerge and attack the foundations of the Torah.

Often it is precisely those who are on the fringes, like the lepers at the edge of the camp, who are most aware of the philosophical and ideological battles that the Torah wages. These two lepers represent two types of conflict between the Torah and foreign cultures. And the Holy Ark, containing the two stone tablets from Mount Sinai, is a metaphor for the Torah itself.

The names of the two lepers were Et and Vahav. What do these peculiar names mean?

The word *Et* in Hebrew is an auxiliary word, with no meaning of its own. However, it contains the first and last letters of the word *emet*, "truth." *Et* represents those challenges that stem from new ideas in science and knowledge. *Et* is related to absolute truth; but, without the middle letter, it is only auxiliary to the truth, lacking its substance.

The word *Vahav* comes from *ahavah*, meaning "love" (its Hebrew letters have the same numerical value). The mixing up of the letters indicates that this is an uncontrolled form of love and passion. *Vahav* represents the struggle between the Torah and wild, unbridled living, the contest between instant gratification and eternal values.

When these two adversaries – new scientific viewpoints (*Et*) and unrestrained hedonism (*Vahav*) – come together, we find ourselves trapped with no escape, like the Israelites in the Arnon Pass. Only the light of the Torah (as represented by the Ark) can illuminate the way, crushing the mountains together and defeating the hidden foes. These enemies may be unnoticed by those immersed in the inner sanctum of Torah. But those at the edge, whose connection to Torah and the Jewish people is tenuous and superficial, are acutely aware of these struggles, and more likely to witness the victory of the Torah.

The crushing of the hidden adversaries by the Ark, as the Israelites entered into the Land of Israel in the time of Moses, is a sign for the future victory of the Torah over its ideological and cultural adversaries in the time of the return to Zion in our days.

Balak

Tents and Dwelling Places[1]

The evil prophet Balaam wanted to curse the people of Israel, but instead found himself blessing them, "How goodly are your tents, Jacob; your dwelling places, Israel" (Num. 24:5). Is the repetition in Balaam's blessing only poetic? Or is there a deeper significance to these two forms of shelter, the *ohel* (tent) and the *mishkan* (dwelling place)?

The Journey of the Soul

As we strive for spiritual growth, we make use of two contradictory yet complementary methods. The first method is our aspiration to constantly improve ourselves. We strive to attain greater wisdom and enlightenment. We seek to continually refine the emotions and ennoble the spirit.

The second method is the necessity to restrain our striving for spiritual growth, in order to assimilate changes and guard against spiritual lapses. We want to internalize our spiritual and ethical gains, and maintain our current level. This means that we must curb the desire for growth, so that our ambitions do not overextend the soul's natural capacity for change.

The *ohel* and the *mishkan* are both forms of temporary shelter. Both relate to the soul's upwards journey. However, they differ in a significant aspect. The *ohel* is inherently connected to the state of traveling. It corresponds to the aspiration for constant change and growth. The *mishkan* is also part of the journey, but it is associated with the rests

---

[1] Adapted from *Olat Re'iyah* vol. I, pp. 42–43.

between travels. It is the soul's sense of calm, its rest from the constant movement, for the sake of the overall mission.

Surprisingly, it is the second method that is the loftier of the two. The desire to change reflects a lower-level fear, lest we stagnate and deteriorate. Therefore, the blessing mentions tents first, together with the name *Jacob*, the first and embryonic name of the Jewish people. The need to stop and rest, on the other hand, stems from a higher-level fear, lest we over-shoot the appropriate level for the soul. For this reason, the blessing mentions *mishkan* together with the name *Israel*, Jacob's second and holier name.

In any case, both aspects are required in order to achieve stable spiritual growth. Balaam's prophetic blessing praises the balanced union of "How goodly are your tents, Jacob," the soul's longing for change, together with the more restful state of "your dwelling places, Israel," restricting growth in order to avoid unchecked advancement, thus enabling the soul to properly absorb all spiritual attainments.

Balak

Eliminating Idolatry[1]

The Weird Worship of Peor

After failing to curse the people of Israel, Balaam devised another plan to make trouble for the Jewish people. He advised using Moabite and Midianite women to entice the Israelite men into worshipping Baal Peor. How was this idol worshipped? The word *Peor* means to "open up" or "disclose." According to the Talmud, the worshippers would bare their backsides and defecate in honor of the idol. The Talmud (*Sanhedrin* 64a) illustrates the repulsive nature of this particular idolatry with the following two stories:

> There was once a gentile woman who was very ill. She vowed: "If I recover from my illness, I will go and worship every idol in the world." She recovered, and proceeded to worship every idol in the world. When she came to Peor, she asked its priests, "How is this one worshipped?" They told her, "One eats greens and drinks strong drink, and then defecates before the idol." The woman responded, "I would rather become ill again than worship an idol in such a [revolting] manner."

> Sabta, a townsman of Avlas, once hired out a donkey to a gentile woman. When she came to Peor, she said to him, "Wait till I enter and come out again." When she came out, he told her, "Now you wait for me until I go in and come out." "But

---
[1] Adapted from *Shemoneh Kevatzim* VIII: 132; IV: 56.

are you not a Jew?" she asked. "What does it concern you?" he replied. He then entered, uncovered himself before it, and wiped himself on the idol's nose. The acolytes praised him, saying, "No one has ever served this idol so consummately!"

Exposing the True Nature of Idolatry

What was the point of this most odious idolatrous practice? In truth, Peor was not an aberrant form of idolatry. On the contrary, Peor was the epitome of idolatry! Other forms of idolatry are more aesthetic, but they just cover up the true ugliness of idolatry. The Golden Calf was the opposite extreme, a beautiful, elegant form of idol worship. But Peor, as its name indicates, exposes the true nature of idolatry. All other forms of idolatry are just branches of Peor, with their inner vileness concealed to various extents.

The repulsive service of Peor contains the key for abolishing idolatry. When the prophet Elijah fought against the idolatry of Baal, he taunted the people: "If Baal is God, then follow him!" The people, in fact, were already worshippers of Baal. What was Elijah telling them?

Elijah's point was that Baal is just a sanitized version of Peor. If Baal is God, then go all the way. You should worship the source of this form of worship – Peor. Elijah's exposure of Baal as just a cleaner version of Peor convinced the people. They were truly revolted by the scatological practices of Peor, and instinctively responded, "Hashem is God! Hashem is God!" (I Kings 18)

Historically, the uprooting of idolatry will take place in stages. The allure of Peor, the purest form of idolatry, was shattered after Moses rooted out those who worshipped Peor at Shittim. That purge gave strength to the men of the Great Assembly who subdued the temptation of idolatry in the time of Ezra (*Sanhedrin* 64a). The final eradication of idolatry's last vestiges will take place in the end of days, through the spiritual power of Moses, whose burial place faced Beit Peor. This obliteration will occur as idolatry's innate foulness is exposed to all.

Why is idolatry so intrinsically vile? The source of idolatry's appeal is in fact a holy one – an impassioned yearning for closeness to God. Ignorance and moral turpitude, however, prevent this closeness and block the divine light from the soul. The overwhelming desire for divine closeness, despite one's moral failings, leads to idol worship. Instead of correcting one's flaws, these spiritual yearnings are distorted into cravings for idolatry. The unholy alliance of spiritual yearnings together with immoral and decadent behavior produces the intrinsic foulness of idolatry. Instead of trying to elevate humanity and refine our desires, idolatry endeavors to debase our most refined aspirations to our coarsest physical aspects. This is the ultimate message of Peor's scatological practices.

True Victory over Idolatry

The Great Assembly in Ezra's time conquered the temptation of idolatry by generally diminishing spiritual yearnings in the world. They did not truly defeat idolatry; rather, they subdued its enticement. In the allegorical language of the Midrash, they cast the temptation of idolatry into a metal cauldron and sealed it with lead, "so that its call may not be heard." Thus, we find that the Talmud (*Sanhedrin* 102b) records a dream of Rav Ashi, the fifth-century Talmudic sage. In his dream, Rav Ashi asked the idolatrous King Menasseh, "Since you are so wise, why did you worship idols?" To which Menasseh replied, 'Were you there, you would have lifted up the hems of your garment and sped after me."

The true cure for this perilous attraction, however, is through greatness of Torah. The highest goal of Torah is the appearance of inner light in the human soul, as divine wisdom is applied to all of the spheres that the soul is capable of assimilating – be it in thought, emotions, desires, and character traits.

Even nowadays, poverty in Torah knowledge results in a weakness of spirit, similar to the spiritual darkness caused by idolatry. The world awaits redemption through greatness of Torah. Then idolatry will be truly defeated, and not merely subdued in a sealed metal cauldron.

Pinchas

Genuine Zealotry[1]

Pinchas... zealously avenged My cause among the
Israelites.... Therefore, tell him that I have given
him My covenant of peace. (Num. 25:11–12)

Why did God present Pinchas, the archetypical zealot, with a
covenant of *peace*? What was the nature of this covenant?

The Prayer of Shemuel HaKatan

The Talmud (*Berachot* 28b) recounts that Rabban Gamliel, who headed the
Sanhedrin in Yavneh after the destruction of Jerusalem, saw the need to
make an addition to the daily prayer. The Jewish people needed heavenly
protection against heretics and informers. But Rabban Gamliel had
trouble finding a scholar capable of composing such a prayer.

In the end, Shemuel HaKatan ("Samuel the modest") agreed to
formulate the prayer, called *Birkat Haminim*. Why was it so difficult to find
a scholar to author this prayer? And what made Shemuel HaKatan so
qualified for the task?

By its very nature, prayer is a medium of harmony and
understanding, full of kindness and love. Any scholar on an appropriate
spiritual level is capable of writing prayers that are fitting for a holy and
wise nation.

A prayer decrying slanderers and heretics, however, touches upon
powerful emotions of hostility and anger. We naturally feel hatred towards

---

[1] Adapted from *Olat Re'iyah* vol. I, p. 278.

our foes and the enemies of our people. To compose a fitting prayer against enemies requires an individual who is utterly pure and holy, one who has succeeded in eliminating all petty hatred and resentments from his heart. In order that such a prayer will be pure, its sole intention must be to limit the damage and correct the evil caused by the wicked, as they impede the world's spiritual and ethical progress. It is for the sake of this pure, unselfish motive that we plead that God vanquish the wicked and foil their evil plans.

Even though one's initial motives are pure, if he is subject to even the slightest feelings of animosity that are naturally aroused when one feels attacked, his thoughts will be tainted by personal hatred, and his prayer will deviate from the true intent. Only Shemuel HaKatan was a suitable candidate to compose this difficult prayer. His life's motto was "Do not rejoice when your enemy falls" (*Avot* 4:9). Shemuel succeeded in removing all feelings of enmity from his heart, even for personal enemies. Only this saintly scholar was able to compose a prayer against slanderers that would convey the feelings of a pure heart, expressing the soul's inner aspirations for complete universal good.

Refining Zeal

From Shemuel HaKatan we see that zealotry is not a simple matter. Zeal must be carefully refined to ensure that it is truly for the sake of heaven. As Rav Kook explained in *Orot HaKodesh* (vol. III, p. 244):

> We need to refine the attribute of zeal, so that when it enters the realm of the holy, it should be a pure zeal for God. Since zealotry often contains some slight influence of human failings, our powers of self-examination must determine its primary motive. We must ensure that it is not based on personal jealousy, which rots one's very bones, but rather a zeal for God, which provides a covenant of peace.

When God gave Pinchas a covenant of peace, He affirmed that Pinchas' act of zealotry – defending the Jewish people from idolatrous influences – was performed with pure motives. Only God could testify as to the purity of Pinchas' zeal, that he had acted solely for the sake of Heaven, without any admixture of pettiness or personal animosity. Pinchas' zeal was purely the product of his burning love for God, an expression of his desire to bring true peace (*shalom*) and perfection (*shleimut*) to the world.

Pinchas

Atonement for the New Moon[1]

The Torah describes the offerings presented for each holiday, starting with those brought on *Rosh Chodesh*, the first day of the lunar month.

> This is the burnt-offering of the new month, for all the months of the year. And one male goat for a sin-offering for God. (Num. 28:14–15)

There is a very peculiar Talmudic tradition about the purpose of the new moon sin-offering. For whom does this offering atone? The Talmud (*Chulin* 60b) explains that this is literally a "sin offering for God." The offering comes to atone for God, as it were, for making the moon smaller than the sun.[2] For this reason, a sin-offering is presented with the appearance of the new moon.

Is it possible to say that God sinned? That God needs atonement?

Restricting the Infinite

This monthly offering relates to the essence of the creation process. The very act of creation is problematic, confining infinite Godliness within the finite boundaries of time and place. This constriction is only possible if there is a continual process of renewal, whereby the physical limits are gradually released, expanding the material boundaries.

---

[1] Adapted from *Olat Re'iyah* vol. I, p. 165.

[2] According to the Midrash, the sun and the moon were initially created the same size. The moon complained, "Is it possible for two kings to rule with one crown?" and was punished by being reduced in size.

In Hebrew, the words "month" (*chodesh*) and "new" (*chadash*) share the same root. The new month signals renewal and advancement.

The animal brought for this sin-offering is a goat. Why a goat? The goat by nature is a destructive animal, devouring not only the leaves but the branches and roots, destroying the foliage and eroding the earth. Within the order of creation, the universe requires destructive forces, in order to break down the limiting borders and push forward the renewal of existence to ever higher levels. In this context, those phenomena that would seem to be purely negative and destructive are redeemed and given cosmic significance.

The principle offering for the new month was not the sin-offering, but an *olah*, an all burnt-offering. The word *olah* means to raise up or elevate. The atonement for the constrictive nature of the physical universe – as symbolized by the reduction in the moon's size – is through the combination of the destructive forces (the goat offering) with the continual renewal and elevation of the world (the *olah* offering).

Matot

Keeping Vows[1]

One who makes a vow should take care to fulfill it:

> If a man makes a vow to God, or makes an oath to
> prohibit [something] to himself, he must not break
> his word. He should do all that he expressed
> verbally. (Num. 30:3)

Oaths and vows are a natural human response in times of intense emotions. Particularly when we sense danger or trouble, we spontaneously begin to bargain with God. We pledge to improve ourselves or repay some undeserved kindness. Why do people act this way?

The Intellect and the Emotions

Two major facets of the soul are the intellect and the emotions. Fortunate is the individual who has succeeded in refining both intellectual and emotional aspects, so that they work together and complement each other.

Torah study and *mitzvot* help us grow in both of these areas. Some *mitzvot* are primarily geared towards developing the intellect. They guide us towards an accurate outlook on the world, and help us focus our powers of analysis and introspection. Other *mitzvot* are more related to our emotional lives. They guard and direct the emotions, refining them so that they will harmonize with the rational intellect.

Where do vows and oaths fit in? They are associated with the realm of emotions. Vows are usually the result of an outburst of feelings – an overpowering sense of holiness, awe, fear, or gratitude – that fill one's

---

[1] Adapted from *Ein Ayah* vol. III, p. 176.

heart and inspire one to make a vow. The Torah admonishes us to be careful to fulfill our pledges. We need to recognize the value of these holy feelings. One who belittles and disregards his vows is in fact rejecting the great benefit of this natural asset, for vows can direct us to live an emotionally refined life that complements our intellectual attainments.

Keeping One's Wife

Rabbi Nathan, the second-century scholar, made a statement that is difficult to understand: "A man loses his wife as punishment for breaking vows" (*Shabbat* 32b). What is the connection between keeping one's vows and keeping one's wife?

The principle differences in the psychological makeup of men and women are rooted in the spheres of intellect and emotion. Women excel in emotional intelligence. They feel more acutely the good and the evil in moral choices, the true and the false in practical studies, the beautiful and the ugly in lifestyles.

Men, on the other hand, are more focused on their intellectual faculties. For them, on the whole, emotions take on a supporting role.

A woman of valor is called "her husband's crown" (Proverbs 12:4). Her talents complement that which is lacking in her husband, namely the emotional component. His powers of introspection are bolstered and sustained by her heightened sense of good and evil, truth and falsehood.

One who disparages the importance of vows, and their usefulness in refining the emotions, has also lost sight of the sublime value provided by a virtuous woman when her talents are properly appreciated. One who disregards his oaths undermines the significance of emotions in life and spiritual growth. Such a person, Rabbi Nathan taught, has "lost" his wife and her unique contribution. His path in life, both spiritual and material, is limited, for only a woman of valor "does him good and not evil all the days of her life" (Proverbs 31:12).

Two Paths to Purity[1]

After the victory over the Midianites, Elazar the High Priest explained to the soldiers how to *kasher* and purify the metal utensils captured in the war:

> As far as the gold, silver, copper, iron, tin and lead are concerned: whatever was used over fire must be passed through fire, and it will be clean. However, it must be then purified with the sprinkling water. (Num. 31:22–23)

The Midianite vessels had become defiled in battle, through contact with death. They needed to be purified, by sprinkling over them water mixed with the ashes of the red heifer.[2] This is the standard process of purification, a process that may take a week to complete.

Instant Purity

There exists a second way to purifying utensils – more drastic, but immediate. One simply makes the utensil unusable by boring a large hole in it. Then it is no longer considered a vessel. When the puncture is

---

[1] Adapted from *Ein Ayah* vol. III, pp. 47–48.

[2] The Talmud (*Avodah Zarah* 75b) explains that the purification referred to in the verse is immersion in a *mikveh*, required for all vessels acquired from gentiles. However, many of the Bible commentators, including Rashi and Nachmanides, understood the simple meaning of the verse to refer to purifying by means of the red heifer ashes.

mended, it is as if a new utensil has been formed, without any residual impurity.

The Talmud (*Shabbat* 15b) relates that the Hasmonean queen Shlomzion (circa 100 BCE) once held a celebration in honor of her son. Tragically, one of the guests died during the party. As a result, the royal cutlery and dishes became ritually impure. The queen wanted to avoid waiting a week to purify them, so she commanded that the utensils be rendered unusable, and then forged anew.

The rabbis informed the queen, however, that her shortcut was not acceptable. Rabbi Shimon ben Shatach – the queen's brother – had already ruled that impure utensils that are broken still retain their original impure state after they are fixed.

What led the Sages to make this decree? They were afraid that the ritual of red heifer ashes would fall into disuse if everyone used the faster method of boring a large hole and then fixing the implement.

How to Rectify an Imperfect World

There is, however, a deeper significance to Rabbi Shimon Ben Shatach's decree. The laws of ritual purity may seem distant from modern life. But upon closer examination, they can have much to teach us – about imperfections in the world, and in each individual.

There are two ways to purify oneself from past follies. The more drastic method is to totally destroy those areas into which evil has rooted itself, and then rebuild from the raw materials left over. This was the method used in the time of Noah, when God purged an utterly corrupt world with the devastating waters of the Flood.

An individual may similarly choose to eliminate deeply rooted personality defects by afflicting body and soul. With the breakdown of his powers, the evil is also destroyed. Then he can rebuild himself in a moral, just fashion.

Given the rampant level of violence and immorality that have become so entrenched among the human race, the world certainly deserves to have been destroyed. Yet, God in His kindness established another method of purification. The preferred path is to gradually rectify moral defects over time, so that even those unbridled forces may be utilized for good. Only in extreme cases is it necessary to purify through destruction.

The rabbinical decree not to purify utensils by breaking them now takes on a deeper significance. We should not become accustomed to this drastic form of purification, which weakens constructive energies as it purges impurities. It is better to use the slower method of red heifer ashes, thereby allowing the vessel to become pure while retaining all of its original strength.

Sefer Devarim – The Book of Deuteronomy

The Special Nature of Deuteronomy

God's divine nature, like all intellectual-prophetic perceptions, is apprehended subjectively, according to one's relation to the matter. After all, everything is grasped through one's personal viewpoint. In all perceptions, there must be some influence of the personal aspects of the one perceiving.

However, the prophecy of the master of the prophets [Moses] transcended this level. He was able to raise himself to such a height as to grasp the pure truth in divine enlightenment. It was as if he was able to stand outside of his own reality and look objectively at "the image of God...."[1]

However, it was fitting that Moses should not lack also that type of prophetic perception that is influenced by one's individual character, since his personal nature was so elevated and uplifting and encompassing....

Perhaps this is the special nature of the book of *Mishneh Torah* [Deuteronomy], as opposed to the other four books of Moses. It is written[2] that the entire Torah was transmitted directly from God,

---

[1] Num. 12:8.

[2] *Megillah* 31b.

but Moses said the curses in *Mishneh Torah* on his own. This indicates that the prophetic level [of Deuteronomy] was similar to that of the other prophets, differing only due to the relatively elevated state of Moses' soul. But it shared with [other prophetic works] the impact of the perceiver's connection to the overall understanding of the cosmos and its Director, as these matters relate to him and his imaginative faculties.

(*Ein Ayah* vol. II, p. 387)

Devarim

The Book that Moses Wrote[1]

Mipi Atzmo

Already from its opening sentence, we see that the final book of the Pentateuch is different from the first four. Instead of the usual introductory statement, "God spoke to Moses, saying," we read:

> These are the words *that Moses spoke* to all of Israel
> on the far side of the Jordan River.... (Deut. 1:1)

Unlike the other four books, Deuteronomy is largely a record of speeches that Moses delivered to the people before his death. The Talmud (*Megillah* 31b) confirms that the prophetic nature of this book is qualitatively different than the others. While the other books of the Torah are a direct transmission of God's word, Moses said Deuteronomy *mipi atzmo* – "on his own."

However, we cannot take this statement – that Deuteronomy consists of Moses' own words – at face value. Moses could not have literally composed this book on his own, for the Sages taught that a prophet is not allowed to say in God's name what he did not hear from God (*Shabbat* 104a). So what does it mean that Moses wrote Deuteronomy *mipi atzmo*? In what way does this book differ from the previous four books of the Pentateuch?

---

[1] Adapted from *Shemuot HaRe'iyah*, *Devarim* 1929.

Tadir versus *Mekudash*

The distinction between different levels of prophecy may be clarified by examining a Talmudic discussion in *Zevachim* 90b. The Talmud asks the following question: if we have before us two activities, one of which is holier (*mekudash*), but the second is more prevalent (*tadir*), which one should we perform first? The Sages concluded that the more prevalent activity takes precedence over the holier one, and should be discharged first.

One might infer from this ruling that the quality of prevalence is more important, and for this reason the more common activity is performed first. In fact, the exact opposite is true. If something is rare, this indicates that it belongs to a very high level of holiness – so high, in fact, that our limited world does not merit benefiting from this exceptional holiness on a permanent basis. Why then does the more common event take precedence? This is in recognition that we live in an imperfect world. We are naturally more receptive to and influenced by a lesser, more sustainable sanctity. In the future, however, the higher, transitory holiness will come first.

The First and Second *Luchot*

This distinction between *mekudash* and *tadir* illustrates the difference between the first and second set of *luchot* (tablets) that Moses brought down from Mount Sinai. The first tablets were holier, a reflection of the singular unity of the Jewish people at that point in history. As the Midrash comments on Exodus 19:2, "The people encamped – as one person, with one heart – opposite the mountain" (*Mechilta*; Rashi ad loc).

After the sin of the Golden Calf, however, the Jewish people no longer deserved the unique holiness of the first tablets. Tragically, the first *luchot* had to be broken; otherwise, the Jewish people would have warranted destruction. With the holy tablets shattered, the special unity of the Jewish people also departed. This unity was later partially restored with the second covenant that they accepted upon themselves while encamped across the Jordan River on the plains of Moab.[2]

The exceptional holiness of the first tablets, and the special unity of the people at Mount Sinai, were simply too holy to maintain over time. They were replaced by less holy but more attainable substitutes – the second set of tablets, and the covenant at *Arvot Moav.*

Moses and the Other Prophets

After the sin of the Golden Calf, God offered to rebuild the Jewish people solely from Moses. Moses was unsullied by the sin of the Golden Calf; he still belonged to the transient realm of elevated holiness. Nonetheless, Moses rejected God's offer. He decided to include himself within the constant holiness of Israel. This is the meaning of the Talmudic statement that Moses wrote Deuteronomy "on his own." On his own accord, Moses decided to join the spiritual level of the Jewish people, and help prepare the people for the more sustainable holiness through the renewed covenant of *Arvot Moav.*

Moses consciously limited the prophetic level of Deuteronomy so that it would correspond to that of other prophets. He withdrew from his unique prophetic status, a state where "No other prophet arose in Israel like Moses" (Deut. 34:10). With the book of Deuteronomy, he initiated the lower but more constant form of prophecy that would suit future generations. He led the way for the other prophets, and foretold that "God will establish for you a prophet from your midst like me" (Deut. 18:15).

In the future, however, the first set of tablets, which now appear to be broken, will be restored. The Jewish people will be ready for a higher, loftier holiness, and the *mekudash* will take precedent over the *tadir.*

---

[2] The Hebrew name for this location, *Arvot Moav*, comes from the word *arvut*, meaning mutual responsibility.

For this reason, the Holy Ark held both sets of tablets; each set was kept for its appropriate time.

Devarim

Elucidating the Torah[1]

> On the east bank of the Jordan, in the land of
> Moab, Moses began to elucidate (*be'er*) this
> Torah. (Deut. 1:5)

Moses and Ezra

The fifth book of the Torah differs from the first four books.
Deuteronomy is not a verbatim transmission of God's word, but a
prophetic work, on par with the writings of other prophets. The final
book of the Torah is called *Mishneh Torah* (Deut. 17:18), for it is Moses'
review and elucidation of the Torah.

A second surge of Torah exegesis took place in the time of Ezra.
"They read in the book of God's Torah, clarified (*mephorash*); and they
gave the sense, and explained the reading to them" (Nehemiah 8:8). Both
Moses and Ezra explained and elucidated the Torah. Their methods of
interpretation, however, differed. Moses' elucidation was a *biur*, while
Ezra's was a *perush*. What is the difference between these two methods?

Two Methods of Elucidation

From the time of Moses until Ezra, the Torah was clarified through the
method of *biur*. This word comes from the root *be'er*, meaning a well of
water. Like a well, the creative outpouring of learning flowed "like an
overflowing spring and a river that never dries up" (*Avot* 6:1). This form
of analysis begins by deducing the underlying principles; then, all of the

---

[1] Adapted from the introduction to *Ein Ayah* vol. I, pp. 14–17.

details may be derived from these fundamental principles, the hidden foundations of the Torah.

Ezra, however, recognized that the innovative *biur*, with its subtle methods of induction and deduction, was not suitable for all periods. In a time of exile, this approach could prove to be dangerous. Political instability and social upheaval diminish the quality of scholarship and peace of mind, thus weakening the nation's spiritual and intellectual capabilities. In such difficult conditions, the method of *biur* could be misused, leading to a subversion of the Torah's true aims.

Therefore, Ezra promoted the approach of *perush*. This is an empirical method of analyzing a subject by examining all of its details. Details are compared to one another, without attempting to determine the underlying principles. The word *perush* comes from the root *paras*, "to spread forth" (see Isaiah 25:11). This form of analysis is less risky, since it limits itself to the material at hand.

Letterforms for the Times

The Talmud (*Sanhedrin* 21b) states that Ezra was a scholar of such stature that the Torah could have been given to Israel through him. While this did not occur, Ezra nonetheless made a revolutionary change in the Torah, by switching the writing in the Torah from the ancient Hebrew script to the square Assyrian script. Why did Ezra make this change in the letterforms?

The two scripts reflect different needs of the nation. During the First Temple period, there was little interaction with other nations, and the Torah did not openly influence the world. The Jewish people dwelled in their own land, and the *kohanim* and the Levites were available to inspect the text of the Torah scrolls and guard them from any scribal errors. When Moses gave the Torah to the Jewish people, a clear script not given to mistakes in transmission was not of paramount importance. The problem of similar-looking letterforms in the ancient Hebrew script was not an issue during the relatively stable era of the First Temple period.

Ezra lived at the beginning of the Second Temple period. This era was essentially a time for the Jewish people to prepare themselves for the long and difficult exile that would follow. Retaining the difficult ancient letterforms would have made it impossible to safeguard the accuracy of the Torah's text. In the centuries of exile and wanderings from country to country, the original Hebrew script would have lead to many mistakes and uncertainties. The sages of the beginning of the Second Temple period, aware of the long exile to come, worked to fortify the spiritual state of the people, despite the future loss of the nation's unifying institutions, such as the Temple, the *Sanhedrin*, and the monarchy. One of the initiatives of that era was Ezra's decision to switch the script to the clear Assyrian script, whose unambiguous letters would prevent confusing similar letters in the text of the Torah.

A Fence for the Torah

The sages of that era made other preparations for the future exile, establishing protective decrees to guard the Torah's laws. "Make a fence for the Torah" (*Avot* 1:1) was the motto of the Great Assembly.

Even though these changes came about due to the needs of the hour, the Jewish people recognized the value and benefits of these decrees. As the nation adopted these holy paths, pure deeds and worthy customs, a net of eternal love spread over them, and they acquired a permanent place in the spiritual life of the nation.

Devarim

Right verses Might[1]

We turned and went up towards Bashan, and Og, king of Bashan, and his people came out to fight against us at Edrei. God told me: "Do not fear him. I will place him and all his people and his land in your hands." (Deut. 3:1–3)

The Battle against Og

Moses gave a terse account of the battle against the fearful giant, King Og, and his people. The Midrash (*Berachot* 54b), however, elaborated greatly upon this amazing event:

> Og said to himself, "How large is the encampment of Israel? Three Persian miles? I will grab a mountain three miles wide, throw it on them and kill them!" So Og took a mountain three miles wide, and lifted it over his head in order to throw it.
> But God brought ants. They ate a hole in the mountain, and the rock crashed down on Og's neck. Og tried to lift it up, but his teeth stuck out in both directions and prevented the rock from lifting over his head.
> Now, Moses was ten cubits [15 feet] tall. He took a hammer ten cubits long, jumped up ten cubits and swung the hammer at Og's ankles, killing him.

[1] Adapted from *Ein Ayah* vol. II, pp. 248–249.

Nice story. But what does it mean? What message were the Sages trying to tell us?

Brute Force versus Spiritual Greatness

The battle between Og and Moses is a metaphor for the struggle between the physical and spiritual realms. Og the giant viewed everything in terms of brute force and power. He was enraged seeing a small, weak people – the Israelites – take on and defeat the Midianites and the Amorites. Og decided he would demonstrate that spiritual power cannot compete against physical strength. He would use the ultimate symbol of brute force – a massive, inanimate mountain – to bury the Jews and all of their pretensions!

The giant lifted the mountain up high over his head. This indicated that the huge rock, as a symbol of brute power, was his crown, his glory, his ultimate value.

"But God brought ants that ate a hole in the mountain." Significantly, Og's downfall was not by means of an even greater physical force. Og's faith in power and might was conclusively shattered by his defeat at the hands of the smallest and most fragile of creatures, the lowly ant.

Overgrown Teeth

At this point, the heavy rock weighed down heavily on Og's shoulders. He began to realize that his trust in physical force was misplaced. His crown had become an oppressive burden. However, it was too late to escape. His teeth, symbolizing his aggressiveness and lust, had grown outwards. His traits of violence and rapacity, like his reliance on brute force, had become an integral part of his life and personality, at the expense of any spiritual inclinations.

Such is the fate of an individual – or a people – addicted to the drug of physical force, living by the power of the fist. In hindsight, such a life of aggression will be a burden and a source of bitter discontent. Old and weak, even if he should now desire to change his ways to a more peaceful existence, he will not succeed. His teeth overgrown, his basic nature has been usurped by the lifelong habits of aggression and savage greed.

Va'etchanan

Cleaving to God[1]

You, who remained attached to the Lord your God, are all alive today. (Deut. 4:4)

What does it mean "to be attached to God"? As the Talmud (*Sotah* 14a) asks, is it possible to cleave to the *Shechinah*, God's Divine Presence, which the Torah describes as a "consuming fire" (Deut. 4:24)? The Sages answered:

> Rather, this means you should cleave to God's attributes. Just as God clothed the naked [Adam and Eve], so too you should cloth the naked. Just as God visited the sick [Abraham after his circumcision], so too you should visit the sick. Just as God consoled the mourners [Isaac after Abraham's death], so too you should console the mourners. Just as God buried the dead [Moses], so too you should bury the dead.

This explanation on how one may cleave to God is the very essence of the Kabbalistic study of the *sephirot*. What is the point in studying the intricacies of God's Names and His manifestations in holy *sephirot*? We learn about God's divine attributes so that we may aspire to imitate them. These studies enable us to follow in God's ways and in this way cleave to Him.

---

[1] Adapted from *Mussar Avicha*, pp. 118–119.

This idea – that we can only attach ourselves to God by imitating His attributes – is a fundamental concept in Judaism. Any other understanding of cleaving to God implies some degree of anthropomorphism or idolatry.

The very existence of ideals, holy aspirations, and ethics in the world and in the human soul mandates the existence of a Divine Source. From where else could they come? Our awareness of the Source of these ideals elevates them, revealing new wellsprings of light and pure life.

Va'etchanan

In Mind and Heart[1]

The *Aleinu* prayer, recited at the conclusion of every prayer service, contains the following verse:

> Know it today and ponder it in your heart: God is the Supreme Being in heaven above and on the earth below – there is no other. (Deut. 4:39)

What is the difference between "knowing it" and "pondering it in the heart"?

Two Stages of Acceptance

Sometimes, people admit that there is a gap between what they know intellectually and what they are ready for emotionally. They will say, "Yes, this makes sense. This is a better way, a healthier way, a truer way. Still, it is not for me. It's too hard; I cannot do it."

Therefore, the Torah emphasizes the importance of two steps. First, we need to recognize the truth. This is the intellectual stage of "*know it today*." This stage is critical, but it is still only on a theoretical level. It must be followed by the second step: to internalize that which the mind comprehends. We need to accept emotionally the ramifications of this understanding, and be willing to act upon it. This is the second stage, to "*ponder it in your heart*."

The second stage of practical acceptance should nevertheless be rooted in the initial step of intellectual comprehension. As the Sages

---

[1] Adapted from *Olat Re'iyah* vol. I, pp. 324–325.

taught (*Berachot* 13a), "First accept the kingdom of Heaven, and then the yoke of [practical] *mitzvot*."

Above and Below

The verse continues by stating that God is supreme in both "the heaven above and on the earth below." What does this mean?

This does not refer to God's unity in the universe, but to our own inner unity when we accept His reign. "Heaven" and "earth" are metaphors for our two major faculties, the mind and the heart. We need to be consistent so that how we act is not detached from what we believe.

In summary, we should accept God's kingship on both levels:

- To understand intellectually – in the "*heaven above*" – using our minds, in cognitive thought and belief.
- And to act upon that wisdom on a practical level – "*on the earth below*" – with our hearts and will, by implementing our understanding in the realm of deed and action.

Va'etchanan

Loving God with All Your Might[1]

You shall love the Lord your God with all your
heart, with all your soul, and with all your
might. (Deut. 6:5)

What does it mean to love God *bechol me'odecha*, "with all your
might"? The Talmud offers two explanations for this phrase.

Thankfulness Even in Misfortune

The first explanation is that, in every situation (*midah*) that God places us,
we should sincerely thank (*modeh*) Him. From here we learn that one
should recite a blessing over bad news as well as good news. When
hearing about death, financial loss, or other tragedies, we need to
acknowledge that God is the true Judge.

How is it possible to thank God for tragedy? And why is this a
form of loving God?

A self-centered individual will look at all circumstances only in the
context of his own narrow interests. From this viewpoint, good and bad
are measured purely by selfish criteria.

However, the individual who can internalize the dictates of his
intellect, and who loves that which his mind tells him to love, will have a
drastically different outlook on good and bad. Happiness and pleasure are
not limited to how events affect him or his immediate surroundings. As a
result of his love of the Infinite, he judges every situation, every

---

[1] Adapted from *Ein Ayah* vol. II, p. 328.

circumstance, in terms of the *klal* – the community, the nation, the universe, all of creation, and beyond.

In the overall picture, evil does not exist. What appears to be evil and bad in a narrow outlook, will ultimately result in greater good in the broader view. If we live our lives in accordance with this insight, we will understand that while a certain situation may be difficult on a personal level, our private suffering enables positive repercussions for the *klal*.

With All Our Possessions

The Sages gave a second explanation for "all your might": to love God with all of your money. We should serve God with all of our possessions.

How does this relate to the first explanation, that we should express gratitude to God in all circumstances of life?

An individual who chooses to reject all material possessions, spurning wealth and comfort in pursuit of an ascetic lifestyle, is living an extremely limited existence. He is incapable of truly appreciating the value of life. What is life worth when it is restricted to poverty and hardship? We can only attain a full measure of love – for life, for the universe, and for God – when we seek to live life to its fullest, albeit in accordance with God's will.

Life is expanded and enriched through material possessions. Money and possessions are called *me'od* ("very"), as they serve to intensify the living experience. The wise individual, living a full, intense life, is deeply aware of the importance of life. He recognizes the greatness of the *klal*, and is willing to sacrifice his life, out of love for God. The richness of his life strengthens his dedication to truth and justice, according to what benefits the *klal*. His soul is full of emotion and feeling, and he can truly feel gratitude for all circumstances of life, whether or not they are in his own personal best interest.

Eikev

Two Loves for *Eretz Yisrael*[1]

The Blessings of Torah Scholars

The Talmud (*Berachot* 50a) gives a litmus test to determine if an individual is truly a Torah scholar: listen to how he recites *berachot* (blessings). Clearly, when *berachot* are recited sincerely, they reflect a proper outlook on life and help instill important traits such as gratitude to God. What is less obvious is that even the detailed laws for blessings reflect fundamental concepts of the Torah. For this reason, Torah scholars are punctilious in their blessings.

Loving the Land of Israel

The following story gives one example of such an exacting approach towards blessings. It also contains an important lesson about love for the Land of Israel.

> Rabbi Hisda and Rabbi Hamenuna were seated at a meal, and were served dates and pomegranates. Rabbi Hamenuna made the blessing over the dates. Rabbi Hisda told him, "Do you not agree that those fruit mentioned earlier in the verse take precedence when reciting the blessing?" Rabbi Hamenuna responded, "Dates are mentioned second after the word *land*, while pomegranates are only mentioned fifth." Rabbi Hisda exclaimed, "If only we had legs of iron to always follow you and learn from you!" (*Berachot* 41b)

---

[1] Adapted from *Ein Ayah* vol. II, pp. 186–187; *Olat Re'iyah* vol. I, pp. 374–377.

The two scholars referred to the verse that praises the Land of Israel for seven grains and fruits: "It is a **land** of wheat, barley, grapes, figs and pomegranates; a **land** of oil-olives and honey-dates" (Deut. 8:8).

Rabbi Hisda felt that the blessing should reflect the order of the produce mentioned in the verse. Thus, pomegranates should come first. Rabbi Hamenuna explained that while the order in the verse is indeed important, there is an even more important factor: how close is the name of the fruit to the word *land* in the verse? Pomegranates are the fifth produce mentioned after the first time *land* appears in the verse; dates, however, are the second fruit mentioned after *land* appears a second time in the verse. In other words, the position of dates in the verse indicates a greater closeness to the Land of Israel; therefore, this fruit deserves to come first.

The thought and care that Rabbi Hamenuna gave to his blessing demonstrates the importance he placed in loving *Eretz Yisrael*. This great love stems from recognizing the unique qualities of the Land – qualities that enable the Jewish people and all of humanity to attain spiritual goals. One who is closer to the Land of Israel, and demonstrates a greater connection to it, comes first for blessing. Such an individual is closer to the perfection that is attained through this special land.

Two Types of Love

Yet, we may ask: why is the word *land* mentioned twice in the verse? Why does the verse divide up the produce of *Eretz Yisrael* into two categories?

There are in fact two types of love for the Land of Israel. One's appreciation for the Land is a function of his spiritual level and awareness. Some value *Eretz Yisrael* because of its unique spiritual qualities. They long "to take pleasure in her stones and love her dust" (Psalms 102:15) in order to fulfill the *mitzvot* that are connected to the Land. They recognize the blessings that *Eretz Yisrael* provides for the spiritual elevation of the Jewish people and the entire world.

Then there are those who appreciate the land for its material benefits. They recognize its value as a homeland for the Jewish people, and work towards settling and rebuilding the land. This form of devotion to the Land of Israel, even though it does not take into account its special spiritual qualities, is nonetheless a good and positive trait.

The verse mentions the word *land* twice, each time followed by a list of produce. This corresponds to the two forms of devotion to the Land of Israel. The first list of produce represents those who love the Land for its elevated, spiritual properties. This list consists of five fruits and grains, corresponding to the Five Books of Moses. This devotion to *Eretz Yisrael* stems from the world of Torah, from an awareness of the spiritual goals of the Jewish people and the entire world.

The second list contains oil-olive, symbolizing knowledge, and the honey-date, symbolizing material contentment. These fruits represent those who appreciate the Land as a place where the Jewish people can be successful in the material spheres of life, whether academic, cultural, or economic.

Rabbi Hamenuna taught us an important lesson: how great is the love for the Land of Israel, even when this love is limited to its physical benefits. When one is connected to the community, all material matters become spiritual ones; the elevated goals will automatically be realized through the bonds of God's people to His Land.

The Pomegranate and the Date

Why does the date take precedence before the pomegranate? Even though the pomegranate belongs to the first group, it is the last fruit in the list. The pomegranate represents those who are aware of the holy qualities of *Eretz Yisrael*, yet in practice remain distant from the Land. These individuals unfortunately take few practical measures to express their love for the Land.

The date, on the other hand, is near the top of the second group. It represents those who only recognize the material benefits of the Land of Israel. Through their efforts, however, they are much closer to the Land, taking practical steps in settling and rebuilding it. Such a person, Rabbi Hamenuna taught, should be strengthened and presented first for a blessing. Devotion to the Land, when promoted in practical, concrete efforts, is a wonderful thing. Thus, we find the Talmud (*Sanhedrin* 102b) states that Omri merited to be king in reward for establishing a city in the Land of Israel, even though his intentions were certainly pragmatic.

"Legs of Iron"

Now we can understand Rabbi Hisda's fervent response, "If only we had legs of iron to always follow you and learn from you!" Rabbi Hisda understood the inner message of Rabbi Hamenuna's teaching. One needs "legs of iron" – courage and fortitude like iron – in order to be able to receive this remarkable message, and appreciate the importance of the material strength of Israel.

Similarly, on the national level, we need "legs of iron," powerful means to build up the physical aspects of the nation. Then we will have the spiritual strength to create a courageous national spirit. "And we will learn from you" – we will follow your path of Torah, and merit inheriting the Land through love and wholeness and inner strength.

Eikev

Blessings over Bread and Torah[1]

Two Blessings of Torah Origin

Most blessings are of rabbinical origin. There are, however, two exceptions to this rule – two blessings that are derived directly from the Torah itself. The first is *Birkat Hamazon*, recited after meals; the second is the blessing said before learning Torah.

The obligation to bless God after eating bread is stated explicitly: "When you eat and are satisfied, you must bless God your Lord...." (Deut. 8:10).

The Sages derived the blessing before studying Torah from the verse: "When I proclaim God's name [or: when I read God's teaching], praise our God for His greatness" (Deut. 32:3).

These two blessings differ not only in the source for our feelings of gratitude – one is for physical nourishment, the other for spiritual sustenance – but also in when they are said. Why is *Birkat Hamazon* recited after the meal, while the blessing for Torah study is recited before studying?

Two Benefits of Food

We derive two benefits from food. The first is our enjoyment from the act of eating, especially if the food is tasty. This is a fleeting pleasure, but it nonetheless deserves to be acknowledged. The primary benefit from eating, however, is the sustenance it gives our bodies, enabling us to

---

[1] Adapted from *Ein Ayah* vol. I, p. 103 (on *Berachot* 20).

continue living. This primary benefit reflects the nutritional value of the food, regardless of its taste.

Our recognition of the principal benefit of eating should take place after the meal, when the body digests and absorbs the food. Since *Birkat Hamazon* expresses our gratitude for physical sustenance, its logical place is at the end of the meal.[2]

Parenthetically, there are also blessings that are recited before eating. These blessings are in recognition of our pleasure in the act of eating itself. We acknowledge this secondary benefit of eating with rabbinically-ordained blessings.

Two Benefits of Torah Study

Torah study also provides us with two benefits. The first is the knowledge acquired in practical areas of *Halachah*, enabling us to live our lives according to the Torah's wisdom.

The second benefit lies in the very act of learning Torah. Torah study in itself is a tremendous gift, even if it does not provide any practical applications. When we learn Torah, the soul is elevated as our minds absorb the sublime word of God.

Which benefit is greater? The Sages taught that the unique sanctity of the Torah itself is higher than all deeds that come from its study. "One who studies Torah for its own sake is raised and uplifted above all actions" (*Avot* 6:1). The benefit of practical knowledge is important, but is only a secondary gain.

Therefore, we recite the blessing over Torah before studying. If the blessing was meant to acknowledge the practical benefit of how to perform *mitzvot*, then it would be said afterwards, since this Halachic knowledge is gained as a result of Torah study. But the blessing over

---

[2] Thus, one may recite *Birkat Hamazon* as long as the food is not totally digested and one does not feel hungry again (*Shulchan Aruch, Orach Chaim* 184:5).

Torah refers to the principle gift of Torah study. When we bless God before studying, we acknowledge the spiritual elevation that we enjoy in the very act of contemplating God's Torah.

Now we can understand why the source in the Torah for this blessing reads, "When I proclaim God's name...." Why does the verse refer to Torah as "God's name"? This blessing requires that we recognize the sublime inner nature of the Torah as "God's name." With awareness of this truth, Torah study can enlighten and uplift us "above all actions."

Eikev

Balancing Torah and Work[1]

Constant Torah Study?

What is the ideal? Should we strive to dedicate ourselves totally to Torah study? Or should we divide our time between Torah study and an occupation?

The Sages debated this issue on the basis of an apparent contradiction between two verses. On the one hand, we are exhorted to study Torah constantly: "This book of Torah shall not depart from your mouth; you shall meditate in them day and night" (Joshua 1:8).

Yet, the Torah also says, "You shall gather your grains, your wine and your oil" (Deut. 11:14) – implying that we should occupy ourselves with working the land and a livelihood. Which is correct?

Rabbi Ishmael explained that the verse exhorting constant Torah study cannot be taken literally. The second verse teaches us that one should combine the study of Torah with a worldly occupation. Rabbi Shimon bar Yochai, however, disagreed:

> Can it be that a person will plow and plant and harvest and mill and winnow, each labor in its season? What will become of Torah? Rather, when Israel fulfills God's will, their work will be performed by others.... And when Israel does not fulfill God's will, they must perform their own labor. (*Berachot* 35b)

[1] Adapted from *Ein Ayah* vol. II, pp. 173–175.

The Nature of the Human Soul

According to Rashi, both scholars agreed that the ideal is full-time Torah study. Rabbi Ishmael, however, took a pragmatic stand that it is better to have a livelihood and not be dependent on charity.

But Rav Kook explained that the disagreement is not a matter of practicality versus an ideal state. Rather, they disagreed about the nature of the human soul and its spiritual capabilities.

Rabbi Shimon bar Yochai held that the human soul is meant to be continually occupied with intellectual and spiritual pursuits. If necessary, we may be forced to deal with mundane matters, but such activity is, in fact, beneath our true potential. The human soul is so elevated that it can only be satisfied with total dedication to study and contemplation.

Thus, the command that "This book of Torah shall not depart from your mouth" should be understood literally. It applies to the complete human being who has not become soiled by sin. Some people may feel a weakness in spirit due to excessive study, but this frailty is only due to flaws in character. As the Jewish people perfect themselves, their work will be performed by others, and their sole desire will be to dedicate themselves to knowing God and His ways.

Rabbi Ishmael, on the other hand, felt that human nature is a composite of both theoretical and practical inclinations. According to his view, occupying oneself with worldly matters in the proper measure is not just a concession to the current state of the world; rather, it meets an innate need of our inner makeup. Rabbi Ishmael came to this conclusion through his observation that most people are not satisfied to spend their days only in study and spiritual pursuits.

Who Was Right?

The Talmud records that many followed the advice of Rabbi Ishmael, and it worked well for them. Those who followed Rabbi Shimon bar Yochai, on the other hand, were not successful.

There may be a select few who feel they are destined for greatness and are happy to delve constantly in wisdom and Torah. However, the Torah was not given to angels; its teachings must be suitable for the majority of people.

While it is difficult to determine the true capacity of the human soul, we can ascertain from empirical evidence that what works for most people is indicative of humanity's true inner nature. Many followed Rabbi Ishmael's counsel and found satisfaction in both their Torah study and their material accomplishments, while those following Rabbi Shimon's opinion felt less successful, due to an internal resistance to constant Torah study. This indicates that Rabbi Ishmael's assessment of human nature is accurate for the vast majority of people. Rabbi Shimon's opinion is only valid for the select few who are blessed with rare spiritual gifts.

The Right Balance

Having ascertained that for most people it is preferable to combine Torah study with an occupation, we still need to determine the proper balance between Torah and work. How should we divide our time and effort between them?

The Talmud (*Berachot* 35b) made the following observation:

> See what a difference there is between the earlier and the later generations. Earlier generations made the study of Torah their main concern and their livelihood secondary to it, and both prospered in their hands. Later generations made their livelihood their main concern and their Torah study secondary, and neither prospered in their hands.

Even in worldly matters, one's sense of contentment and happiness is influenced by his spiritual state. A person who has acquired virtuous character traits, a strong faith and an awe of heaven is protected against many of the aspects of life that can lead one astray and that make life's burdens so overwhelming. Such a person is content with his portion in life. For this reason, the earlier generations who made Torah study and ethical pursuits their principle concern, were successful in both their spiritual and material endeavors.

However, one who has not properly developed his ethical nature, since he concentrated all of his energy on his livelihood, will never be content with what he has acquired. His flawed character traits will lead him to chase after ill-advised cravings. Even if he succeeds in amassing great wealth, he will not be satisfied and will never feel true peace of mind.

Quality, not Quantity

Rav Kook concluded with a very significant remark. The amount of time devoted to a particular activity is not the sole factor in determining that this is our main pursuit in life. What truly matters is our mindset. That which we consider to be the central focus of our life, even if we are unable to devote most of our time to it, constitutes our principle activity.

"The Word of *Shemitah*"[1]

The Sabbatical year is more than just a cessation from agricultural labor. It is called *Shemitah*, the year of remission, since all outstanding debts are cancelled during this year.[2] What happens if a debtor insists on repaying his loan? The Mishnah (*Shevi'it* 10:8) teaches:

> If a debtor wants to repay a loan during the seventh year, the lender only needs to formally declare, "I am canceling the debt." If the borrower replies, "Nonetheless, I am paying it back," the lender may accept repayment. This is learned from the verse, "This is the *word* of *Shemitah*" [i.e., it is sufficient to verbally cancel the debt, even though it is actually repaid]. (Deut. 15:2)

The Mishnah concludes that not only may a debtor repay his loans, but that it is praiseworthy to do so.

What is the purpose of the *Shemitah* year debt-remission? Why is it sufficient if only lip service is given to canceling debts? Why did the Sages praise debtors who insist on paying back loans?

---

[1] Adapted from *Ein Ayah* vol. II, p. 404.

[2] A legal loophole to avoid debt remission was devised by first-century scholar Hillel. He designed the *pruzbul*, a legal device that enabled lenders to collect debts by transferring their loans to the public court.

Repairing Social Ills

The seventh year serves to rectify the social ills and inequalities that accumulate in society over time. When poorer segments of society borrow from the wealthy, they feel beholden to the affluent elite. "The debtor is a servant of the lender" (Proverbs 22:7). This form of subservience can corrupt even honest individuals in their dealings with the rich and powerful.

The Sabbatical year comes to correct this situation of inequality and societal rifts, by removing a major source of power of the elite: debts owed to them.

However, the Torah stresses that a healthy and successful society is not achieved via annulment of private assets and redistribution of wealth. It is only the extreme cases of inequality and social injustice that the Torah seeks to remedy by remitting private debts, a partial repair of social inequalities once every seven years.

Nonetheless, it is important that the cure itself does not lead to detrimental side effects, namely the belittling of personal rights of property and ownership. Therefore, the Torah allows the cancellation of debts to be limited to formalities, a technical declaration of remission – "This is the word of *Shemitah*." Just the verbal expression of the right to be released from all financial obligations may suffice to neutralize the feelings of dependence and obsequiousness towards the wealthy lender.

The Torah does not seek to reduce the borrower's sense of honesty and integrity. Therefore, the debtor may reject the offer of remission, out of a sincere desire not to benefit from the wealth of others. In fact, the Sages praised this honorable insistence on repaying loans.

Private and Public Redemption[1]

When Did the Exodus Occur?

At what time of day did the Jewish people leave Egypt? The Torah appears to contradict itself regarding the hour of the Exodus. In Deut. 16:1 we read, "It was in the month of spring that the Lord your God brought you out of Egypt *at night.*" Clearly, the verse states that the Israelites departed in the night. However, the Torah previously stated in Num. 33:3 that they left during the daytime: "*On the day* after the Passover sacrifice, the Israelites left triumphantly before the eyes of the Egyptians."

So when did they leave – during the night, or in broad daylight, "before the eyes of the Egyptians"?

Two Stages of Redemption

The Talmud in *Berachot* 9a resolves this apparent contradiction by explaining that both verses are correct. The redemption began at night, but it was only completed the following morning.

After the plague of the first-born struck at midnight, Pharaoh went to Moses, pleading that the Israelites should immediately leave Egypt. At that point, the Hebrew slaves were free to depart. Officially, then, their servitude ended during the night.

However, God did not want His people to sneak away "like thieves in the night." The Israelites were commanded to wait until daybreak, before proudly quitting their Egyptian slavery. Thus, the *de facto* redemption occurred during the day.

---

[1] Adapted from *Ein Ayah* vol. I, pp. 43–44.

Night and Day

Rav Kook explained that there is an intrinsic correlation between these two time periods – night and day – and the two stages of redemption.

The initial redemption at night was an inner freedom. Egyptian slavery was officially over, but their freedom was not yet realized in practical terms. The joy of independence, while great, was an inner joy. Their delight was not visible to others, and thus corresponded to the hidden part of the day – the night.

The second stage of redemption was the actual procession of the Jewish people out of Egypt. This was a public event, before the eyes of Egypt and the entire world. The consummation of their freedom took place at daybreak, emphasizing the public nature of their liberation from Egyptian bondage. As the sun shone, "the Israelites marched out triumphantly" (Ex. 14:18).

Food for Thought[1]

Gifts of Meat

One of the lesser-known ways that the Torah provides for the support of the *kohanim* in their holy activities is through gifts of certain cuts of meat:

> This shall be the *kohen*'s due from the people: when an ox or sheep is slaughtered for food, they shall give the *kohen* the foreleg, the jaw, and the maw.[2] (Deut. 18:3)

Rabbi Hisda's Offer

While this gift belongs to the *kohanim*, they do not have to eat it themselves. The Talmud (*Shabbat* 10b) recounts that Rabbi Hisda, fourth-century Babylonian scholar and a *kohen*, found an original use for his gifts of meat. Rabbi Hisda held up two portions of priestly gifts and announced, "I will give this beef to whoever will come and teach me a new dictum of Rav."[3]

The scholar who won the prize was Rava bar Mahsia, who quoted Rav's statement that one should inform his neighbor when giving him a gift.

---

[1] Adapted from *Ein Ayah* vol. III, pp. 14–15.

[2] The last of a cow's four stomachs.

[3] The great Talmudic scholar and leader of Babylonian Jewry, Abba Aricha (160–248 CE), was known simply as *Rav* ("the Master") due to his stature as the preeminent scholar of his generation.

Why does the Torah reward the *kohanim* with gifts of meat? And is there some connection between the prize offered by Rabbi Hisda and the dictum quoted by Rava bar Mahsia?

Permission to Eat Meat

To answer these questions, we need to examine the moral dilemma regarding the slaughter of animals for food. The Torah expresses a certain reservation in the matter; its acquiescence to allow eating meat appears to be a concession to the baser side of human nature. Thus, the Torah adds the otherwise superfluous phrase, "When you desire to eat meat" (Deut. 12:20), implying that when you have a strong craving for animal flesh, you need not suppress this desire. Were it not for this craving, however, it would be preferable to refrain from eating meat.

Why then are we allowed to kill animals for food? The Torah recognizes that, given our current state of weakness, both moral and physical, we would be unable to perfect ourselves if we were to deny ourselves those foods that give us strength. Merely for the sake of our physical welfare, we would not be justified in taking the life of an animal. In time, however, the spiritual advance of humanity will bring about the overall elevation of the entire universe, including the animals. Therefore, it is reasonable that the animals should also make their contribution during this interim struggle, until the world attains its desired goal.[4]

Meat and Wisdom

Given this understanding of the Torah's attitude towards eating meat, it is clear that this consent is linked to mankind's intellectual and moral progress. This is particularly true regarding the development of new knowledge in Torah and wisdom, which has a direct impact on advancing the world.

---

[4] See "*Noah*: Permission to Eat Meat."

For this reason, we find the Sages counseled, "An ignoramus should not eat meat" (*Pesachim* 49b). Since an ignoramus does not contribute to the world's spiritual advance, he is not justified in taking an animal's life for his food.

This also explains the purpose of the gifts of meat that the Torah decreed be given to the *kohanim*. The major source of income for the *kohanim* are tithes, which (by Torah law) are only taken from basic staples – grain, oil, and wine. Why did the Torah also give these cuts of meat, a nonessential food of indulgence, to the *kohanim*? This confirms the premise that the Torah permitted meat in order to promote the activities of scholars and holy teachers, so that they may expand their wisdom and help advance the world's spiritual growth.

For this reason, Rabbi Hisda used his portions of beef as a reward for a new teaching. Particularly regarding beef, the Talmud (*Baba Kama* 72a) ascribes properties of increased intellectual powers. Rabbi Hisda wanted to use his gift of meat for its true purpose, to gain wisdom and new Torah knowledge, so he announced, "I will give this beef to whoever will come and teach me a new dictum of Rav."

But why did Rabbi Hisda hold up *two* portions of beef?

Rabbi Hisda realized his efforts to amass the sayings and wisdom of Rav would be rewarded doubly. First comes the benefit gained by learning any new word of wisdom. The second benefit is the result of collecting together all of the statements of an eminent scholar. By bringing together all of the sparks of light that illuminate his teachings, we can uncover a complete picture of the great individual's unique approach, enabling us to follow in his spiritual path.

Private versus Public Good

Our last question was why did Rava bar Mahsia relate to Rabbi Hisda this particular dictum, that one should inform his neighbor when giving him a gift?

320

Rav's statement deals with an interesting moral dilemma. On the one hand, a person who truly loves doing *chesed* and helping others prefers that his actions go unnoticed. In this way, the beneficiary will not express his appreciation, and the kindness is performed in a completely sincere and altruistic manner.

On the other hand, it is important for the moral development of the world that people develop and deepen their powers of appreciation. The trait of *hakarat hatov* brings genuine good to the world, uplifting our lives. So, which value should prevail: the ethical benefit of the individual, or the moral need of the world?

Rav taught that the overall benefit of the world takes precedence over that of an individual. Thus, when giving a gift, the recipient should be informed.

This teaching neatly corresponds to the moral dilemma regarding eating meat. A sensitive individual will feel some moral aversion to the slaughter of animals, even for food. The Talmud (*Baba Metzia* 85a) relates that Rabbi Yehudah HaNasi was punished when he failed to show proper sensitivity towards a calf about to be slaughtered, telling it, "Go! For this purpose you were formed." Such a spiritual giant should have been appreciative of all ethical sensitivities. Even though the world may not yet be ready for vegetarianism, these aspirations should nevertheless be given their due place.

But in the end, as with the case of giving a gift, the spiritual needs of society come first. The need to permit meat in order to promote humanity's intellectual and spiritual progress takes precedence over any private moral considerations.

Shoftim

The Murderer's Admission[1]

We all live a double life. There is our external world: our relationships with friends and family, our jobs, and our place in society. And we have our inner world: our private thoughts and feelings, our introspections and contemplations. We are influenced by both spheres, and we need them both.

One of the positive aspects of the outside world is the sense of worth and respect that society bestows to the individual. The Sages placed great value on human dignity, even waiving rabbinical prohibitions when one's dignity is at stake (*Berachot* 19b).

Honoring Criminals

What about criminals? Do they also deserve respect and honor?

The Talmud (*Makkot* 12b) raises an interesting question regarding people who have killed unintentionally. Accidental manslaughters are penalized with exile to one of the designated cities of refuge. What if the people in the city of refuge wish to honor the murderer is some way, perhaps with a public position – may he accept? Or would doing so negate the very purpose of exile? After all, one of the principle aspects of this punishment is loss of recognition and place in society. To what extent must the murderer suffer public disgrace in order to atone for his criminal negligence?

---

[1] Adapted from *Ein Ayah* vol. II, p. 404.

Accepting Responsibility

The Talmud answers that the murderer must state clearly, "I am a murderer." His inner truth must be public knowledge. He may not hide from the heinous crime he committed, albeit unintentionally. He cannot pretend as if the murder never took place.

The Sages derived the need for the criminal to openly admit his crime from the verse, "This is the word of the murderer" (Deut. 19:4). His response to the offers of society must be as one who has committed manslaughter.

The murderer must not let social honors distract him from the private soul-searching which he must undertake. He needs to attend to his inner world of emotions and introspection, and avoid being caught up in the rush of public life. He should reject social honors by announcing, "I am a murderer."

If the people choose to accept him despite his past, then he is permitted to accept the honor. Respect from the community is a positive value that should not be denied, even from criminals. This respect should not be allowed to cover up the terrible truth of manslaughter. It should not negate or desensitize the murderer's inner sense of justice. But if he demonstrates responsibility for his actions, and his moral sensibilities are strong and healthy, then the external influence of social acceptance and honor will be a positive factor in his ultimate rehabilitation.

Ki Teitzei

The Rebellious Son – Preventive Medicine[1]

Only Theoretical

Is there really a death penalty for rebellious children? Even in Talmudic times, it was clear that the severe punishment for the "wayward and rebellious son" (Deut. 21:18–21) is only "on the books."

> There never was, nor will there ever be, a child who meets all of the legal qualifications of the "wayward and rebellious son." Why then was this law written? So that you may study it and receive reward [for the Torah learning, despite its lack of practical application]. (*Sanhedrin* 71a)

Does this law serve no other purpose other than as a theoretical area of study?

Preventative Medicine

While field of medicine has made tremendous strides over the centuries, it is widely recognized that among its greatest successes have been in the area of preventive medicine. Efforts to ensure clean air and water, sewage treatment, public education on healthy lifestyles and food, and immunization against infectious diseases, have been the most important factors in fighting disease and increasing life expectancy.

We should similarly appreciate the benefit of the Torah and its *mitzvot* in terms of the most effective assistance: preventing harm and ruin.

---

[1] Adapted from *Otzerot HaRe'iyah* vol. II, p. 187.

Thus, God promised, "If you obey God... keeping all His decrees, I will not strike you with any of the sicknesses that I brought on Egypt. I am God, your Physician" (Ex. 15:26). The healing powers of the Torah should be compared to preventive medicine. It provides a healthy lifestyle that does not leave room for affliction. God did not promise that He will cure us of sicknesses of Egypt. Rather, by faithfully following the Torah, we will not be visited by those maladies.

What does this have to do with the hypothetical "rebellious son"? By educating the people about the draconic punishment for the rebellious child, the Torah helps prevent this tragic breakdown in family and society from occurring in the first place. This is what the Talmud means by "Study it and receive reward" – the very study of the subject is its own reward. As each generation is educated about the dangers of the "rebellious son" and absorbs the message of the gravity of the offense, this deplorable situation is avoided.

Teaching For Free

We often take for granted the truly important things in life, such as peace, freedom, mental and physical health. They safeguard our happiness and well-being, yet we only properly appreciate them in their absence. Inconsequential matters, on the other hand, are just the opposite. They come to our attention only when they are present and visible. As the Talmud (*Sotah* 8a) teaches, "The evil inclination only rules over what the eyes can see."

This explanation can shed light on why one should not accept payment for teaching Torah.[2] The most vital aspects of life, protecting our health and well-being, cannot be procured with money. Thus, a doctor who heals a sick patient may request remuneration for his services, but a

---

[2] "Just as I [Moses] taught for free, so too, you should teach for free" (*Nedarim* 37a). See, however, *Shulchan Aruch Yoreh Dei'ah* 246:5, that teachers may draw a salary as compensation for time lost to gainful employment.

person who chases away a lion and averts damage to his neighbor's possessions may not demand a reward. What is the difference? The doctor may be paid for after-the-fact healing, but the greater benefit – preventing potential injury – must be provided free of charge.

This is the lesson of the "rebellious son," the Torah's preventive medicine to safeguard familial and social order. "Study it and receive reward."

Ki Teitzei

Rationale for *Mitzvot*[1]

Are we capable of understanding the true reasons for the Torah's commandments? Or should we be satisfied with the simple rationale that we perform *mitzvot* in order to fulfill what God wants us to do?

> If you come across a bird's nest.... You must first send away the mother, and only then may you take the young. (Deut. 22:6–7)

At first glance, the *mitzvah* to chase away the mother bird seems clearly to be an expression of Divine compassion for His creations. In fact, that is exactly what Maimonides wrote in his *Guide for the Perplexed* (III: 48). However, we find the Talmud (*Berachot* 33b) explicitly states: "One who says in his prayers, 'May Your compassion extend to us as it does for the mother bird'... should be silenced."

Maimonides explained that this Talmudic statement is according to the opinion that we should not seek explanations for *mitzvot*. According to this position, the Torah's *mitzvot* may only be understood as an expression of God's Will and His divine decrees, and are beyond the grasp of the human intellect.

Two Forms of Serving God
It is possible, however, to offer an alternative explanation. When we serve God with our minds and intellect, it is proper to seek rationale for *mitzvot*. Such pursuits contribute to the intellectual realm, to the realm of Torah

---

[1] Adapted from *Ein Ayah* vol. I, p. 160.

study. Understanding is achieved empirically, as we try to discern the underlying principles from the myriad details. It is thus fitting to analyze each individual *mitzvah*, and attempt to understand its function and reason; and each individual analysis will then contribute to our overall understanding of the Torah.

Yet, we also seek perfection in our emotional service of God. And in the emotional realm, the details tend to obstruct and confuse. Especially when we serve God in prayer, our incentive should be a general desire to fulfill God's will. This universal motivation, simple and uncomplicated, applies equally to all *mitzvot*.

The distinction between our intellectual and emotional service of God surfaces in the difference between Torah study and prayer. One who prays, "May Your compassion extend to us as it does for the mother bird," is confusing what should be the straightforward, simple emotions of noble service with complex calculations regarding the underlying rationale of *mitzvot*. Such in-depth analyses may be appropriate in our investigative efforts when studying Torah, but they obstruct the purer, more natural service of God that is appropriate when praying.

Investigations into the reasons for *mitzvot* belong in the philosophical inquiries of the *Guide for the Perplexed*. One who does this during prayer, however, "should be silenced."

Free Will versus Causality[1]

The Torah commands us to set up a guardrail (*ma'akeh*) to prevent people from falling off the roof. This is a straightforward *mitzvah*, if there ever was one. Nonetheless, a deeper look into this *mitzvah* leads us to a complex philosophical topic. To what extent are events pre-determined, and to what extent do we have free will? To what degree are we responsible for our actions?

"The One Who Is Falling"

> When you build a new house, you must place a guardrail around your roof. Do not allow a dangerous situation in your house, for the one who is falling could fall from it. (Deut. 22:8)

The language in the verse is awkward. What does it mean, "the one who is falling"? Is not the Torah warning against a possible future event? Or has he already started to fall? The Talmud (*Shabbat* 32a) explains as follows:

> This person [who fell] was predestined to fall since the six days of Creation. That is why the verse refers to him as "the one who is falling." Reward is brought about through a person of merit, while punishment is brought about through a person of guilt.

---

[1] Adapted from *Ein Ayah* vol. III, p. 172.

This Talmudic statement needs to be examined. If the one who fell was supposed to fall anyway, why should I bother with the guardrail? He would have fallen anyway! Where do free will and personal responsibility enter the picture?

Two Systems Governing the Universe

When we witness the phenomenon of cause and effect in the world, we are lead to ponder the extent of our personal freedom to act versus underlying, pre-ordained causes. It is important to note that, while free will assumes complete freedom of action, this does not negate the possibility of requisite causes.

We recognize in the economic and political spheres that, despite freedom of personal initiative, there exist overall factors that may neutralize any such attempts at change. For example, the initiative to setup a high-tech company in a backward, third-world country may fail due to lack of infrastructure and skilled labor, political corruption, etc. This is also true in the moral and spiritual realms. We have complete freedom of action and choice, but other underlying factors may negate the actual outcome of our actions. Even when great changes do occur, they too may be simply part of the overall divine plan.

In some cases, the discerning eye will detect the effects of actions of free choice, while in others, we see the footprints of pre-ordained causes. In fact, both of these systems – freedom of choice and causality – are tools by which the universe is governed. Together they achieve the overall universal goal, as it says in Isaiah 16:5, "With kindness and truth, the throne will be established."

Means and Ends

We may divide all activity into means and ends.[2] Means do not make a permanent impression on the world on their own accord; their significance is due to what they cause. Means relate primarily to the power of free choice. There exist a variety of means that may lead to a particular end; if a goal is not attained through one medium, it will be achieved by another. Ultimate ends, on the other hand, relate to pre-ordained causes.

Now we can better understand the Talmudic principle, "Reward is brought about through those with merit, and punishment through the guilty." This is the "magical" connection between the two systems, freedom and causality. Through the act of free will by some individual – the means – the appropriate pre-ordained goal, be it reward or punishment, is achieved. In the case of the guardrail, it is the free will of the house-owner, who failed to erect a *ma'akeh*, that led to the punishment of the one predestined to fall.

---

[2] In specific instances, this distinction may not be obvious, as a particular action may be a means in one aspect and a goal in another.

Ki Tavo

Be Happy![1]

The Torah portion opens and closes with the same theme: *simchah* (joy). It begins with the *mitzvah* of offering *bikurim* (first-fruits) in the Temple, an exercise in appreciating what God has given us, as it says, "You shall rejoice in all the good that the Lord your God has granted you and your family" (Deut. 26:11).

Afterwards, the Torah describes the terrible trials that will befall the Jewish people if they are unfaithful to the Torah's teachings. This section concludes with the root cause for these punishments: "Because you did not serve the Lord your God with joy (*simchah*) and contentment (*tuv levav*)" (Deut. 28:47).

Not only does God expect us to keep the *mitzvot*, but we are to perform them with joy and contentment. What is the difference between these two emotions?

Joy and Contentment

Simchah and *tuv levav* are two distinct levels of happiness. Interestingly, they are the result of contradictory perceptions.

What is the source of *tuv levav*? This is a sense of satisfaction that we feel good about our service of God. We pray, study Torah, and perform *mitzvot* out of a feeling that we are doing what we were created to do. As one of God's creations, it is natural for us to serve Him. We are grateful to have been blessed with the intellectual and spiritual capabilities needed to worship Him through Torah study and *mitzvot*.

---

[1] Adapted from *Mussar Avicha*, p. 32.

Simchah, on the other hand, comes from the perception that some unexpected boon has befallen us. We feel joy in serving God when we are aware of the tremendous privilege in being able to connect to God – a gift far beyond our true level. Awareness of this amazing gift, while at the same time feeling that our service is appropriate and suitable, allows us to feel both *simchah* and *tuv levav*.

Cultivating Joy

How does one attain a true sense of *simchah* in serving God? The secret to developing and enhancing our feelings of joy is to reflect on two thoughts:

- Appreciating the significance and wonder of every medium – such as Torah and *mitzvot* – that allows us to connect with the Master of the universe.
- Recognizing the divine source of our soul and its inherent holiness, even though it may have become soiled through contact with the material world.

We experience genuine joy in serving God when we are able to thoroughly internalize these two insights.

First Fruits, Led by an Ox and a Flute[1]

The Mishnah in *Bikurim* (3:2–3) describes the impressive procession of Jewish farmers, as they brought their first-fruits to Jerusalem:

> How were the first-fruits brought up to Jerusalem? Farmers from surrounding towns would gather in the district capital, and camp out in the main square. In the morning, the officer would call out, "Let us rise and ascend to Zion, to the House of God!"... An ox walked in front of the procession, its horns covered with gold and a crown of olive-twigs on its head. A flute would be played before them, until they drew near to Jerusalem.

What was the significance of the ox? Why the golden horns and olive-twig crown? And why was the flute chosen for musical accompaniment?

Labor, Prosperity, and Wisdom

Most nations understand the value of labor and productivity. They strive to create a social framework for honest, productive living. Progressive nations aspire to two additional goals: national wealth and wisdom. Through their prosperity, they are able to enlighten the world with their wisdom and knowledge.

The ox, the classic beast of burden, represents the value that society places on productive labor. The ox walked proudly in front of the

---

[1] Adapted from *Ein Ayah* vol. II, p. 413.

farmers who brought their first-fruits – an impressive symbol of their solid, respectable way of life.

The ox's horns were plated with gold, a sign that, while riches may be acquired in many ways, the most honorable route is through honest, productive labor.

Why was the ox crowned with olive-twigs? Olives and olive-oil symbolize enlightenment and wisdom. The only oil used in the Temple Menorah, a symbol of light and wisdom, was refined olive-oil. Thus, the ox's olive-twig crown indicates that our aspirations should not be limited to labor and wealth. The crowning goal of our efforts should be wisdom.

Why the flute?

Long ago, the flute was played not only at weddings and other happy occasions, but also at funerals. Its mournful notes helped evoke emotions of loss and grief.

The ox, with its gold horns and olive-twig crown, was a metaphor for productive labor, prosperity, and wisdom. Yet, these three measures of success may be used for both good and evil. Hard labor can oppress and darken the human spirit. Wealth can lead to overindulgence in physical pleasures, desensitizing the spiritual faculties of the heart. Knowledge too may be misused for destructive and evil purposes. The flute, a symbol of both joy and sorrow, signified the moral ambiguity inherent in these aspirations.

Yet, if the procession is leading towards Jerusalem – "God's word [will come] from Jerusalem" (Isaiah 2:3) – we are confident that these three assets will be used for elevated goals. Then the flute, which may also accompany unhappy occasions, will ring out in joy before them, "until they draw near to Jerusalem."

Ki Tavo

Tithing in the Proper Order[1]

Twice every seven years, the Torah enjoins us to declare that we have properly tithed our produce:

> When you finish taking all the tithes for your produce... you should declare before the Lord your God: I have removed all the sacred portions from the house. I have given to the Levite, the stranger, the orphan and the widow, according to all the instructions that You commanded me.
> (Deut. 26:12–13)

What are these tithing instructions that God prescribed? The Mishnah in *Ma'aser Sheini* (7:11) explains that this refers to tithing in the proper order. The first tenth, *ma'aser rishon*, is distributed to the Levites. Only afterwards should the second tithe, *ma'aser sheini*, be set aside to be consumed by the owner in Jerusalem.

Why is the order so important? What does it matter which *ma'aser* is apportioned first?

The Mishnah teaches us an important lesson in how we should fulfill out moral obligations. The Torah wants to impress upon us the importance of executing our duties in the correct order and appropriate time. If the hour is right, our efforts will bring about consummate good in the world. However, when irresponsible and rash individuals attempt to

---

[1] Adapted from *Ein Ayah* vol. II, p. 406.

address problems before their time, their actions often turn out detrimental, and prevent much good.

Four Levels of Responsibility

For example, our primary responsibility is for the welfare of our family. Only afterwards come moral obligations to the nation. Next comes our concern for all human beings, and lastly, for all creatures.

Only after taking care of our family should we turn towards the needs of our nation. Fortunate is the individual whose obligations towards his people are such that he has the opportunity to also work for the good of all humanity.

The prophets spoke of a future era when humanity will no longer need to help one another. Spiritually, there will be no need to teach others, "For all will know Me, both small and large" (Jeremiah 31:34). None will require physical assistance, since "The lame will leap like deer and the tongue of the mute will sing" (Isaiah 35:6) and "He will swallow up death forever" (Isaiah 25:8). Nor will economic support be required, as "There shall be no needy among you" (Deut. 15:4). At such a time, what will we do with our natural inclination to help others? Who will require our aid?

At that time, we will turn to the creatures beneath us, to care for them and enlighten them, until "the cow and the bear will graze together" (Isaiah 11:7). Mankind will then be revealed as a benevolent king watching over all creatures.

Moral Recklessness

Sadly, there are those so troubled by the woes of the world – war, ignorance, oppression – that in their haste to rectify the world's problems, they ignore the needs of their own families and nations. They only bring about greater sorrow, and have neglected those closer to themselves. Likewise, some hasten to help the animals, disregarding the distress of people in front of their eyes. These rash individuals cause great evil in their attempts to alleviate problems before their time.

For this reason, the Torah instructs us to declare that we have properly fulfilled our moral obligations – tithing our produce – in the correct order and in the appropriate time.

Nitzavim

Two Levels of *Teshuvah*[1]

The Torah portion of *Nitzavim* is always read before Rosh Hashanah, a fitting time to speak about reflection and repentance. Often we have a strong desire to make changes in our lives. We want to be better parents, better spouses, and better people. We aspire to greater spirituality in our lives, to devote more time to Torah study, to be more thoughtful in our interpersonal relationships. And yet, circumstances may make such resolutions very difficult to keep. Our goals may seem unattainable, and our personality faults beyond correction.

National *Teshuvah*

The Torah describes the national *teshuvah* (repentance) of the Jewish people as they return to their homeland and their faith:

> Among the nations where the Lord your God has banished you, you will reflect on the situation. Then *you will return up to the Lord your God...* He will gather you from among the nations... and bring you to the land that your ancestors possessed....
> God will remove the barriers from your hearts... and you will repent and obey God, keeping all of His commandments... For *you will return to the Lord your God* with all your heart and soul.
> (Deut. 30:1–10)

---

[1] Adapted from *Olat Re'iyah* vol. I, p. 335; *Orot HaTeshuvah* 17:2.

Twice, the verses state that "you will return to God." Is there a purpose to this repetition? A careful reading reveals a slight discrepancy between the two phrases.

After reflection in the exile, the Jewish people will return to the land of their fathers. Here the text says, "you will return *up to* God," using the Hebrew word *ad*.

After returning to the Land of Israel and God removes the barriers of their hearts, they will learn to fully love God and keep His commandments. This time the Torah says, "you will return *to* God," using the preposition *el*.

Two Stages of *Teshuvah*

How do these two forms of national return differ? What is the difference between *ad* and *el*?

The first *teshuvah* is a physical return to their homeland, to their language, and to their national essence. This is returning "up to God" – approaching, but not fully attaining. Thus the Torah uses the preposition *ad*, indicating a state of "up to, but not included in the category" (a Talmudic expression, *"ad, velo ad bichlal"*). This is a genuine yet incomplete repentance, obscured by many veils.

After this initial return, the Jewish people will merit divine assistance that "will remove the barriers from your hearts." This will enable the people to achieve the second stage of return, a full, complete *teshuvah* all the way "to God." This is an all-embracing return to God "with all your heart and soul."

Thoughts of *Teshuvah*

It is important to recognize and appreciate these different levels of *teshuvah*. This lesson is also true on a personal level. We should value even partial efforts to change and improve. The Sages praised even *hirhurei teshuvah*, the mere desire to improve (*Pesikta Rabbati* 44). Perhaps we are unable to fulfill our spiritual aspirations to the extent we would like. Nonetheless, we should view our desire to change and improve as tools that purify and sanctify, leading us on our way to attaining complete spiritual elevation.

Nitzavim

Bridging the Generation Gap[1]

The time will come, the Torah assures us, when God will bring the Jewish people back to the land of their ancestors. In the Land of Israel, they will learn to fully love God and keep His commandments:

> God will remove the barriers from your hearts and from your descendants' hearts, so that you will love the Lord your God with all your heart and soul. (Deut. 30:6).

Why does the verse mention both "your hearts" and "your descendants' hearts"? Do the parents and children have different hearts?

In fact, their hearts *are* different. Each generation has its own intellectual, emotional, and spiritual yearnings. Each generation has its own hurdles and barriers to be overcome. While the fundamental content of the Torah does not change – it is still the same divine Torah from Sinai – its style and exposition must meet the needs of the day.

The prophet Elijah, harbinger of the redemption, will know how to reach out to each generation in its own language. He will succeed in bringing them together, and thus fulfill his mission to "restore the heart of fathers to the children, and the heart of the children to their fathers" (Malachi 3:24).

---

[1] Adapted from *Otzerot HaRe'iyah* vol. II, p. 369; *Igrot HaRe'iyah* vol. II, p. 226.

Torah for Our Time

Rav Kook was profoundly disturbed by the widespread abandonment of religious observance by the young people of his time. He repeatedly called for the creation of a renascent literature to reach out to the younger generation. In a letter from 1913, for example, he wrote:

> We must translate our entire sacred treasury according to the contemporary style of writing. Almost the entire body of Jewish knowledge and sentiments must be made accessible to the people of our time.

In the days of the return from Babylonian exile, Ezra switched the script of the Torah from the paleo-Hebrew characters to the letters that we use today, the more aesthetically pleasing Assyrian script (*Sanhedrin* 21b). One reason for doing so was in order to help his generation appreciate and connect to the Torah. We live in a similar age, when the exiled Jews returning to their homeland are often detached from their spiritual heritage. Ezra's initiative is an apt metaphor for the current need to present the Torah in a language and style suitable for our time, while preserving its inner content.

Vayeilech

The Song of Torah[1]

Near the end of his life, Moses commanded the people, "Now write for yourselves this song and teach it to the Israelites" (Deut. 31:19). This verse is the source-text for the obligation of each Jew to write a Torah scroll.[2] But why did Moses refer to the Torah as a "song"? In what way should we relate to the Torah as song?

Studying *Mussar*

A young scholar once wrote Rav Kook a letter probing certain philosophical issues, raising questions that had eluded him. Rav Kook was delighted to see the young man immerse his talents analyzing the philosophical aspects of Torah, unlike most Torah scholars who dedicate themselves solely to Talmudic and practical *Halachic* studies. Exploring abstract philosophical issues, Rav Kook stressed, is especially important in our times.

Nonetheless, Rav Kook urged the young scholar to approach this field only after a prerequisite study of *mussar* texts.

> You should first acquire expertise in all moralistic
> tracts that you come across, starting with the easier
> texts. Great scholars, wise-hearted and

---

[1] Adapted from *Igrot HaRe'iyah* vol. I, p. 94.
[2] *Sanhedrin* 21b. However, the *Shulchan Aruch* (*Yoreh Dei'ah* 270:2) quotes the opinion of Rabbeinu Asher (the *Rosh*) that "Nowadays it is a *mitzvah* to write books of the Pentateuch, Mishnah, Talmud, and their commentaries," since we no longer study directly from Torah scrolls. (The commentaries debate whether there is still a *mitzvah* to write a Torah scroll, see *Shach* and *Taz* ad loc.)

> exceptionally pious, wrote this literature from the heart. Many subjects of philosophical inquiry cannot be fully grasped until one's emotions have been properly prepared.

In other words, it is important to precede the analysis of Torah philosophy with the study of simpler texts that clarify the unique holiness of Torah. What is the function of this preparatory study? By studying *mussar*, we gain a proper appreciation and reverence for the subject at hand. Only after this emotional preparation are we ready to delve into an intellectual analysis of Torah thought.

Engaging the Emotions

It is for this reason, Rav Kook explained, the Torah is called a "song." Just as the beauty of song stirs the heart, so too, the special power of *mussar* literature lies in its ability to awaken our inner sensitivity to the divine nature of Torah. This emotive preparation is essential, as only the pure of heart are successful in penetrating the philosophical foundations of the Torah.

While ethical works do not engage the intellect to a high degree, they nonetheless enable the soul to recognize its inner foundations. Of course, one should not be content with reading moralistic literature, but should continue with in-depth, analytical study of the Torah and its worldview.

Ha'azinu

How Do We Serve God?[1]

> When I proclaim God's name, ascribe greatness to
> our God. (Deut. 32:3)

How does one go about "ascribing greatness to God"? The book *Ikvei HaTzon*, first published in Jaffa in 1906, contains two of Rav Kook's most philosophical essays, *Da'at Elokim* and *Avodat Elokim*. These stimulating articles discuss the very core of religious belief. Who is God? How can we relate to Him? How do we serve Him?

Anthropomorphism in the Torah

It is surprising that the Torah often uses anthropomorphic expressions, attributing to God human emotions (anger, pleasure), senses (seeing, hearing) and even physical attributes ("outstretched arm"). Nothing could be further from the teachings of Judaism, and yet, the Torah uses such expressions freely. In fact, it is precisely the combination of these anthropomorphic descriptions together with the application of our faculties of reason and logic that can bring us to the highest and purest insight into God and Godliness (*Elokut*).

It is critical, however, that we do not limit our concept of God to a simplistic understanding as implied by a literal reading of the Torah. When a generation advances in general knowledge and makes significant strides in science and philosophy, and yet remains with a primitive understanding of God, widespread rejection of religion is a foregone conclusion.

---

[1] Adapted from *Ikvei HaTzon*, pp. 142–156.

The same holds true for our mental picture of *avodat Elokim,* service of God. This term is commonly understood as simply a synonym for religion and ritual worship, but it too needs to be clarified.

Our perception of how one serves God is influenced by our concept of God. On its simplest, most literal level, such a service denotes the labor of a servant as he serves his master. A person well-versed in ethics and general knowledge, but with a poorly-developed understanding of God, will likely feel tremendous inner opposition to this interpretation of serving God. He will naturally rebel against such servitude – why should I willingly forfeit my freedom and independence? However, as we refine our understanding of what *Elokut* is, this concept will also be refined.

Ascribing Greatness to God

We should not be afraid of advances in modern science and philosophy. On the contrary! All progress in knowledge and wisdom helps elevate the holy light of Torah, allowing it to shine with a purer radiance. The intellectual upheaval from new ideas helps clarify and refine our comprehension of Torah. These advances grant to all a more accurate understanding – an understanding that was previously the purview of the select few.

A more profound insight into God and His service was already known to the spiritual giants of past generations; but our generation's need to explain and bring sublime matters down to the level of general knowledge now allows all people to grasp these refined concepts. This advance in knowledge of the general public signifies the gradual fulfillment of Isaiah's prophecy, "All your children will be knowledgeable of God" (54:13).

The remedy for our times is to elevate God's name – i.e., our conception of *Elokut* – in sublime feeling and expansive thought. Our understanding of *Elokut* needs to be at least on par with the other great ideals of the day. This was Moses' charge, "When I proclaim God's name, ascribe greatness to God." We need intensive intellectual labor in the Torah's esoteric teachings in order to refine and elevate our concepts of God and His service.

When Moses asked God for His name, God responded, "I will be Who I will be" (Ex. 3:14). What does this unusual name mean? This indicates that our concept of God changes and develops over time. According to each generation's advance in ethics and knowledge, the light and powerful beauty of God's holy name is revealed.

Renewed Study of *Aggadah*

It is incumbent upon the greatest scholars, and all who are blessed with talent and interest in elevated spiritual studies, to concentrate their intellectual efforts in the study of divine wisdom, including the *Aggadah*, the homiletic and allegorical teachings of the Talmud and Midrash.

The Sages wrote in *Chagigah* 14a that "bread" is a metaphor for *Halachah* (Jewish law), while "water" refers to *Aggadah*. Unfortunately, the study of *Aggadah* has long been forsaken. There is a great hunger in the land, "not a hunger for bread, nor a thirst for water, but to hear the words of God.... On that day, the beautiful young women and men will faint in thirst" (Amos 8:11, 13). This faintness is not due to famine. The basic staples exist – scholarly Talmudic research and practical *Halachic* study. Still, the youth are faint from thirst. They lack the water needed to revive their hearts and minds. The refreshing fountains of *Aggadah* must be opened before them. This is the sacred duty of great scholars, who have acquired Torah, awe and love of God, within their hearts.

Actualizing the Godly Ideals

It is well known that even God's holy names do not truly reflect His essence. Rather, these names are the divine ideals, God's ways and paths, His desires and will, His *sephirot* and holy attributes. Some of this Godly content is ingrained within the human soul, "whom God made straight" (Ecclesiastes 7:19). The most powerful desire planted in the depths of the soul is the drive to realize this hidden light, to actualize our innate aspirations for goodness and progress. We constantly strive to rectify the breach between the infinite perfection of the Godly ideals on the one hand, and the imperfect reality of life, for the individual and the community, on the other. This natural drive of the soul is the enlightened concept of *avodat Elokim*: the labor of children, acutely aware of their inner connection to their Father, the Source of good and life and enlightenment.

We may possess a sublime and refined image of God, but if we view *avodat Elokim* as the worship of some divine object, without recognizing the aspect of inner idealism in the service itself, then we have relegated this service to a primitive state that can only relate to objects. The preferred understanding of service to God must be expanded to reflect all human efforts to realize the Godly ideals, as we strive to integrate these ideals within the frameworks of our personal lives, our nation, all of humanity, and the entire universe.

Circling Back to the Simple Understanding

If serving God means the worship of a servant to his Master, then we are relating to an object. This can become an idolatrous concept, just as anthropomorphic expressions can lead to idolatrous misconceptions. In general, the notion that we can objectively perceive our surroundings is simplistic, belonging to the primitive stage in human intellectual development which fails to differentiate between objects and their perceived characteristics.

Yet, at the same time, this same understanding of *avodat Elokim* may also be the most sublime. When we realize that we can only perceive reality in a subjective fashion, according to its appearance to us but not its true essence, we may then conclude that the relationship that is the deepest and truest is our inner connection to God. It becomes apparent that even the relationship to our own selves is subjective, while our connection to *Elokut* is the very essence of life and the truth of reality.

Just as the perception of *avodat Elokim* as the service of a divine Object implies the ultimate realness of this connection to God, so too, the physical characteristics that the Torah attributes to God hint at the inner truth that God alone is the true, objective reality. As Maimonides wrote in *Yesodei HaTorah* 1:3,

> The Torah's statement, "There is none besides Him," means that, besides God Himself, no other existence can be compared to God's true existence.

Nonetheless, this elevated concept cannot lead to more than a dim inner emotion. It cannot create powerful feelings and great deeds. The rich treasury of thought and reason must be built on the basis of Godly ideals, through our descriptive and subjective connection to God via His attributes and manifestations. Yet, we find that the literal concept of divine service, relating to God as an object, is at once the most childish and most sublime.

One who speaks about God's essence will sense an unaccountable darkness and sadness. This is because any attempt to relate to God's essence puts our own existence in doubt. If, however, we do not speak of God as an object, but refer to the abstract property of *Elokut* and Godly ideals, we will be filled with strength and happiness. In this understanding of God, we find an expression for our most powerful inner drive, namely, our quest for justice and kindness and truth.

Vezot HaBerachah

The Full Cup of Blessing[1]

The centerpiece of a Jewish ceremony is usually a glass of wine. Weddings, circumcisions, *kiddush* on the Sabbath – all make use of wine, a symbol of joy.

The Talmud (*Berachot* 51a) teaches that this cup of wine should be filled to the brim. "Whoever says the blessing over a full cup is given a boundless inheritance" and "is privileged to inherit two worlds, this world and the next." The Sages derived this reward of a "boundless inheritance" from Moses' blessing to the tribe of Naphtali before his death: "He shall be filled with God's blessing, inheriting [land] to the west and to the south" (Deut. 33:23).

Why is it important to fill the ceremonial glass to the brim? Why should this act grant us boundless riches and an inheritance in this world and the next?

The Pursuit of Riches

One might think that if we sincerely desire to live life according to our true spiritual goals, then we should make do with only our barest needs. We should distance ourselves as much as possible from the distracting pursuit of luxuries. And yet, the desire for an expansive lifestyle is ingrained in human nature. It is natural to delight in greater wealth, nicer homes, and fancier cars. There must be some inner purpose to this innate human nature.

---

[1] Adapted from *Ein Ayah* vol. II, pp. 225–226.

In fact, the pursuit of riches is only a negative trait when its sole objective is self-gratification. Wealth and material possessions serve no purpose if there are acquired only for our own personal benefit. But if we utilize our energy and joy of life for that which is good and proper, than it is unnecessary to restrict these natural tendencies. On the contrary, a generous and kind-hearted individual can contribute much more to the world when he is blessed with wealth.

A full cup of wine represents an abundance of riches. The Sages praised filling a wine-glass to the brim – on condition that the glass is a *kos shel berachah*, a ceremonial cup used for *mitzvot* and good deeds. With such a "cup of blessing," it is proper to pursue a life of wealth, as we recognize that material blessings are a vessel, a tool to perform *mitzvot* and help others, both physically and spiritually.

Boundless Inheritance

One who pursues riches only for his own benefit has set for himself very limited goals. How much joy can all the pleasures of the universe generate when they are confined to one individual? But one who seeks financial success in order to help others – there is no end to the benefit of the wealth he acquires. Therefore, the Sages taught that a full ceremonial cup is indicative of a "boundless inheritance."

In addition, if we recognize that God is the source for all blessings, then being showered with material wealth helps us develop the important trait of gratitude. Our resolve to serve God and help others is strengthened, and we become loyal emissaries of God in spreading kindness in the world.

Inheriting Both Worlds

For most people, there is a clear dichotomy between physical and spiritual pleasures. This world and the next are separate, even competing, realms.

But if our love for this world is based upon the good that we can benefit others, then the pursuit of material riches is also a spiritual pursuit, and there is no longer any contradiction between the love of this world and the World to Come. Life in this world becomes a spiritual life, filled with the pure ideals of loving-kindness and generosity. This is "the inheritance of two worlds" that the Sages ascribed to one who fills his *mitzvah* wine-glass to the brim.

Vezot HaBerachah

Why Keep *Mitzvot?*[1]

Why do we keep *mitzvot?* What should be our motivation for observing the Torah's precepts?

In an article in *Orot HaKodesh* entitled "Three Levels of Holy Service," Rav Kook analyzed different motivations in serving God. He discerned three levels, which he categorized as (1) the service of the Levites, (2) the service of the *kohanim*, and (3) the highest level, the service of Moses, God's servant.

The External Service of the Levites

The most prevalent incentive to serve God is analogous to the service of the Levites. The Levites received tithes "in exchange for their work" (Num. 18:21). The motivation for this divine service is personal gain. *Mitzvot* are valued for their material, psychological, and spiritual benefits. As this service of God becomes more refined, it no longer focuses on the reward. Yet, it remains based on simple, straightforward discipline.

The Levite service is a proper conduit to spread the Torah's teachings in the areas of ethics and Jewish law. Nonetheless, it is an external form of serving God. The word *Levite* means "associate,"[2] as the Levites did not participate in the inner Temple service. They served as guards at the gates – on the outside. They lifted their voices in song, but

---

[1] Adapted from *Orot HaKodesh* vol. III, pp. 201–202.
[2] See Num. 18:4.

the song of the Levites was a musical accompaniment to the actual Temple service.

The Altruistic Service of the *Kohanim*

Superior to the Levite service is that of the *kohanim*. The *kohanim* performed an inner service of God. They worked inside the Temple. This is the mystical service of holy *tzaddikim*, who are the foundations of the world. These saintly souls concern themselves with the secrets of the universe. They seek to "nourish" the supernal spiritual worlds by giving strength and greatness to God's Divine Presence. Because of the altruistic nature of the priestly service, the Torah describes it as a gift: "This is the *gift* of service that I have given you as your priesthood" (Num. 18:7).

The Service of Moses, God's servant

The highest level is the service of Moses. The *Zohar* refers to Moses as *ra'aya meheimna*, "the faithful shepherd," for his concern was solely for the people under his charge. This sublime level of selflessness transcends all spiritual realms. It goes beyond the efforts of the righteous to nourish and increase them. In accordance with the flawless purity of his intentions, Moses' prophetic visions were seen through a "clear lens," an *aspaklaria me'irah*. Compared to this brilliant prophetic gift, all other divine blessings are like the weak light of a candle in the blazing midday sun.

At the end of his life, Moses merited the title "God's servant": "It was there in the land of Moab that *God's servant* Moses died, at God's word" (Deut. 34:5).

A servant of God is always ready to serve and influence, without any thought of benefit or gain. He is not even motivated by the reward of noble, spiritual blessings. By virtue of his pure and selfless service, Moses merited to be called "God's servant." "Moses rejoiced in the gift of his portion, for You called him a 'faithful servant'" (from the Sabbath morning prayers).

Bibliography

Ein Ayah – commentary on Talmudic Midrashim, arranged according to the book *Ein Ya'akov*.[1] Rav Kook began writing on tractate *Berachot* while serving as rabbi in Zaumel. He wanted to publish *Ein Ayah* while in Jaffa in 1906, but he lacked sufficient funds for the undertaking. He continued to add material over the years, penning his final entry (two-thirds the way through tractate *Shabbat*) in Jerusalem in 1934 (he passed away the following year). As in his other early work, *Midbar Shur* (which was similarly delayed before being printed), this commentary reflected his fervent belief that our generation needs to deepen its understanding of the Torah's philosophical principles. Rav Tzvi Yehudah Kook made use of some of these commentaries in *Olat Re'iyah*. Published by HaMachon al shem HaRav Tzvi Yehudah Kook (Jerusalem 1995).

Igrot HaRe'iyah – three-volume collection of letters written by Rav Kook between the years 1886 and 1919. Published by Mossad HaRav Kook, Jerusalem, 1962. A fourth volume for the years 1920–1925 was published by HaMachon al shem HaRav Tzvi Yehudah Kook (Jerusalem 1984).

Ikvei HaTzon – booklet of essays about the new generation and a philosophical understanding of God and serving Him. First printed by Rav Kook in Jaffa in 1906. The small book "made a profound impression on the writers and intellectuals of the Second Aliyah, who were concentrated in Jaffa."[2] Republished by Mossad HaRav Kook (Jerusalem 1982).

---

[1] A compilation of Aggadic material from the Talmud by Rabbi Jacob ben Solomon ibn Habib, first published in 1516.

[2] Rabbi Simcha Raz, *An Angel Among Men* (translated by Rabbi Moshe Lichtman), p. 405. See also p. 387, where Rabbi Tzvi Yehudah Kook writes (in a letter to

Midbar Shur – sermons written by Rav Kook while serving as rabbi in Zaumel and Boisk in 1894–1896. One of Rav Kook's first writings, but mysteriously lost. Finally printed by HaMachon al shem HaRav Tzvi Yehudah Kook (Jerusalem 1999).

Mo'adei HaRe'iyah – a blend of stories and writings of Rav Kook about the holidays by Rabbi Moshe Tzvi Neriah. Published by Moriah (Jerusalem 1982).

Mussar Avicha – ethical tract on awe of Heaven and divine service. First printed by Rabbi Tzvi Yehudah Kook in 1946, but it was written some fifty years previous. Published by Mossad HaRav Kook (Jerusalem 1979).

Olat Re'iyah – two-volume commentary on the prayer book. Rav Kook began this project while in London during WWI, and continued after his return to Jerusalem. However, he only wrote as far as midway through the introductory psalms (*Pesukei deZimra*) of the morning prayers. Rabbi Tzvi Yehudah Kook completed the work by collecting appropriate texts from various unpublished writings, and printed it in 1939, several years after his father's death. Published by Mossad HaRav Kook (Jerusalem 1983).

Orot – collection of essays, many analyzing Israel's national rebirth. The book was arranged by Rabbi Tzvi Yehudah Kook, and first published in 1920.[3] Despite rabbinical controversy concerning certain passages in the book, Rabbi Tzvi Yehudah taught that this work is, in comparison to Rav Kook's other writings, his "Holy of Holies." Published by Mossad HaRav Kook (Jerusalem 1982).

Yosef Chaim Brenner) that the philosophical underpinnings for some of the essays may be found in the writings of Prof. Herman Cohen.

[3] For a detailed account of the *Orot* controversy, see Rabbi Bezalel Naor, *Orot* (New Jersey: Aronson, 1993), pp. 14–44.

Orot HaKodesh – expositions on divine service, prophecy, the spiritual experience, etc., collected and organized from Rav Kook's diaries (see below, *Shemoneh Kevatzim*) by his student, Rabbi David Cohen (known as "the Nazir"). The *Nazir* spent twelve years preparing the four-volume work, considered by many to be Rav Kook's magnum opus. Published by Mossad HaRav Kook (Jerusalem 1985).

Orot HaTeshuvah – on the repentance of the individual, the nation, and the cosmos, first published in Jerusalem in 1925. Rav Kook wrote the first three chapters, while the rest were collected from his writings and organized by Rabbi Tzvi Yehudah Kook. Rav Kook emphasized the importance of studying this book; he himself would review it during the month of Elul as a spiritual preparation for the High Holidays. Published in Jerusalem, 1977.

Orot HaTorah – short work on the metaphysical "importance of Torah, its study, and practical guidance" (from the cover page). Rabbi Tzvi Yehudah Kook collected these writings on the subject of Torah, five years after his father's passing, in order to create a work similar in nature to *Orot HaTeshuvah*. Published by Choshen (Jerusalem 1973).

Otzerot HaRe'iyah – five volumes of writings collected from various sources, together with a number of indexes and summaries of Rav Kook's writings, by Rabbi Moshe Yechiel Tzuriel. Published by Yeshivat HaHesder Rishon LeTzion (2002).

Rosh Milin – mystical reflections on the Hebrew alphabet and vowels. Rav Kook composed this short treatise while in London during World War I. It is considered to be one of Rav Kook's most difficult works. Published by Yeshivat HaChaim veHaShalom (Jerusalem 1972).

Shabbat Ha'Aretz – Halachic treatise on the laws of the Sabbatical year and a legal defense of the *Heter Mechirah*, with a forward discussing the significance of the Sabbatical year. Rav Kook wrote the book in just eight days, printing it in Jaffa in 1910 in preparation for the coming Sabbatical year. Republished by Mossad HaRav Kook (Jerusalem 1979).

Shemuot HaRe'iyah – based on Rav Kook's *Se'udah Shelishit* (third Sabbath meal) discourses in Jerusalem, which weaved together Halachah, Midrash, Jewish philosophy, and Kabbalah. After the Sabbath, Rabbi Frankel would write down from memory summary notes of these long, intricate discourses. Edited and arranged by Rabbi H. Yeshayau Hadari, some were printed by the Dept. of Torah Education and Culture in the Diaspora (Jerusalem 1994).

Shemoneh Kevatzim – the "eight notebooks," Rav Kook's spiritual diaries from 1904, when he became rabbi of Jaffa, until his return to Jerusalem in 1919 after being trapped in Switzerland and England during the First World War. These eight volumes served as the raw material from which *Orot HaKodesh* (as well as much of *Orot*, *Orot HaTeshuvah*, starting from chapter 4, and *Orot HaTorah*) was compiled. Published in Jerusalem, 2004.

Timeline for Rabbi Abraham Isaac HaKohen Kook

5625 (1865)	Born in Greive (now Griva), Latvia, on the sixteenth of Elul.
5644 (1883)	At age 18, studied for a year and a half at the famed Volozhin yeshivah (headed at that time by Rabbi Naftali Tzvi Berlin, the "Netziv").
5645 (1885)	Married Batsheva, the daughter of Rabbi Eliyahu David Rabinowitz-Teomim (known as the "Aderet"), then rabbi of Ponevezh (later chief rabbi of Jerusalem).
5648 (1888)	Appointed rabbi of Zoimel (Zaumel), Lithuania, at the age of 23. During his stay in Zoimel, Rav Kook's first wife died. His father-in-law, the Aderet, convinced him to marry Raiza-Rivka, daughter of the Aderet's twin brother.
5655 (1895)	Became rabbi of Bausk (now Bauska).
5664 (1904)	Arrived in *Eretz Yisrael* on the 28th of Iyar. He served as rabbi of Jaffa and the surrounding settlements for the next ten years.
5665 (1905)	Published the first chapters of *Orot HaTeshuvah*, Rav Kook's original thoughts on the topic of repentance, as well as *Eder Hayakar* and *Ikvei Hatzon*.
5670 (1910)	(Sabbatical year) Published *Shabbat Ha'Aretz*, defending the *heter mechirah*.
5674 (1914)	Went to Europe for *Agudat Yisrael* convention in Berlin. Unable to return to Israel due to the sudden outbreak of World War I, Rav Kook spent two years in St. Gallen, Switzerland.
5676 (1916)	Served as rabbi of Machzikei HaDat congregation in London during the war. Published the mystical treatise *Rosh Milin*.
5679 (1919)	Returned to *Eretz Yisrael*. In Tevet 5680, he accepted the position of Chief Rabbi of Jerusalem. Two months earlier, his twelve-year-old daughter Ether Ya'el had died tragically after falling down a flight of steps.

5680 (1920)	Rabbi Tzvi Yehudah Kook edited some of his father's writings, publishing them in the book *Orot*.
5681 (1921)	Established Chief Rabbinate in pre-state Israel, becoming Chief Rabbi together with Sephardic Chief Rabbi Yaakov Meir.
5684 (1924)	Established the Mercaz HaRav yeshivah in Jerusalem, unique among the yeshivot at that time in its religious philosophy and positive attitude towards Zionism.
5695 (1935)	Passed away on the 3rd of Elul, in Jerusalem, several days before his 70th birthday.

Glossary of Hebrew Terms

Akeidah – the Binding of Isaac

Amidah – literally, "standing," the central prayer recited quietly while standing

Avot – the Patriarchs Abraham, Isaac, and Jacob

berachah (pl. *berachot*) – blessings

birkat hamazon – grace after meals

bitachon – the trait of reliance in God

brit milah – ritual circumcision

chatat – sin-offering

chametz – leaven, forbidden during the Passover holiday

chesed – kindness

Eretz Yisrael – the Land of Israel

hakarat hatov – sincere appreciation

Halachah – Jewish law

ketoret – incense

kohen (pl. *kohanim*) – priests, descendants of Aaron

luchot – the stone tablets upon which the Ten Commandments were engraved

Mishkan – the Tabernacle

mohel – ritual circumciser

mitzvah (pl. *mitzvot*) – one of the 613 commandments of the Torah

parah adumah – the red heifer used for purification

Sanhedrin – the supreme court of judges

Shemitah – the Sabbatical year, when farm-land was not worked once every seven years

taharah – ritual purity

tefillin – phylacteries, worn on the arm and forehead

terumah – "heave-offering" of produce given to the *kohanim*

teshuvah – repentance

tzaddik (pl. *tzaddikim*) – righteous person

tzitzit – ritual strings that are tied to each corner of a four-cornered garment

yeshivah (pl. *yeshivot*) – institute for Torah study

Index

Rabbi Abraham Isaac Kook (1865-1935), the celebrated first Chief Rabbi of pre-state Israel, is recognized as being among the most important Jewish thinkers of all times. His writings reflect the mystic's search for underlying unity in all aspects of life and the world, and his unique personality similarly united a rare combination of talents and gifts. Rav Kook was a prominent rabbinical authority and active public leader, but at the same time, a deeply religious mystic. He was both Talmudic scholar and poet, original thinker and saintly tzaddik.

After graduating with a B.A. in Mathematics from Yeshiva University (New York), **Rabbi Chanan Morrison** studied for several years at Yeshivat Mercaz HaRav, the Jerusalem yeshiva founded by Rav Kook in 1924. He was ordained after completing rabbinical studies in the Ohr Torah Stone (Efrat) and Midrash Sephardi (Jerusalem) rabbinical seminaries.

Rabbi Morrison taught Jewish studies for several years in Harrisburg, PA, before returning to Israel. He and his family subsequently settled down in Mitzpe Yericho, an Israeli community in the Judean Desert.

In an effort to maintain contact with former students, Rabbi Morrison began emailing weekly articles on the weekly Torah portion based on the writings of Rav Kook. Over the years, this email list grew at a phenomenal rate; it now benefits thousands of readers from all over the world. He is frequently featured on the Torah section of the Arutz Sheva website and his work can be read on his own website at http://ravkook.n3.net.